Pride Against Prejudice

THE BIOGRAPHY OF LARRY DOBY

Joseph Thomas Moore

CONTRIBUTIONS IN AFRO-AMERICAN AND
AFRICAN STUDIES, NUMBER 113

GREENWOOD PRESS

NEW YORK · WESTPORT, CONNECTICUT · LONDON

Library of Congress Cataloging-in-Publication Data

Moore, Joseph Thomas.
  Pride against prejudice.

  (Contributions in Afro-American and African
studies, ISSN 0069-9624 ; no. 113)
  Bibliography: p.
  Includes index.
  1. Doby, Larry. 2. Baseball players—United
States—Biography. 3. Segregation in sports—
United States. 4. Afro-American baseball players—
Case studies. I. Title. II. Series.
GV865.D58M66 1988   796.357′092′4 [B]   87-17743
ISBN 0-313-25995-X (lib. bdg. : alk. paper)

British Library Cataloguing in Publication Data is available.

A paperback edition of *Pride Against Prejudice:
The Biography of Larry Doby* is available from
Praeger Publishers (ISBN 0-275-92984-1).

Library of Congress Catalog Card Number: 87-17743
ISBN: 0-313-25995-X
ISSN: 0069-9624

First published in 1988

Greenwood Press, Inc.
88 Post Road West, Westport, Connecticut 06881

Printed in the United States of America

The paper used in this book complies with the
Permanent Paper Standard issued by the National
Information Standards Organization (Z39.48-1984).

10 9 8 7 6 5 4 3 2 1

Copyright Acknowledgment

Grateful acknowledgment is made to the following for permission
to reprint previously published material.

Excerpts from *The Souls of Black Folk* by W.E.B. Du Bois. Copyright © 1973.
Reprinted by permission of Kraus-Thomson Organization Ltd., White Plains, N.Y.

For the late Ben Marmo,
and for Joan, whose encouragement
brackets my lifelong interest in Larry Doby

Contents

Preface   ix

Acknowledgments   xiii

1. The Photograph of 1948   1

2. Black Bottom   5

3. The North Star   13

4. The End of Innocence   19

5. From Mog-Mog to Newark   29

6. Pioneer   39

Illustrations *(following page 65)*

7. The Most Significant Player in the League   67

8. Prime Time   87

9. "A Load Off My Back"   109

10. "Gaijin"   123

11. Another Robinson   131

12. Veeck, Again   147

13. Major League Manager   155

14. Pride Against Prejudice   167

Appendix: Larry Doby's Career Statistics 179

Bibliographical Notes 183

Index 187

Preface

To begin the preface of the biography of one man with reference to another may seem peculiar, but because Larry Doby has lived his life in the shadow of Jackie Robinson, it seems a necessity to do so. Robinson has been the subject of a voluminous literature. Fifteen books, parts of at least 23 others, innumerable magazine and newspaper articles, even a Broadway musical, make Robinson one of the most storied athletes in history.

Certainly Robinson deserves it. His symbolic importance to black Americans, and his significance in the social history of the United States, is unquestioned here, and richly told elsewhere. As Jules Tygiel put it, Robinson's "triumph had ramifications that transcended the realm of sports, influencing public attitudes and facilitating the spread of the ideology of the civil rights movement."[1]

Robinson's is not the whole story, of course; nor will the addition of Doby's make it complete. But Doby's story has not been told at all, even though he followed Robinson into the major leagues by just 11 weeks, and subsequently became the second black man to manage there, and the second former major league player to play in Japan. The point is that Doby's story has been neglected, unduly so, for a variety of reasons.

Foremost, of course, is that Robinson *was* first. He played in New York, not Cleveland. He became a spokesperson for a large segment of black America, while Doby remained publicly silent. He played on a team immortalized as "The Boys of Summer," not the mortal Indians. He was enshrined in the Hall of Fame, while Doby was not. And in a society where most people cannot name the most recent, or perhaps even the current, vice-president of the United States, we relegate number two to an often undeserved obscurity.

Nevertheless, Larry Doby is a significant American. He, as much as Robinson, was a civil rights pioneer. After all, he integrated the American

League at a time when it dominated the National League, and probably therefore was better known to most Americans. In at least one sense he may be more significant than Robinson, for it will be argued here that Doby was a more typical person, and a more typical baseball player, than Robinson. Doby's story, then, is the story of the many black men who followed them into major league baseball, whereas Robinson's was a more singular experience.

Thus, this book. It is an attempt to rectify the neglect of Larry Doby, and as such, it takes sides. I hope that the reader will understand that motivation. And I hope, as well, that the reader will see that nothing here is intended to tell Doby's story at the expense of Jackie Robinson's, or any of the other men, black and white, who shared importantly in pioneering the integration of the sport which, in the late 1940's and 1950's, deserved its sobriquet as America's "national pastime." And I hope, finally, that the reader will see that although this book takes sides, it does not deny Doby's critics their voice. Some of the most vilifying columns in the history of American sports journalism have not gone unreported in this book.

There are other motivations behind this book as well. I grew up with the legend of Larry Doby. He was the hero of four sports at Eastside High School in Paterson, New Jersey, while I, living in a small town nearby, heard people who saw him play reminisce about his exploits. For example, my late brother-in-law, Ben Marmo, a baseball entrepreneur and scout for the Philadelphia Phillies, told Doby stories to his friends while I listened. And, when I began to work on the rewrite desk in the sports department of Paterson's *Morning Call*, I learned firsthand how my editor there, Bob Whiting, wrote his scoop that Doby had signed a contract with Cleveland.

Still later, when my career evolved into the formal study of history, and sports history became a newly-respectable academic calling because of the importance that sports had assumed in American life, I knew that Doby's was a story worth telling.

With all that in mind, I obtained Doby's approval to research and write his biography. I believe that his approval was vital. Without it, many people who knew him well would not have talked to me at all, or in the way they did. The late Bill Veeck and his wife, Mary Frances, for example, spent the better part of two days and submitted to two lengthy telephone conversations in response to my questions. With the exception of the reasons for firing Doby as manager of the Chicago White Sox after the 1978 season, both spoke candidly about Doby, and about other people in baseball who were vital to the story.

This, then, is an authorized biography. However, unlike many such arrangements, I hasten to assure the reader that Doby never asked me to change a word as he read the manuscript during its various stages. If I have gone too far in praising him, the causes for that are my own: I do admire what he did, and who he is. If I have not gone far enough in criticizing him, the causes for that are also my own. I have tried to write my belief that it is time to let the historical record show that Jackie Robinson had a full partner in 1947 and thereafter, when he and Doby integrated a segment of American life.

If any one person has not received proper credit in this book, it is Helyn Doby. She, in a role fully comparable to that of Rachel Robinson, contributed the stability and support which her husband needed, and depended upon, to face in public the racial prejudice which she experienced more privately. It was she who provided the home which her husband did not have in his youth. And it was she who, in the quiet tradition of the "baseball wife," raised their five children, largely alone, while he lived the nomadic life of a professional baseball player. Because this is a biography of her husband, Helyn Doby seldom appears here, revealing by her absence another form of prejudice—sexism—which she also faced. But her contribution to what her husband did is no less significant for the infrequent appearance of her name on these pages.

Finally, in those few weeks when Jackie Robinson was the only black man in the major leagues, it was, as Tygiel has written, "a great experiment." When Larry Doby went to bat at Comiskey Park on July 5, 1947, the "experiment" ended, but two courageous men, and the great game, continued on. Although prejudice would linger, their country would never be quite the same again.

NOTE

1. Jules Tygiel, *Baseball's Great Experiment* (New York: Oxford University Press, 1983), p. viii.

Acknowledgments

I am grateful to many people for their assistance with this book. Robert Beckwith of the History Department at Montclair State College criticized the manuscript in its earliest and most crucial stage. Another colleague, Kenneth Olenik, translated articles from Japanese into English. Librarians in Camden, South Carolina, Cleveland, Columbia, South Carolina, Cooperstown, New York, Newark, New Jersey, New York City, Paterson, New Jersey, and at Montclair State College facilitated my research. The National Endowment for the Humanities enabled me to have a summer to concentrate on research and writing. Montclair State College provided a sabbatical leave, and a grant for research assistant Vernon Woody. Monte Irvin opened many a door for me from his post as assistant to former commissioner of baseball Bowie Kuhn. I am deeply indebted to all of the people quoted in this book, whose names appear in the notes, and to many other people whose interviews could not be cited but which provided me with essential background material. Most of all, I am indebted to Larry Doby himself. As we traversed a life which has had its full measures of pleasure and pain, he neither exalted his triumphs nor sought sympathy for his wounds, leaving me always free to fulfill my obligations as his biographer.

PRIDE AGAINST PREJUDICE

1

The Photograph of 1948

On the evening of October 9, 1948, Americans watching the evening news in those early days of television saw an extraordinary picture flash before their eyes. A black man and a white man, smiling joyously, were hugging each other in the clubhouse of a major league baseball team in Cleveland, Ohio. The next day, a photograph in many morning and afternoon newspapers confirmed what Americans had seen the night before.

For those who may have shaken their heads in disbelief that such a pair embraced in full view of a battery of photographers, there were 81,897 fans, the highest total in World Series history, who saw in person what the black man, outfielder Larry Doby, and the white man, pitcher Steve Gromek, had done on the field.

Gromek, pitching for the American League champion Cleveland Indians, limited the National League champion Boston Braves to just one run in nine innings. Doby hit a pitch from Johnny Sain far over the fence in right center field. Their heroics gave the Indians a 2–1 victory, a 3–1 lead in games, and brought them within one game of becoming world champions.

And so it was that a black descendant of captured West African slaves who were forced into labor in the state of South Carolina, and a white descendant of Eastern European immigrants who had traveled voluntarily to work in the state of Michigan, had suddenly become linked as momentary heroes in the long history of baseball.

Forty years later, the photograph of Doby and Gromek is commonplace. Hardly a day goes by that Americans do not see their televised sports idols, black and white, celebrating together. But Doby and Gromek were among the first, and they couldn't have picked a better time.

In the autumn of 1948, the American people were in the middle of one of the most bitter presidential election campaigns of the twentieth century.

During the summer, Hubert H. Humphrey, the young mayor of Minneapolis, had challenged the delegates to the Democratic National Convention. "I say the time has come," Humphrey declared, "to walk out of the shadow of states' rights and into the sunlight of human rights." Shortly thereafter, when the Democrats voted to accept Humphrey's challenge by making a strong civil rights plank a part of their party's platform, the southern wing of the party walked out. They formed the States' Rights party, promptly nicknamed the Dixiecrats.

Few attentive Americans missed the meaning of what happened. "States' Rights" were code words for denying equal rights to black Americans on the grounds that individual states, and not the federal government, should define the rights of citizens. It was a tired old argument which ought to have been settled by the Civil War, but wasn't.

While the Indians battled the Braves for supremacy of the baseball world in 1948, the Dixiecrats battled for the supremacy of the white race over the black. Their standard bearer, J. Strom Thurmond, then the governor of South Carolina, tried to convince his fellow Americans of the righteousness of his cause. Yet, earlier that year, the president of the United States, Harry S Truman, saw the necessity, and found the courage, to ask Congress to protect the safety of black Americans against lynch mobs.

If a presidential election campaign is the proper place to argue over the rights of black Americans, the baseball diamonds of America may seem to be an unlikely place. Students of the subject have long known, however, that sport in all societies serves as a reflection of each society. The game of baseball, America's "national pastime," had always been both a reflection of society, and an instrument of social change. After a brief period of integration in the early 1880's, the game had been rigidly segregated for 60 years. In 1947 it became, again, a battleground of "the American dilemma," race. In this sense, then, baseball was very much like a political campaign. In both, the debate about race had waxed and waned.

After the invention of the box score, however, baseball slowly became different from politics. In politics, feelings were often more important than facts. In baseball, a game increasingly based on numerical standards, facts had become more important than feelings. It became inevitable, then, that a man like Larry Doby would play in the World Series. He had his batting average, .301, to prove objectively that he deserved to play for the Cleveland Indians. Now he had affirmed his worth by hitting the home run that won a World Series game.

After the World Series, Doby and Gromek returned home. Doby went to Paterson, New Jersey, and Gromek to Hamtramck, Michigan, both industrial cities. Doby, at first, got a hero's welcome in his adopted home city—a motorcade, speeches, applause. A few months later, when he tried to fulfill a portion of the American dream by investing his World Series check in a house in a nicer neighborhood, he had to ask the mayor for help. Gromek, after the cheers died down, had a parallel experience.

"I got some static when I got home," Gromek remembered. "A couple of friends and I went over to see a fella we knew who owned a bar in Hamtramck. We walked in, and I saw a guy I had known for more than 10 years, a guy I had played ball with. I said hello, and he ignored me. So I asked the guy behind the bar—I knew him, too, because this was my old neighborhood—I asked him, 'What's the problem?'

" 'Oh Christ,' he said, 'it's the picture you took with Larry Doby. He's all upset about it.' And I said, 'Why?' He said, 'I don't know. Don't ask me, ask him.'

"So then the guy told me, 'Jesus, you could have shook his hand!' But then this other friend of mine said, 'If I was in Steve's shoes, and Doby did what he did, I would have kissed him!' And I said, 'That's right. We played together, and Larry and I were friends. Hell, that was the greatest thrill I ever had in my life, winning a World Series game.'

"But the guy didn't want to talk about it, and I haven't talked to him ever since. It's just one of those things. He didn't like that picture, but my other friend did."[1]

In the bar in Hamtramck, Gromek shrugged and said, "What the hell, Larry wins a World Series game for me and I'm not going to show my appreciation?"[2] But in the real estate market in Paterson, Doby could not simply shrug. From the time of his birth in the Black Bottom section of Camden, South Carolina, through his integration of the American League in 1947 just 11 weeks after Jackie Robinson's more celebrated entry into the National League, Doby could never, in his heart, afford the luxury of Gromek's indifference to disapproval.

After the World Series of 1948, Larry Doby went on to a career lasting 11 more seasons. He played in one more World Series, collected a half-share check for another, played in five All-Star games, and was named to the American League team a sixth time. At various times, he led his league in home runs, runs batted in, and slugging percentage. He fielded his position capably. Later, he became the second former major league player to play in the Japanese baseball leagues. After retirement as a player, he developed into a highly regarded batting instructor. In 1978, he achieved the distinction of becoming the second black man ever to manage a major league baseball team. In the 1980's, he is an executive with the New Jersey Nets of the National Basketball Association. For more than 40 years, longer than any other famous American athlete save the late Jesse Owens, Doby has lived the life of a proud black man—not simply a man—in American national sport.

Yet of all the plaques, trophies, rings, and mementos awarded to him over the years, he cherishes his 1948 picture with Steve Gromek the most. "That's the one I like best," he says. "It was exciting to me then, and it's still exciting to me now.

"The picture was more rewarding and happy for me than actually hitting that home run. It was such a scuffle for me, after being involved in all that segregation, going through all I had to go through, until that picture. The picture finally showed a moment of a man showing his feelings for me.

"But the picture is not just about me. It shows what feelings should be, regardless of differences among people. And it shows what feelings should be in all of life, not just in sports. I think enlightenment can come from such a picture."[3]

A few weeks after the 1948 World Series, Doby found reasons outside of baseball to be hopeful about the future. The Dixiecrats carried only four states, all of them in the south. In the political upset of the century, President Truman, civil rights program and all, defeated his principal rival, Republican Governor Thomas E. Dewey of New York.

As he read the results of that election, Doby remembers, he noted that the Dixiecrats carried his native state of South Carolina, and he thought about his boyhood there. In a Jim Crow state which took pride in black humility, and in humiliating black pride, Doby somehow had combined humility and pride. Each would prove to be a blessing and a curse. His life became, slowly and relentlessly, a story of pride against prejudice.

NOTES

1. Telephone interview with Steve Gromek, October 9, 1981.
2. Ibid.
3. Personal interview with Larry Doby. In most of the quotations attributed to Larry Doby, the source will be a personal interview and thus will not bear a note. Exceptions will be cited. These personal interviews began in November 1979 and continued until the spring of 1987.

2

Black Bottom

The origins of the black Dobys of South Carolina are shrouded by more than two centuries of time, and slavery. They are difficult, perhaps impossible, to trace. Two possibilities emerge.

The first is from the family's oral tradition, currently kept by Betty Lytelle Cooke and Mary Kathryn Cooke Johnson, cousins of Larry Doby. It says that their earliest remembered black ancestor, Burrell Doby, was born a slave "somewhere in Georgia." According to this story, Burrell remembered that he and his older brother, as little boys, were playing in their master's yard when "someone came along and bought the brother and left Burrell. He never saw that brother again. Burrell grew up, bought his freedom, and migrated to Camden [South Carolina]. He started buying up land, land, land."[1]

The second explanation of Burrell Doby's origins depends on educated guesses and on the written record. Burrell's black ancestors were probably captured and enslaved somewhere in West Africa, probably between 1619, when the first slaves were brought to North America, and 1808, when the slave trade legally ended. His white masters came from England before the Revolutionary War began in 1775.[2] By 1852, when Burrell was born (in South Carolina, according to the Census of 1900),[3] three white men named Doby owned slaves in the Camden area of Kershaw County. One of these three men may have been Burrell's master.

But it is not possible to tell which one. James Cureton Doby's holdings included 230 slaves when his estate was settled in 1858, but the names of only 23 slaves remain. James's two sons, Joseph William Doby and Alfred English Doby, owned 57 slaves between them. Neither of their estate packets include Burrell's name.[4]

The early history of Burrell Doby thus seems lost. The weight of the evidence, however, makes James Cureton Doby likely to have been Burrell's master. The large number of slaves he owned supports his probable ownership. And the story told by Larry Doby's cousins, Betty and Kathryn, would make their grandfather Burrell six years old at the time when James Cureton Doby's estate was settled, making Burrell a little boy when "someone came along and bought the brother and left Burrell."

After the Civil War ended in 1865, Burrell Doby does not appear in the U.S. Census until 1880. Then he appears as a free man, a sharecropper in West Flat Rock Township near Camden. He had married Molly Bailey, the daughter of Anthony and Sarah Bailey, in 1878. A search of Census records and the archives of the State of South Carolina reveals only that Molly's parents were also born in South Carolina.[5]

With tools valued at three dollars and livestock, including one mule, worth $100, Burrell and Molly harvested 90 bushels of Indian corn from 11 acres in 1880. At the marketplace in Camden their year's labor brought them $190,[6] at least half of which went to the landowner. Nevertheless, Burrell and Molly Doby, 15 years after being freed from bondage, had made their start.

They had also begun a family of eight children: Anna arrived in 1876, just months before federal troops were finally withdrawn from South Carolina. Preston, Emma, Margaret, Johnnie, William, and Alice Lytelle followed before the last child, David Jonathan, was born in 1897.[7] By the time of their deaths, Burrell and Molly owned 23 acres, free and clear, on 1903 Campbell Street in Camden.[8]

They also owned at least one book, *Up From Slavery*, by Booker T. Washington. On its flyleaf, Burrell wrote a simple inscription in a bold hand: "Burrell Doby."

The hours, days, and years of toil which enabled a black man and woman to acquire land, and at least bare literacy, in the State of South Carolina in the late nineteenth and early twentieth centuries can hardly be imagined. Burrell and Molly's lives were the unconscious but real basis of their grandson's struggle, some 25 years after they died, to breach the racial barriers which surrounded America's national sport.

David Doby, the baby of Burrell and Molly's family, did not see the most arduous years of their struggle. Certainly, though, he knew that the Dobys were one of the most prosperous black families in Camden. Yet, with one of America's oldest horse races, the Carolina Cup, as well as the polo fields of the luxurious Kirkwood Hotel, in his neighborhood, it is not surprising that David became a stable hand. He groomed the horses of the wealthy northern families who wintered in the mild Camden climate.[9]

During World War I, David Doby served for five months in the Army's 156th Depot Brigade and in Company G of the 810th Pioneer Infantry. After his honorable discharge a month after the war ended on November 11, 1918,[10] David returned to his work grooming polo ponies and saddle horses. At the time of his marriage to Etta Brooks in 1922, he spent his summers in Saratoga, New York, and his winters in Camden, working for the Branham family.[11] In his leisure time, David played baseball. He became, according to Richard DuBose, a key figure in black baseball in South Carolina for 60 years, "the greatest hitter I ever saw."[12]

Etta Brooks met David Doby while playing ball in the road in front of her mother's house on Market Street in Black Bottom, Camden's poorest section.[13] Her mother, Augusta Brooks Allison, had been born to a white man named William Brooks and to former slave Lucy Collins in 1877 in Camden. The fair-skinned Augusta, termed a mulatto in the 1900 Census,[14] married a black man named Charles Allison in 1905. Etta never knew her father, who died early in 1907, and so she grew up as Etta Brooks. She was so naive at the time of her marriage to David Doby that when Judge McDonald asked, at the wedding, "Etta, have you been playing around?" she replied, "Oh yes. Football and baseball."[15]

After their marriage, Etta and David lived occasionally with his parents on Campbell Street, adjacent to the golf course of the Kirkwood Hotel, but usually with Etta's widowed mother in Black Bottom. It was there that their only child, Lawrence Eugene, was born on December 13, 1923, in the tiny frame house at 710 Market Street.[16]

David's long absences in the north and Etta's ties to her strong-minded mother soon ruined their marriage, however. Lawrence, called "Bubba" by everyone, found himself increasingly under the care of his grandmother, Augusta Brooks.[17] In fact, he thought his name was Bubba Brooks. When his mother migrated alone to Paterson, New Jersey, to work as a domestic, he became more completely the child of "Miss 'gusta."[18]

While under his grandmother's roof, little Bubba began, barefoot, to roam the dirt roads of Black Bottom and nearby neighborhoods. He absorbed, unconsciously, the habits, customs, and values expected of a black boy living in the Carolina Piedmont. He had to learn that the race-ridden southern culture severely restricted his freedom to travel, talk, and even think. He had to learn just "how far to go with white folks." By the time he was seven years old, in 1930, he had acquired feelings which would cause him to be misunderstood by some people for the rest of his life.

But for reasons of its local history, Camden did not crush him with the ugly racism of a state which accepted the lynchings of black men. Camden, a town of about 7,000 people in the 1920's, had become a resort for the wealthy, who included among their number William F. Buckley's mother and Bernard Baruch.

As Larry's cousin Kathryn explains it, "Camden at that time was unique. We didn't have the problems that people in other parts of South Carolina would encounter." Instead, Kathryn remembers, "Camden was made up of what we used to call 'truebloods,' people with money, people with breeding, and culture. Our livelihood came from those people. We didn't have what you would call the 'redneck' type that much in Camden." During trips to the local stores, "you could go in the front door. The only places you couldn't go in were your bus station and railroad station, where you saw the signs 'White' and 'Colored.' I personally encountered racial segregation when I moved to New York, and I got a liberal dose of it there."[19]

When young Bubba Brooks began to attend the public Jackson School in Camden, he found it segregated, of course, as required by a state constitution which said that "no child of either race shall ever be permitted to attend a school provided for children of the other race." The Supreme Court of the United States added its blessing in 1896, in *Plessy v. Ferguson*, when it adopted the "separate but equal" doctrine which permitted segregation. Yet the climate of terror and hatred promoted by heirs to the racist traditions of South Carolinians John C. Calhoun, Pitchfork Ben Tillman, and Cole L. Blease seldom openly frightened the black population of Camden.

Almost without regard to the old traditions of the state which was the first to secede from the Union at the start of the Civil War, life with Miss 'gusta went well for Bubba Brooks for a couple of years after his mother went north. Miss 'gusta regarded him, and he considered himself to be, the man of the house. With his help, she did laundry for a white family. Bubba made pickups and deliveries with his small red wagon, delivered blocks of ice to wealthy white families, tended to the vegetable patch, fed the chickens, chopped wood for the stove, and occasionally picked cotton for $1.00 for a 12-hour day. Miss 'gusta also had a pig "on halves" with a nearby black farmer; Bubba fed it slop as it wallowed in the rich mud of Black Bottom.

During these formative years, Bubba Brooks began also to acquire the air of dignity which anyone who has ever met Larry Doby notices. With few exceptions, his relatives were proud people, and it must have been passed on. When he was five years old, he and his friends would claim the coins that patronizing white people would throw from their horse-drawn carriages into the dirt of Market Street. But when his friends would then approach the carriages so that the whites could rub the wooly heads of the children "for luck," Bubba would remain at the side of the road, holding himself aloof from any further degradation. The scene foreshadows his adult reactions to "Amos 'n' Andy," Satchel Paige, and to a thousand incidents in his life.

As he looks back, Larry Doby regards Miss 'gusta with affection and respect. "Even though I was expected to be the man of the house," he says, "she was very strict with me. She sent me to a lady named Miss Dickerson to learn how to read and write before I went to Jackson School. She would even inspect my ears every Saturday after my bath in an old tin tub, which she put in front of the fireplace when it was cold outside.

We always had enough to eat, even though we seemed to have rice and sardines a lot.

"She made me go to church with her all the time. I liked what I heard in the Twenty-third Psalm and the Ten Commandments. Somehow I got the feeling that the church helped black people to be themselves. I liked that feeling. I think my grandmother did, too."

Bubba's youthful instincts were right. In most black churches in the south, the ministers preached salvation, not damnation. Bubba couldn't go as far down the salvation road as his grandmother could, though. One night she "got religion" while little Bubba didn't feel a thing.

The years with Miss 'gusta came to an abrupt end during the pivotal summer of 1934. Bubba overheard whispered conversations that Miss 'gusta was losing her mind, and might lose her house for failure to pay the rent. One night, when she fled from the house through her bedroom window, Bubba pursued his grandmother out the back door to bring her back. At about the same time, when a male friend who had moved in with Miss 'gusta struck her, Bubba defended her, only to be beaten himself. Crying, he ran a couple of blocks to the home of his Aunt Alice, his father's sister, for temporary shelter.

Notified of her son's plight, Etta returned briefly to Camden from her job in New Jersey and agreed to let Bubba live with her sister-in-law, Alice, and Alice's husband, James. Etta may have had little choice, because Miss 'gusta had to be taken to a hospital.[20]

That same summer, on August 16, 1934, after Etta had gone back to New Jersey, David Doby died. On a day off from his work as a groom at a riding school in New Rochelle, New York, he went fishing on Lake Mohansic in Westchester County, about 37 miles north of New York City. There, in the words written on his death certificate, he died from "Asphyxiation by drowning while fishing from a rowboat."[21] He was 37 years old.

Surprisingly, although perhaps not, neither Larry Doby nor his relatives now remember the arrival of David Doby's body in Camden, or a burial service. Yet Doby's second wife, Juanita Kirkland, sent the body to Camden for burial in segregated Cedar Cemetery, next to the graves of his father and mother, Burrell and Molly. The U.S. Army, in recognition of David Doby's service during World War I, provided the simple stone which marks the grave.

The dramatic summer of 1934 came to its conclusion when Bubba's new guardians, Aunt Alice and Uncle James Cooke, enrolled him in the sixth grade at Browning Home-Mather Academy, a thriving and respected black mission school of the Methodist Church. He went under his real name, Lawrence Eugene Doby.

And so, at the age of 10, Bubba Brooks changed his name, address, and school. At home with Aunt Alice, born Alice Lytelle Doby, he heard Doby family stories which he had never heard before. In Uncle James, Bubba met a strong male role model, a successful carpenter and contractor, who wore a dress shirt and necktie under his pressed overalls. White candidates for public office sought his support, knowing that it would help to win that handful of votes held by Camden's few black voters.[22]

At Mather Academy, Bubba (he was still called by that name) tried to catch up with the learning he had neglected at Jackson School. He played organized sports for the first time, heard occasional addresses to the student body by Mary McLeod Bethune, one of the most noted of black educators, and noticed that, while there were many fights at Jackson, the students at Mather got along with each other.

A measure of the impact of Mather Academy on its students can be found in the fact that many alumni return for reunion dinners 40 years after graduation. There, the school's remarkable white principal, Lula Bryan, long since retired, still remembered the first names of her students, whether they were "poor, or po'." She certainly would not forget Lawrence Doby: she was the first person to call him by his given name.[23]

Baseball provided a focal point for black life in Camden in the 1920's and 1930's. Etta, Larry's mother, remembers it as the most important event on Saturdays.[24] Often, Richard DuBose took his teams in a homemade trailer, hitched to his Model T Ford, to the state capital, Columbia, and to other towns in the Piedmont which had black teams. After World War II, at about the time when Doby and Jackie Robinson broke the color line in the major leagues, DuBose broke two traditions at one time in Camden, racial and religious. His teams played integrated Army teams from Fort Jackson and Fort Bragg on Sundays, despite the resistance of local segregationists and a formal letter from the Catholic Archdiocese of Atlanta. "We'd take in almost $1,000 at the gate," DuBose remembers. "Those stands were packed and ramstacked. Packed and ramstacked."[25]

DuBose and Larry Doby have very different memories of David Doby. DuBose's are vivid and numerous, of David as a first baseman and a great hitter. Larry's are embodied in just a single incident. "We were at a field called Dusty Bend. I remember being with my father at a game, but I can't remember seeing him play. After the game, we went over to my Grandmother Molly's house. I remember that we drank lemonade and ate ice cream. That's the last I ever remember seeing my father."

Doby's four years with his Aunt Alice and Uncle James, from 1934 to 1938, were perhaps the happiest years of his life. Emotionally supported by them and their five children, educated by the capable teachers and coaches at Mather Academy, and trained to play baseball by Richard DuBose, he felt successful and popular. These happy years, though, could not make up for the turmoil of his first 10 years of life. It would be a rare child, indeed, who could experience so many changes without enormous and lasting emotional consequences.

Even so, after a visit with his mother's sister, Aunt Lucille, in Columbus, Ohio, during the summer of 1935, Doby longed to return to Camden. Before leaving for a summer in Paterson after the close of school in 1936, the 12-year-old boy expressed his feelings in a small autograph book:

> Dear Classmates
> School is about to close
> I hope you all will have a loving summer
> Which I know you will have
>   Close with
>   Love and kisses
>   Lawrence E. Doby[26]

Doby's awareness of the world beyond Camden expanded in other ways besides visits to Ohio and New Jersey. Richard DuBose would sometimes lie about Lawrence's age and let him play when his senior team visited nearby towns for games. Mather Academy's coaches would take him to games away from Camden as the team water boy.

In 1937 and 1938, Lawrence made summer visits to Paterson, where his mother spent her weekly day off from her work as a domestic in the wealthy suburb of Ridgewood. Paterson's public playground facilities exceeded anything he had seen in South Carolina, and an occasional "knothole gang" excursion to Yankee Stadium added excitement. He saw Lou Gehrig and Tony Lazzeri, he remembers, but didn't try to copy them when he got back to Paterson. He preferred then, as he does now, to remain "plain me."

Despite the excitement of three summer visits to Paterson, Lawrence always looked forward to his return to the familiar sights, sounds, tastes, and smells of Camden in September. However, after his graduation in 1938 from Mather's eighth grade, his mother insisted, against his tearful resistance, that he remain in Paterson to attend Eastside High School. She knew that promising young black men didn't stay in segregated South Carolina in the depression years of the 1930's. Because she could be with him only on "maid's day off," she arranged for him to live with an old friend from Camden in an integrated neighborhood at the intersection of Carroll and Harrison Streets.[27]

And so Lawrence's life in South Carolina abruptly and permanently ended. Ready or not, he began a new phase of his life. Many years later, after his career as a player, coach, and manager in the major leagues, Doby could evaluate his childhood. "When I look back, I think that my years in Black Bottom, before I moved in with my aunt and uncle, were a lot like my years in baseball: I could be me, but it was hard.

"But in the summer of 1934, when I found out I was a Doby, I felt more important, more proud of myself. I had the feeling that my life was new. But I also knew I had been me all the time. In a way, I came upon my true self. Living with the Cookes, it was just easier to be me.

"Then, when my mother kept me in Paterson, I was lonely living alone. But I just kept trying to be me."

NOTES

1. Personal interview with Mary Kathryn Cooke Johnson, November 28, 1980.

2. Charlotte Boykin Salmond Brunson, *Kershaw County Cousins* (Columbia, S.C.: R. L. Bryan and Co., 1978), p. 199.

3. U.S., Bureau of the Census, Report of the Census of 1900, Vol. 3, E.D. 46, Sheet 6, Line 6 (Washington, D.C.: U.S. Government Printing Office, 1901).

4. Estate packets, Kershaw County Court House, Camden, S.C., Apartment 21.

5. U.S., Bureau of the Census, Report of the Census of 1880, Farm Schedule 2, p. 8, S.D. 3, E.D. 73 (Washington, D.C.: U.S. Government Printers, 1883).

6. Ibid.

7. Johnson, loc. cit.

8. Deed recorded in Kershaw County Court House, Camden, S.C., January 15, 1906.

9. Johnson, loc. cit.

10. State of South Carolina, *Official Roster of South Carolina Soldiers, Sailors and Marines in the World War, 1917–18*. Vol. 2 (Colored Section) (Columbia, S.C.: South Carolina Adjutant General's Office, 1929), p. 1304.

11. Johnson, loc. cit.

12. Personal interview with Richard DuBose, November 29, 1980.

13. Personal interview with Etta Brooks Doby Walker, November 3, 1980.

14. U.S. Bureau of the Census, Report of the Census of 1900, loc. cit.

15. Walker, loc. cit.

16. Walker, loc. cit., and affidavit of birth of Lawrence Eugene Doby, Kershaw County Court House, Camden, S.C.

17. Johnson, loc. cit.

18. Walker, loc. cit.

19. Johnson, loc. cit.

20. Ibid.

21. New York, State Department of Health, Bureau of Vital Records, Albany, N.Y. Death Certificate no. 51920.

22. Johnson, loc. cit.

23. Personal interview with Lula B. Bryan, November 28, 1980.

24. Walker, loc. cit.

25. DuBose, loc. cit.

26. Larry Doby, Diary, May 1936.

27. Walker, loc. cit.

3

The North Star

The city which claims it produced Larry Doby is itself the product of the genius of Alexander Hamilton. Between the two men lie a tumult and a shouting which gave Americans Samuel Colt's six-shooter, the locomotives which linked the Atlantic and Pacific Oceans, a vice-president of the United States, textiles of almost every variety, the engine for Lindbergh's flight, poets William Carlos Williams and Allen Ginsberg, comedian Lou ("Who's on First?") Costello, the first practical submarine, at least two famed assassins, a secretary of the treasury, an anarchist strike, and Leaping Sam Patch, the only man to survive the Niagara Falls and the Passaic Falls without a barrel. Few American cities can lay such diverse claims to distinction as "The Silk City," Paterson, New Jersey.

When Doby became a permanent resident of Paterson in the summer of 1938, he did not know that Hamilton first saw the industrial potential of the 70-foot waterfall on the Passaic River in 1791. Doby did know, however, that the city's 140,000 residents, red brick factories, and their adjacent tenement houses removed him from the resort atmosphere of horsey Camden by far more than the Mason-Dixon line.

Life in an industrial city like Paterson is not lived from horizon to horizon, but in neighborhoods. Doby's was the poorer end of Twelfth Avenue, below the tracks of the Susquehanna Railroad. Without exhortation or design, but probably out of necessity, the Jewish, white Catholic, and black Protestant kids went to Public School 6 together. In the Newman Playground, and on Twelfth Avenue itself, everybody played with everybody. Or at least that's how everybody remembers it.

Lawrence—he still wasn't called Larry—soon found acceptance in his new neighborhood. At a makeshift playground on Twelfth Avenue he took his turn in the continuous pickup games of basketball and stickball. An old timer who lived across the street didn't mind an occasional broken window, so long as the kids chipped in to pay for it. In a coincidence that defies the laws of probability, the old timer was Charlie Jamieson, called "Chuck" in Paterson, center fielder for the Cleveland Indians in the 1920 World Series.[1]

The white men who now remember Doby's arrival from the south recall that he always dressed well, and didn't have a deep southern accent. A black man, Wendell Williams, then "The King of the Kids" and later a school principal in Paterson, recognized the type. He always regarded Doby as a "geechee," a black South Carolinian, usually from sophisticated Charleston, who feels he's special, superior. "Their concept of self is such that they don't accept ordinary achievements," Williams says. "They tend to be more successful, they plan, they have objectives. In their terms, they're 'taking care of bidiness,' " pronounced to rhyme with business, which it also means. "For example, South Carolinians dominated the black churches in Paterson. But they didn't admit their origins because they were not proud of the roles they had to play there."[2]

Two of Doby's closest black friends have slightly different memories of their old neighborhood. To Russell Hapgood, "We had a unison with each other."[3] To Ben Veal, later to be Doby's brother-in-law, there was a certain amount of friction.[4] For one of Doby's closest white friends, the late Adolph Bagli, it was more a recognition of difference than friction.[5]

In this atmosphere, Doby began to make his way. His athletic talents won him acceptance and friends. Quickly they found out that Lawrence was somehow different. "Every kid on Twelfth Avenue had a nickname," Bagli pointed out, "but Larry Doby never got one. Except 'Avenue,' but that was like calling him 'Brother.' "[6]

Paterson's Eastside High School offered a contrast to the Twelfth Avenue street life. It was the kids themselves who created street life. At Eastside, however, adults were in charge.

Eastside High School in the depression decade of the 1930's had a reputation as one of New Jersey's finest academic schools. Many in its student body of approximately 1,200 teenagers were in its "classical" curriculum, meaning that they studied Latin and algebra and went on to college. Others, either less affluent or less academically capable, enrolled in general, industrial arts, or commercial courses. The school as a whole typified urban high schools throughout the northeast in its mixture of religions and races. Doby was one of only about 25 black students in the school. By means he cannot remember, he was slotted into the commercial curriculum, where a poor black boy might be prepared to work as a clerk or a stock boy in one of Paterson's many businesses.

It didn't matter to him, though. Lawrence took a much livelier interest in sports than studying. By the time he finished his scholastic athletic career he had won 11 varsity letters, in football, basketball, baseball, and track, and repeatedly achieved all-New Jersey recognition in all but track.

Along the way, he heard reports that some of Eastside's coaches had quotas for black players, rumors that Eastside's state champion football team would not be invited to a postseason bowl game in Florida because of his presence on the team, and insults from fans and rival players directed at the color of his skin.

His world between 1938 and 1942 was not limited to Eastside High School, however. He played recreation league basketball for a team named the Colored Eagles, thereby coming under the influence of Wendell Williams. Williams urged a radical racial militance on his players, but they didn't understand his message: they didn't share his level of black self-awareness, and they had not read or even heard of black leaders such as W.E.B. Du Bois, Marcus Garvey, or even New Jersey's own Paul Robeson. Neither did they know, as Williams spoke to them in the casual atmosphere of Newman Playground, that he and other black adults in the community had in mind a whole program and strategy for economic and social justice. At the same time, Williams could not know that one of his listeners would some day be a silent crusader for Williams's very objectives.

"It may have been a blessing that we didn't understand Wendell Williams about a quota system," Doby says. "If we had a chip on our shoulders, the white kids wouldn't understand us because they themselves would not treat us in a way that would cause us to behave in the militant way Williams wanted."

"I have no resentment that Larry didn't want to take on the racists," William says. "But one of the easiest ways not to is to say they're not there. It's a tactic of survival."[7]

After Doby outgrew recreation league basketball, his exploits brought him to the attention of the famed Harlem Renaissance, a professional team which won the National Basketball Tournament in 1938. As an unpaid substitute player when the "Rens" played Sunday night games in nearby Passaic, he saw, for the first time, black men making a living as professional athletes.

In the spring and summer, Doby played for as many as three semi-professional baseball teams at a time. Most important were the Smart Sets, a well-known black team whose shortstop had been Monte Irvin, now a member of baseball's Hall of Fame. Manager Pat Wilson must have discerned the emotional needs of the youthful Doby, for he soon assumed a relationship with the boy which came as close to a father-son relationship as Doby was ever to have.

To climax his career at Eastside, at an assembly program before graduation in June 1942, Doby received his tenth and eleventh varsity letters, and yet another ovation from the student body. Yet, for all the acclaim, Doby seldom relaxed the personal defenses which he had constructed as a boy in South Carolina. Al Kachadurian, a teammate in both football and baseball, got to know him so well that when Doby's mother was hospitalized and could not do his laundry, Mrs. Kachadurian washed Larry's and Al's together. Yet Kachadurian never felt that he could slap Larry on the back after a nice play. Neither could anyone else get too close.

Doby's temperament presented problems to people who wanted to befriend him. Kachadurian says, "I remember distinctly that if things didn't go just right, he'd sulk. Deep down he's a warm-hearted guy. But you didn't know if he was sulking at you personally, or whether he was sulking inwardly at himself."[8]

"I was not sulking at anybody, individually or collectively," Doby says today. "Kachy misread that, and a lot of other people misread that. That's been the history of my career. But nobody ever discussed it with me. Nobody asked."

When it was suggested that his manner may have dissuaded people from asking, Doby unburdened himself. "This is the first time it ever came out for me to explain. I had been alone most of my life. I had gotten accustomed to that. Not that I wanted to be alone. You learn to live with being alone." Few of Doby's teammates knew that during his four years at Eastside, he had lived in four different houses, with four of his mother's friends. Rejecting the persistent description of him as a "loner," he says, "I looked at it from the independence standpoint. I wasn't lonely. But I was unhappy at the situation that caused me to be alone."

Doby also had to feel Paterson's racism in the years just before the entry of the United States into World War II. He had to sit in the third balcony, well known as "Nigger Heaven," when he attended a movie and vaudeville show at the Majestic Theatre. He knew, as did his future brother-in-law, Ben Veal, that "You had to be careful where you went. You couldn't sit downstairs in any of the movies. You couldn't eat at Bickford's Restaurant downtown."[9]

Doby also knew, as Veal did, that he had to be home in his Twelfth Avenue neighborhood after dark. Any black person walking in the white sections of the city at night would be stopped by the police. At the same time, though, Doby remembers no abuse by the police in his own neighborhood.

At Eastside, the coaches, with the exceptions of track coach Bob Dimond and baseball coach Al Livingstone, showed their prejudice in various ways. Football coach Dave Ross would assume a friendly air in the presence of blacks, but, as Wendell Williams recalls, "He'd take on a southern accent when he talked to black players—'How y'all.' But he wouldn't do that with Larry. Larry knew what The Man was up to and could sidetrack it. He was always alert to any assaults on his personality or any belittling. You didn't do that to Larry."[10]

Basketball coach Henry Rumana never seemed consistent in his relations with blacks. On the one hand he seemed to like everybody, but on the other hand he would call his black students "Nicodemus." He never invited Doby to the summer camp he owned for a job as a counselor. When Ben Veal was at Eastside, he noted that he, Max Friedman, and Joe Taub, the latter two Jews, all proficient athletes, were also not invited to work at the camp. (Taub, who later befriended Doby as the owner of the New Jersey Nets of the National Basketball Association, will be discussed later.) Yet here, again, Doby suffered no pain. He never even knew that Rumana owned a camp until years later, when Veal told him.[11]

Robert "Spooks" Smith and Russ Hapgood, both black, had been much more popular among their teammates than the reserved Doby. As Adolph Bagli observed, "Spooks knew his place. He knew he was black. Larry sometimes didn't know he was black. Spooks accepted his place on earth, his position. But Larry at times didn't understand that he was black." "Baggy" also remembered what it was like to play at schools like Passaic, where fans would yell "Amos 'n' Andy!" at black players. He indicated no sense of contradiction in his observations.[12]

In comparing his two black friends, Kachadurian observed that "Russ Hapgood was a different type of black man from Larry. Russ was more of a ghetto black guy, fun, more relaxed. He was one of those black guys that everybody adored. You could hug him, kiss him. With Larry, it was always 'Don't touch me.' It came from his background somewhere."[13] Indeed it did, but Doby never told Kachadurian about Black Bottom.

Kachadurian, who indicated no awareness of his stereotyping of Hapgood, nevertheless treasures his associations with Doby, partly because he never again had a black teammate in college at Lafayette, Swarthmore, or Columbia, and acknowledges prejudice against blacks: "They had two strikes against them in those days. They had to be better to make the team."[14]

In Wendell Williams's view, Doby was "an angry kid, but he didn't know it."[15] If Doby was angry, he did not show it in his face. Kachadurian describes the Doby of those days as showing little emotion during games, and "social calmness" at team parties at Kachadurian's house. He, and his teammates, Kachadurian says, saw a "stoic look" when Doby was criticized during practice.[16]

As Doby rehearsed for the graduation ceremony at Eastside in June 1942, he contemplated a career as a physical education teacher and coach. He felt that he had succeeded not only in athletics, but also in his unspoken efforts to be himself, "plain me." He had chosen to be neither militant, as Wendell Williams wished, nor gregarious, in the manner of Russ Hapgood. Just a few years later, Williams would be replaced by Jackie Robinson, and Hapgood by Satchel Paige, in a triangular symbolism which a larger American public was to see, but only dimly to understand.

NOTES

1. Group interview with the late Adolph Badagliaccia (Bagli), Ed Bradley, Fred Casale, and others, December 12, 1980.

2. Personal interview with Wendell Williams, January 5, 1981.
3. Personal interview with Russell Hapgood, December 12, 1980.
4. Personal interview with Dr. Benjamin Veal, December 29, 1980.
5. Bagli, loc. cit.
6. Ibid.
7. Williams, loc. cit.
8. Personal interview with Al Kachadurian, December 17, 1980.
9. Veal, loc. cit.
10. Williams, loc. cit.
11. Veal, loc. cit.
12. Bagli, loc. cit.
13. Kachadurian, loc. cit.
14. Kachadurian, loc. cit.
15. Williams, loc. cit.
16. Kachadurian, loc. cit.

4

The End of Innocence

As Larry Doby carried his high school diploma from the graduation platform at Eastside High School on June 24, 1942, applause mixed with the grim reality of World War II. That summer, a Japanese gunboat shelled the coast of Oregon. In Europe, Allied air raids began to crumple the cities of the Third Reich. The lives of all Americans, including Doby, would be changed forever by the war.

Even before his graduation, Doby had taken steps which would transform his life. On May 31, a young man bearing the alias "Larry Walker" played his first professional baseball game, at Yankee Stadium in New York City. In a Negro National League four-team doubleheader, "Walker" hit a single in four at bats during an 8–3 victory for the Newark Eagles over the New York Cubans.[1]

It was a festive day for the 17,000 mostly black fans. They saw promising young catcher Roy Campanella help the Baltimore Elite Giants defeat the Philadelphia Stars in the first game, 5–3. To start the second game, the future middleweight champion of the world, Sugar Ray Robinson, threw out the first ball.[2]

At the time of his professional baseball debut, Doby did not know that the same black newspapers which reported his debut with the Eagles pressured the commissioner of baseball, Judge Kenesaw Mountain Landis, to end white baseball's half-century-old color line. Neither did Doby know that a minor league owner named Bill Veeck planned to buy the Philadelphia Phillies with the as yet unannounced intention of breaking that color line.

Notwithstanding the events that swirled about him, "Walker" played sensationally a week later at Parkside Stadium in Philadelphia. He collected six of Newark's 27 hits in a 13–0 win over the Stars. One of his hits was a home run, and he scored four runs.[3] The Pittsburgh *Courier*, an important black paper, later reported that Walker "showed considerable hitting power."[4]

The owners of the Eagles, Effa and Abe Manley, offered their youngest player $300 to play until college started in September, identifying him as "Larry Walker from Los Angeles" to protect his amateur status. Thus New York's *Amsterdam Star-News* told its mainly black readers that the "addition of Larry Walker of Los Angeles" would improve the Newark team.[5] The *New Jersey Afro-American*, a subsidiary of the nationally distributed Baltimore *Afro-American*, published a two-column headline declaring, "Signing of Larry Walker Rejuvenates Newark Eagles."[6]

The Eagles needed rejuvenation. They had some of the greatest players in all of baseball, black or white, in their lineup: third baseman Ray Dandridge was admitted to the Hall of Fame at Cooperstown in 1987; shortstop Willie Wells and pitcher Leon Day probably should be there. But the Homestead Grays, with future Hall of Famers Josh Gibson and Buck Leonard, were ahead of the Eagles in the standings.[7]

Doby closed his first season with the Eagles in a mid-September four-game series against the powerful Grays. In the first black baseball game at Ebbets Field in Brooklyn since 1935, "Larry Walker" had three hits in seven at bats and scored two runs in a doubleheader. The following day, at Ruppert Stadium in Newark, "Walker" singled twice, tripled, stole a base, and scored a run in seven at bats in two games.[8]

After that final series against the Grays, Doby could look back on his initiation into professional baseball with satisfaction. He remembers playing in about 50 games, for which only 26 box scores could be found. In those 26 games, he had 36 hits in 92 official at bats for a .391 average. It seems reasonable to suppose that in the games for which no published records exist, he played equally well.

Throughout most of the summer of 1942, while Doby played segregated baseball, black leaders continued to pressure the commissioner of baseball and the owners of the Pittsburgh Pirates and Philadelphia Phillies to lower the color barrier. They became especially angry when they read, in mid-July, that Joe Engel, president of the Chattanooga Lookouts of the Southern Association, had signed Ho Sing Ping, a Chinese player. Called "George Ho" by Engel, the new player's contract had been purchased from Hartford of the Eastern League.[9] It had now become clear that the color line barred only one of humanity's three races from Organized Baseball.

A few days after the transfer of Ho Sing Ping, Leo Durocher, the manager of the Brooklyn Dodgers, heated the racial pot to the boiling point. *The Daily Worker*, a Communist newspaper which delighted in exposing racial prejudice, quoted Durocher as saying that a "grapevine understanding or subterranean rule" barred blacks from baseball.[10]

In reaction, Commissioner Landis called Durocher to his office, one of many such trips "Lippy Leo" would make during his stormy career in baseball. After their meeting, Landis issued a formal statement to the press, claiming that "Negroes have not been barred from baseball by the commissioner and never have been during the 21 years I have served as commissioner."[11] In an interview, Landis claimed further that there was "no rule, formal or informal, or any understanding, written, subterranean or sub-anything," to keep black players out.[12]

Few observers, white or black, believed Landis. Butts Brown, in a black newspaper, applauded Landis but said, "There still exists such a thing as an implied 'Gentleman's Agreement' which will keep everything at status quo."[13] Chester Washington wrote in the *Courier* that baseball was engaging in a "perennial practice of buck-passing on the issue of color."[14]

Harry Keck, sports editor of a white paper, termed Landis's statement a "big sugar-coated pill" and "malarky." "Why lie about it," Keck asked his readers in Pittsburgh, "and say white is black, or vice versa, and expect the fans to believe it just because the great Judge Landis says so?"[15]

The *Courier*, pursuing the story for its black readers, asked William E. Benswanger, president of the Pittsburgh Pirates, about signing a black player for his team. "There is no rule of any sort, written or unwritten, barring Negro players," Benswanger said in an echo of Landis. "No one has approached me on such a proposition. . . . [I]t might be a good thing for the game to add the Negro stars to the various big league teams. I certainly am not against it."[16]

Benswanger then wobbled. The national wire services quoted him on July 27, 1942, as having invited Roy Campanella and Sam Hughes of the Baltimore Elite Giants and Dave Barnhill of the New York Cubans to an August 4 tryout at Pittsburgh.[17] The invitation seemed to be confirmed by a telegram, published in the Norfolk, Virginia, *Journal and Guide*, from the sports editor of *The Daily Worker*, Nat Low, to the three players: "Have just arranged with William Benswanger, President Pittsburgh Pirates, a tryout for you with team in Pittsburgh soon. Congratulations. Won't you please get in touch with me so that we can make full arrangements."[18] Three days later, on July 30, Benswanger denied that he had made the invitation.[19]

On the same day as Benswanger's denial, Leland Stanford "Larry" MacPhail, president of the Brooklyn Dodgers, said that he had no intention of following Pittsburgh's lead:

First, there is no real demand for Negro baseball players.
Second, how many of the best players in the Negro circuit do you suppose would make the National or American Leagues? Very few.
Third, why should we raid those circuits and ruin their games?

Fourth, I have talked with some of the leading Negroes. Ask them what they think of breaking down the custom.

Concluding, MacPhail exposed the baseball establishment:

Judge Landis was not speaking for baseball when he said there is no barrier: there has been an unwritten law tantamount to an agreement between major league clubs on the subject of avoiding the racial issue.[20]

The next day, the New York *Amsterdam Star-News* quoted Alva T. Bradley, president of the Cleveland Indians, as agreeing to give tryouts to "Negro players."[21] A week earlier, Cleveland manager Lou Boudreau had told the local *Call and Post*, a black weekly, that "it was all up to Bradley." "I've played with Negroes in school competition," Boudreau explained. "I have seen many players who I believe are very good."[22]

The issue of race in baseball had three more gasps left in it before dying out in 1942. Two weeks after MacPhail's statement, the National League president, Ford Frick, responded to a question from the Pittsburgh *Courier*. "If a contract for a colored player came across my desk today," Frick stated, "I would approve it, providing it was otherwise in order. There is nothing in the rules of baseball that I know of, that would permit any other action."

"This is really a social problem, not a baseball problem," Frick claimed. "In fact, if I thought that the inclusion of Negroes in baseball would end racial discrimination in America, I would start right out today and crusade for it."[23]

About a month later, on the same weekend that Larry Doby played so well in the back-to-back doubleheaders against the Homestead Grays, the manager of the Cleveland (formerly Cincinnati) Buckeyes of the Negro National League announced that the Indians of the American League had decided to delay tryouts for three Buckeyes players until the start of the 1943 season.[24]

The next episode implicated Commissioner Landis, demonstrating conclusively that the autocratic judge's hands were not clean when he issued his pious mid-summer statements about the absence of a color barrier. Bill Veeck, the owner of the Milwaukee Brewers of the American Association, a top minor league, exposed Landis and the owners of the teams in the National League beyond all redemption. But Veeck did not tell his story until many years later.

During the 1942 season, Veeck began to negotiate to buy the Philadelphia Phillies from Gerry Nugent. After the season ended, having assembled the financial backers he needed, Veeck arranged to close the deal in Philadelphia. But on his way from Milwaukee, Veeck "decided that on my way I would stop and tell Judge Landis what I had planned to do."

But the next morning, upon his arrival at the offices of the Phillies, Veeck "suddenly discovered" that "the ball club had been sold. In fact, to the National League! And Nugent said, 'What are you going to do, sue me?' And I said, 'I don't know.' And so there went my first idea of having some black players in Organized Baseball. So I guess I am somewhat ahead of Mr. Rickey."[25] (Branch Rickey, as president of the Brooklyn Dodgers, did not sign Jackie Robinson to a contract until October 1945.)

The race issue in baseball still had one final episode in 1942. In December, during meetings of club owners from the major leagues under the gavel of Landis at his offices in Chicago, the commissioner denied a request from a committee representing the Chicago Council of the Congress of Industrial Organizations (CIO). The union committee had asked that the owners conduct a hearing on admitting black players into white baseball. Landis replied that, under baseball regulations, all subjects must be submitted to him well in advance of any scheduled meeting.[26]

Although the integration of baseball dominated the sports pages of the black press in late July and early August of 1942, Larry Doby does not recall that the subject ever came up for open discussion among his teammates on the Eagles. Nor does Leon Day, one of the veteran stars of the team.[27] It seems likely that the older players had long since learned not to raise their hopes too high. They knew how to protect themselves from hurt as black men in white America. It was a knowledge that they quietly passed along so that their young rookie would also be protected.

As the 1942 season drew to a close, Doby bid goodbye to the men who had made him feel so comfortable with the Eagles. The time had come to begin his freshman year at Long Island University (LIU), where, under legendary coach Clair Bee, the Blackbirds had become one of college basketball's most successful teams. In the season prior to Doby's freshman year, they had won 25 games and lost only two.[28] "But the main reason for going to LIU was that I was in love," Doby says. He had been dating one of Eastside High School's prettiest girls, Helyn Curvy, since he was a sophomore and she a freshman. "Being close to Paterson allowed me to come home on weekends to see her."

Before leaving for LIU, Doby took care to inquire about his chances of being drafted into military service. As a result, a friendly official on his local draft board saw to it that Doby's papers were placed on the bottom of the priority pile. Upon his arrival on campus, he found that he would be living in an all-black YMCA. True to his accustomed reaction to such treatment, he felt little conscious insult. LIU was a commuter college, without a team dormitory. Most of its players were from New York City, only a subway ride from classes and the gym. The only black players who preceded Doby there, Dolly King and Eddie Younger, both lived in the city.

Doby remembered that back in Paterson, the YMCA admitted black children only during certain hours on Saturday. Here, in Brooklyn, with its large black population, it was a facility especially for blacks. Given these circumstances, he accepted his segregated status, refusing to connect it with messages he had heard from Wendell Williams four years before. Instead, he directed his energies to basketball and to attending classes in biology, English, history, math, and physical education.

By the time Clair Bee called the first practice, the military draft had claimed five of his top players, opening the way for Doby to play as the first substitute off the bench. But in November, his own draft status abruptly changed: the man who had put his papers on the bottom of the pile in Paterson transferred to Washington, D.C. Concerned, Doby took his problem to Bee, who could offer no help, and to friends, who put him in touch with Henry B. Hucles, basketball coach at Virginia Union College in Richmond.

With players also drawn mainly from New York City, Hucles had developed Virginia Union into the LIU of black college basketball. In fact, the schools had played each other during the previous season. But they could not play at Madison Square Garden because Ned Irish, its basketball promoter, would not invite black college teams to perform there.[29]

Informed that because Virginia Union had an ROTC program he might be able to complete his freshman year, Doby told Coach Bee of his decision to transfer. "He treated me real well," Doby says. "As a matter of fact, when he knew that I might be drafted he gave me $10 for transportation home. He wished me luck, and said I could come back when the war was over to finish my education."

At Virginia Union, as it turned out, Doby was limited to practicing with the team in December and January. Rival coaches in the Colored Intercollegiate Athletic Association (CIAA) (Howard, Hampton, North Carolina A & T, Winston-Salem Teachers College, Shaw, Johnson C. Smith, North Carolina College, West Virginia State College, and Virginia State) knew that Doby had attended LIU, and Hucles therefore carefully observed eligibility requirements. In late February Doby appeared in a college game for the first time. As a substitute guard, he scored four points in a 63–57 victory over Virginia State.[30]

Doby continued to play as a substitute in Virginia Union's remaining few games, helping his team to the CIAA championship.[31]

A month after the end of basketball season, Doby received his draft call with the famous opening line from Uncle Sam: "Greetings." Soon he and many of his high school friends boarded a military train in Newark, imbued with the camaraderie so common among young men going off to war. When they got off their train in Chicago, though, naval officers directed white recruits in one direction and black recruits in another. Suddenly, without warning, the rigid military discipline compelled Doby into a confrontation with overt racism for the first time in his life. Thereafter, he could never suppress the thoughts and feelings forced upon him by the Navy that day. In fact, they would often rise to the surface throughout the rest of his life.

From Chicago, Doby and the other black men traveled to Camp Robert Smalls, the black section of the Great Lakes Naval Training Station. There, 1,000 black men per month became apprentice seamen. Of that number, 950 were assigned to mess duty, washing pots and pans, peeling potatoes, swabbing the deck, hauling away garbage. The 50 men who escaped mess duty after eight weeks of basic training qualified for advanced instruction as "technical specialists." Many of them later performed the most dangerous job in the Navy—handling ammunition. Another portion of the 50 worked on all-black construction and labor battalions.

Doby, however, got lucky. At Camp Smalls, named for a black sailor who captured a Confederate ship during the Civil War and delivered it to the Union Navy, Doby's superior officers noted his physical fitness and athletic skills. He became a physical education instructor for other black recruits.

A closer look at Camp Smalls provides a glimpse of the status of blacks in the military services during World War II. The Navy had assigned Lieutenant Commander David W. Armstrong to overall command of the black recruits at Great Lakes. His father, a Civil War general for the Confederacy, founded Hampton Institute as an industrial school for blacks. He himself was a graduate of Annapolis, a trustee of Hampton, and an ardent segregationist.[32]

Armstrong observed National Negro History Week by hanging twelve large murals depicting the few black men who had performed heroic deeds in the Navy. He established the Midwest Servicemen's Leagues for black baseball and basketball teams, and organized two military bands and dance orchestras, a glee club, a choir, and a quartet.[33] Armstrong allowed just one exception to his policy of racial separation. Since he did not organize a black football team, and since Ozzie Simmons, a black star from the University of Indiana, was a sailor at Great Lakes, Armstrong allowed Simmons to play on its otherwise white team.[34]

Armstrong had other ideas, as well. He required the black sailors to learn and recite a creed, written under his direction, dealing with the advancement of the Negro race, and required them to sing spirituals on Sunday evenings, even though some of the northern blacks had never heard them before.[35]

Doby remained under Armstrong's command from July 1943, until August 1944. He spent his mornings leading calisthenics for successive classes of recruits, and his afternoons playing basketball and baseball with men who were good enough to make the Camp Smalls teams. Sometimes they would travel to other military bases in the north central states to play other black teams. Once, the baseball team played before a large crowd in Cleveland Stadium.

Lifelong friendships proved to be the chief benefit of Doby's stay at Great Lakes. Buddy Young and Marion Motley, who became two of professional football's greatest running backs after the war, were now his buddies. Doby met Arthur "Choker" Grant, a gifted semiprofessional basketball player from Cleveland. Three years later, Arthur and Doris Grant invited him to live in their Cleveland home.

During the last five months of 1944, the Navy stationed Doby at Treasure Island in San Francisco Bay, at Ogden, Utah, and at San Diego. Meanwhile, the U.S. fleet defeated the Japanese navy in the Battle of Leyte Gulf, the greatest naval engagement of World War II. As General Douglas MacArthur prepared his forces to invade the Philippine Islands, the Navy decided it needed Doby in the Central Pacific Ocean, on a coral atoll named Ulithi.

For Admiral William "Bull" Halsey, Ulithi was his "barn," where floating drydocks, supply and repair ships, and hospital ships provided support for invasions of Japanese-held islands. Ulithi's stock of fuel for ships and airplanes supplied the largest aircraft carrier task force ever assembled, in support of the invasion of Iwo Jima in 1945.

Doby remained at Ulithi for a full year, until January 1946, five months after Japan surrendered. On the atoll's largest island, Mog-Mog, he organized various games for the visiting sailors. At night, Doby and other black seamen were often called to unload ships. The dining rooms, social functions, and recreation programs were integrated, but at night the Navy segregated blacks and whites in separate sleeping quarters.

On this tiny island, 900 miles from the bloody beaches of Iwo Jima, Doby pondered his baseball skills in conversations with Mickey Vernon, the renowned first baseman of the Washington Senators. Vernon, director of recreation, noticed that Doby could kick and throw a football farther than anybody on the island. He also saw Doby's power at bat and his defensive agility on the baseball diamond, prompting letters to his father and to Clark Griffith, the owner of the Washington Senators, reporting his observations.[36] After the war, Vernon continued their friendship with a gesture that a baseball player would appreciate most. "He sent me a gift of some bats when I started the 1946 season with the Eagles," Doby says. "It was a gift I'll never forget."

The world in 1946 was not the same world it had been when Doby graduated from high school in 1942. Then, an athlete known for his punching power, Joe Louis, threw a longer shadow than any other black athlete. But in 1946, a minor league baseball player named Jackie Robinson shared the spotlight with Louis.

NOTES

1. *Amsterdam Star-News* (New York), June 6, 1942.

2. Ibid.

3. *Tribune* (Philadelphia), June 13, 1942.

4. *Courier* (Pittsburgh), June 20, 1942.

5. *Amsterdam Star-News*, June 13, 1942.

6. *New Jersey Afro-American* (Newark), June 20, 1942.

7. Ibid.

8. Ibid., September 12, 1942.

9. *Courier*, July 18, 1942.

10. *The Daily Worker*, cited in *New Jersey Herald News* (Newark), July 25, 1942.

11. Ibid.

12. *The Sporting News* (St. Louis), March 3, 1948.

13. Butts Brown, "In the Groove," *New Jersey Herald News*, July 25, 1942.

14. Chester Washington, "Sez Ches," *Courier*, July 25, 1942.

15. Harry Keck, cited in the *Courier*, July 25, 1942.

16. William E. Benswanger, cited in the *Courier*, July 25, 1942.

17. *Evening News* (Newark), July 27, 1942.

18. *Journal and Guide* (Norfolk), July 15, 1942.

19. *Evening News*, July 30, 1942.

20. Ibid.

21. *Amsterdam Star-News*, August 1, 1942.

22. Lou Boudreau, *Call and Post* (Cleveland), cited in *Amsterdam Star-News*, August 1, 1942.

23. Ford Frick, cited in the *Courier*, August 8, 1942.

24. Parnell Woods, *New Jersey Afro-American*, September 12, 1942.

25. Personal interview with Bill Veeck, April 23–24, 1980.

26. *Journal and Guide*, December 12, 1942.

27. Personal interview with Leon Day, June 23, 1980.

28. *New York Times*, December 10, 1942.

29. *Amsterdam Star-News*, March 27, 1943.

30. *Journal and Guide*, February 27, 1943.

31. *Journal and Guide*, March 20, 1943.

32. Dennis Nelson, *The Integration of the Negro into the U.S. Navy* (New York: Farrar, Straus and Young, 1951), p. 31.

33. Ibid., pp. 32–35.

34. Personal interview with Arthur Grant, January 9, 1981.

35. Nelson, *The Integration of the Negro*, pp. 32–34.

36. Telephone interview with Mickey Vernon, April 25, 1981.

5

From Mog-Mog to Newark

In a sense, Larry Doby's ascent to national fame began while he sat under a tropical sky on the coral speck named Mog-Mog in 1945, launched by a news report that changed the course of American social history. He remembers it well.

"It came on the radio one night in October while we were sitting there, that Mr. [Branch] Rickey had signed Jackie [Robinson] to a contract with Montreal. I didn't know much about Montreal at that time, but I knew it was in the International League because the Eagles played in the same park the Newark Bears [the International League farm team of the Yankees] played in.

"Then I felt I had a chance to play major league baseball. Everybody had said to me that I could. As a matter of fact, Mickey Vernon and Billy Goodman told me that on Ulithi. [Goodman later batted .300 in 16 seasons in major league baseball, including a league-leading .354 for the Boston Red Sox in 1950.] My main thing was to become a teacher and coach somewhere in New Jersey, but when I heard about Jackie, I decided to concentrate on baseball. I forgot about going back to college."

With his plans changed, Doby welcomed his honorable discharge from the Navy in January 1946. After a visit with his mother, with Helyn Curvy (his future wife), and with other old friends in Paterson, he gladly accepted Monte Irvin's invitation to join him and pitcher Barney Brown for two months of winter baseball with the San Juan Senators in Puerto Rico. The $500 per month salary wouldn't be hard to take, either, after two and one-half years on Navy pay.

The two months in Puerto Rico further convinced Doby to pursue a career in baseball. All the skills which he displayed with the Newark Eagles as a rookie in the summer of 1942 returned. By the time he and Irvin joined the Eagles at their spring training camp in Jacksonville, Florida, in early April, both were ready to play ball, Doby as the second baseman and Irvin as the shortstop.

Against their mounting sense of excitement, Doby, Irvin, and the other stars of the Eagles steeled themselves for probable disappointment. Robinson's presence in Montreal's training camp had released intense feelings among all black Americans, yet their own feelings remained guarded. Doby recalls their mood: "One of the things that was disappointing and disheartening to a lot of the black players at the time was that Jack was not the best player. The best was Josh Gibson. I think that's one of the reasons Josh died so early—he was heartbroken.

"There were many others better than Jackie—Satchel Paige, Buck Leonard, Willard Brown, Biz Mackey, Willie Wells, Ray Dandridge, Leon Day, Mule Suttles, Dick Seay, Ed Stone, Piper Davis, and Monte."

The players in the eastern Negro National League and midwestern Negro American League had reason to talk about the future in subdued tones. They knew that the commissioner of baseball, Judge Landis, implacably opposed integration right up until his death in late 1944. They also knew that the new commissioner, Albert B. "Happy" Chandler, had been Governor and U.S. Senator from the Jim Crow state of Kentucky.

The black players did not know that behind-the-scenes pressure had been brought to bear on Chandler shortly after he took office early in 1945. In a letter dated April 27, 1945, marked "Personal and Confidential," Larry MacPhail, now president of the influential New York Yankees, addressed the problem of segregation: "Rickey and myself think we have a possible solution along the lines of cooperation in the establishment and operation of strong Negro leagues."[1]

Another kind of pressure arrived on Chandler's desk at his home in Versailles, Kentucky, in a letter dated May 5, 1945, from J. G. Taylor Spink, general manager of *The Sporting News*, baseball's "bible." Addressing the commissioner as "My dear Happy," Spink arrogantly told Chandler that he was enclosing a copy of an editorial on the subject of integration "which took care of the situation."[2] The editorial, dated August 6, 1942, stated that both black and white teams "prefer to draw their talent from their own ranks" and did not want "to run the risk of damaging their own game." It went on to cite the "tragic possibilities" of a beanball or spiking incident, the role of "agitators, ever ready to seize an issue that will redound to their profit or self aggrandizement," and the decline of quality and gate receipts in black baseball if the best players left black baseball to play in the American and National Leagues.

Spink's editorial reached this patronizing conclusion:

Of course, there are some colored people who take a different view, and they are entitled to their opinions, but in doing so they are not looking at the question from the broader point of view, or for the ultimate good of either the race or the individuals in it. They ought to concede their own people are not protected and that nothing is served by allowing agitators to make an issue of a question on which both sides would prefer to be let alone.[3]

Spink was right on at least one count: there were some "colored people" who took a "different view." On the same date as Spink's letter to Chandler, Joe Bostic, in his "Scoreboard" column in Harlem's *People's Voice*, called for "positive action" from baseball executives.[4]

By October 1945, Chandler had made his decision. He did not oppose Branch Rickey's signing Robinson to a contract to play for the Montreal Royals in the International League in 1946. Apparently Chandler had lined up support, or at least silence, within Organized Baseball. His private papers contain just one letter of opposition, from Thomas H. Richardson, then president of the minor Eastern League.[5]

Before Larry Doby and his Newark teammates began to assemble for spring training in March 1946, they had new reasons for doubt about following Robinson. In late January, Commissioner Chandler told reporters in Texas that he had been asked by J. B. Martin, president of the Negro American League, and Tom Wilson, president of the Negro National League, for help in strengthening their leagues. The two presidents also asked Chandler, in the presence of Will Harridge, president of the American League, and Ford Frick, to become commissioner of "colored baseball."

"I told them to get their house in order," Chandler told the Texas press, and then come to him with a petition for recognition. He added, "The colored leagues favor keeping their own boys, and with their leagues on a sound basis, with a contract like the one we use, they expect those boys to want to stay in their own class."[6]

Martin, from his offices in Chicago, immediately charged that his statement to Chandler was "misinterpreted." Martin said that he and Wilson were indeed anxious to strengthen the structure of their leagues, "but we certainly do not desire to hamper our boys who have a chance to advance in organized baseball."[7]

A week later, the hopes of all black players took a second leap when the president of the Montreal Royals announced the signing of Johnny Wright, a 27-year-old pitcher for the Homestead Grays.[8] Before March ended, they saw yet another breach in the color line, in another sport—the Los Angeles Rams had signed Kenny Washington, who is usually regarded as the first black to appear in the modern National Football League.[9]

In the midst of such ferment, 19 members of the Eagles boarded their private bus in Newark on April 1 for the trip to spring training in Jacksonville. Don Newcombe, a 19-year-old pitcher who had had a fine rookie season in 1945 with the Eagles, was mysteriously absent,[10] but the Eagles found out why during their journey south: Branch Rickey had added

Newcombe and Roy Campanella, catcher for the Baltimore Elite Giants, to his growing collection of black players, now numbering four.

Immediately, the co-owner of the Eagles, Effa Manley, reacted. After first expressing her elation that one of her players had signed with the Dodgers, she protested Rickey's failure to pay her for Newcombe. "What will become of colored baseball leagues if players are picked out by major league owners without consulting the team management?" she asked.[11]

After three weeks under the Florida sun, the Eagles barnstormed north to Newark. For their season's opening game against the visiting Philadelphia Stars, Mayor Vincent J. Murphy declared Sunday, May 5, as "Newark Eagles Day" at Ruppert Stadium.[12] It was a day that Larry Doby, and a young boy sitting in the stands with his father, would long remember. Doby broke a scoreless tie in the sixth inning when he scored from first base on an infield out.[13] The young boy in the stands, Leroi Jones, later to become one of America's leading poets and playwrights as Leroi Jones and Amiri Baraka, watched the Eagles win that day. In his *Autobiography*, Jones wrote,

the specialest feeling was when my father took me down to Ruppert Stadium some Sundays to see the Newark Eagles, the black pro team. Very little in my life was as heightened (in anticipation and reward) for me as that. What was that? Some black men playing baseball? No, but beyond that, so deep in fact it carried and carries memories and even a *politics* with it that still makes me shudder.

The Eagles, Jones said,

would have your heart out there on the field. . . . And we were intimate with them in a way and they were extensions of all of us, there, in a way that the Yankees and Dodgers and what not could never be!

We knew that they *were* us—raised up to another, higher degree. . . .

Reflecting on the significance of the Eagles to Newark's black community, Jones observed that "we all communicated with each other and possessed ourselves at a more human level than was usually possible out in cold whitey land."

Away from Ruppert Stadium, the Eagles gathered at the Grand Hotel where, Jones wrote,

You could see Doby and Lennie Pearson and Pat Patterson or somebody there and I'd be wearin my eyes and ears out drinking a Coca-Cola, checking everything out. . . .

In the laughter and noise and colors and easy hot dogs there was something of us celebrating ourselves. . . . We was cheering for Mule Suttles or seeing Larry

Doby make a double play. We was *not* clowns and the Newark Eagles laid that out clear for anyone to see![14]

Through May and June the Eagles shared space on the sports pages of the black press with Jackie Robinson, and with Joe Louis, the most prominent black man in America in 1946. The long-awaited rematch between Louis and his challenger, Billy Conn, overshadowed all other sports stories in the spring and early summer. Meanwhile, the Eagles slumped in late May, then won nine straight games and 14 out of 15 to win the first half championship of the Negro National League by the Fourth of July.[15]

Doby batted .339 over the first half. Above him among the batting leaders were three men who would go on to the Hall of Fame in Cooperstown: Monte Irvin led with .409, followed by James "Cool Papa" Bell and Josh Gibson of the Grays at .405 and .357.[16]

The "experiment" with Robinson at Montreal continued without undue notice until July. In a game there, Robinson accused Eddie Robinson of the Baltimore Orioles, then a minor league team, of kicking him in the back on a force play at second base. "If I did, it was an accident," Eddie explained.[17]

Sometime in the summer of 1946, Doby and Helyn Curvy decided to marry. While Doby's ancestry can be traced back to slavery in South Carolina, Helyn's background is more complex, and in some ways more interesting. The Curvys moved to Paterson from Hillburn, New York, where they had been part of the secluded Ramapo Mountains community known as the "Jackson's Whites."[18] These isolated people, who could see the distant skyline of New York City from their mountain enclaves, were a mixture of Native Americans ("Indians"), blacks who had escaped from slavery, free blacks, white English women who had been brought to North America by a Captain Jackson to provide sex to British troops during the Revolutionary War, mercenary German soldiers who had deserted their employment by the British, and assorted renegades who were trying, for whatever reasons, to escape conventional society.

The Curvys had moved from the rural mountains to industrial Paterson seeking work, and soon established themselves as one of the city's most cohesive and successful black families. At the time of her marriage, Helyn had already been a racial pioneer. She was the first black person to be employed by the New Jersey Bell Telephone Company in Paterson, and possibly anywhere else in the Bell System.[19]

Larry and Helyn set the date for August 10 at 1 P.M. in the Baptist church at the corner of Harrison and Graham Avenues in Paterson. After a small reception, they traveled to Trenton, New Jersey, where the Eagles had a night game against the Baltimore Elite Giants. A honeymoon would have to wait.

The highlight of the summer for Negro baseball came a few days after the wedding, when the best players from the Negro National and American Leagues met in a pair of All-Star games. The Nationals, with an awesome lineup that included Buck Leonard and Josh Gibson from the Grays and Doby, Irvin, and Day from the Eagles, won both games.

In the first game, played before 45,474 fans at Comiskey Park in Chicago, Doby connected for one hit in three official at bats, made three putouts and three assists in a 4–1 game. Five days later, before 16,268 fans at Griffith Stadium in Washington, D.C., Doby had four hits in four at bats in a 6–3 triumph. He scored twice, made an error, and turned in the game's best defensive play.[20]

As the regular season moved on toward Labor Day, Doby and the Eagles mounted a 12-game winning streak to add the second half championship to their first half title, thus avoiding a playoff series.[21] Doby, whose average had fallen as low as .323,[22] raised it to .348 at season's end. Irvin remained near the .400 level throughout and closed with a .395 average.[23] In comparison, Jackie Robinson, in a league about equal to the Negro leagues in quality of play, won the batting championship in the International League with an average of .349.[24]

To climax the 1946 season, the Eagles faced the Kansas City Monarchs in the Negro World Series. It opened at New York's historic Polo Grounds, home of the National League Giants, before 19,423 fans on September 17, and ended eleven days later in Newark when the Eagles won for the fourth time in a seven-game series. In between, the teams played the second game at Ruppert Stadium in Newark; the third and fourth at Blues Stadium in Kansas City, home of the Monarchs; the fifth at Comiskey Park in Chicago; and the sixth at Newark.

The series in general, and Game Two in particular, revealed the status of black sport in American history: it had an itinerant quality, deep roots, and a focus on baseball and boxing. The schedule showed how black teams had to travel far and wide to attract gate receipts. Before Game Two, Joe Louis, at the peak of his fame after knocking out Billy Conn and Tami Mauriello that summer, threw out a silver ball in a ceremony honoring 90-year-old Benjamin F. Holmes of Orange, New Jersey. The ball dated back to 1888, when Mr. Holmes and the Cuban Giants of Trenton, New Jersey, won the first "colored world championship."[25]

For the seven-game series, Doby batted .272. He connected for three singles, a double, a triple, and a home run; drove in five runs; scored six times; and stole three bases. Irvin led the offense with a .462 average on 12 hits, including three home runs, and drove in eight runs.[26] The pair also excelled on either side of second base. In fact, Doby ended Kansas City's championship hopes in the ninth inning of the seventh game when he took a throw from the outfield and tagged out a runner at second base for the second out, and caught a pop fly for the final out of the series.[27]

At the conclusion of the Negro World Series, attention turned to Jackie Robinson and the Montreal Royals in their Little World Series against the Louisville Colonels, and of course to the World Series between the St. Louis Cardinals and the Boston Red Sox. But black baseball had staged its own show, its last, as it turned out, before the integration of major league baseball.

After the Negro World Series, Doby didn't get to drive his first new car, a blue Ford convertible, for very long. Opportunity called in the form of a contract to play winter baseball again for the San Juan Senators in the Puerto Rican League. By this time, though, his traveling companion was not Monte Irvin, as it had been after he got out of the Navy, but Helyn. The trip was their honeymoon, delayed by baseball since their marriage in August.

As Doby prepared to depart for Puerto Rico, the integration of baseball proceeded in fits and starts, as it always had. The owners of the Eagles, New York Cubans, and New York Black Yankees met with the attorneys for the National League to explore a working relationship between the Negro National League and the white National League. Their meeting came about when prior efforts by Branch Rickey to organize a United States League composed of black players, operating in cooperation with Organized Baseball, failed for lack of players and ball parks. But this meeting failed, too, over the difficult obstacle of territorial rights.[28]

Thus, at least two attempts to incorporate black baseball into "separate but almost equal" status with the white minor leagues collapsed.

Before heading for Puerto Rico, Doby, Irvin, and Len Pearson, bulwarks of the Eagles, joined the Jackie Robinson All-Stars for a couple of games against a major league team composed mainly of players from the Cincinnati Reds and Pittsburgh Pirates. In honor of Pirate great Honus Wagner, they were called the "Honus Wagner National League All Stars."

The black players had more than postseason money on their minds. They also wanted to prove themselves at least equal to major league players. But it would not be a clear-cut comparison, because Robinson hired left fielder Marv Rackley and shortshop Al Campanis from his Montreal Royals team, and pitcher Mike Nozinski, who had played with Roy Campanella and Don Newcombe all summer at Nashua, New Hampshire. Rackley, Campanis, and Nozinski were white.

Since these were exhibition games, few were reported in detail in the press. Irvin and Doby played in at least two games. In the first, at Forbes Field in Pittsburgh, home of the Pirates, the Robinsons beat the Wagners, 6–4, with the help of a two-run triple by Doby. In the second, the Robinsons whipped the Wagners again, 10–5, at Comiskey Park in Chicago. In the absence of a box score, it could be learned from a report of the game that Doby drove in one run with a sacrifice fly and collaborated with Robinson on a bases-filled double play.[29]

The results of these two games would not have surprised author John Holway. He found that, in games between black and white professional teams between 1920 and 1939, the black teams won 186 games and lost only 93.[30]

As 1946 ended, the *New Jersey Afro-American* published the results of a poll of black sportswriters. Asked to name the "No. 1 athlete of 1946," they awarded Jackie Robinson 25 points and Joe Louis 19.[31] It was a startling result. Louis had been America's most prominent black person for more than 10 years. His first round knockout of Max Schmeling in 1938 had become one of the most political events of the decade of the 1930's. His rematch against Billy Conn in that very same year of 1946 had been the subject of conversations in bars and barracks through all the years of World War II. But Robinson, the baseball player, had nudged Louis, the boxer, aside.

Shortly after Larry and Helyn Doby celebrated New Year's Day, 1947, in Puerto Rico, the Negro National League began to organize for the coming season. By appointing a new president, Episcopal minister Dr. John W. Johnson, and by giving him independent powers, the league's owners demonstrated new determination. Either they would strengthen the league against piracy by the likes of Branch Rickey, or they would so organize as to be ready to establish a formal working relationship with white baseball.[32]

Doby continued to perform for the San Juan Senators when the news came in late February that the Dodgers had called Robinson, Campanella, Newcombe, and pitcher Roy Partlow to their training camp in Havana, Cuba. Meanwhile, he kept up his batting pace on the diamonds of Puerto Rico, finishing among the top hitters with an average of .358, and second in home runs with 14.[33]

By April 1, Larry and Helyn returned to Paterson for a brief visit before his departure for spring training in Florida with the Eagles. The players had a happy reunion in Newark as they boarded their deluxe new bus for the trip to Jacksonville. As they posed for a departing photograph below the words NEGRO WORLD CHAMPIONS, painted in light blue letters the length of the white bus, rumors flew that Doby and Irvin had signed contracts with the Brooklyn Dodgers.[34] They were, of course, not true.

When the Eagles returned from Jacksonville to Newark to open their 1947 season in early May, three days of heavy rain forced the cancellation of gala opening day festivities.[35] Instead, they opened against the weak Black Yankees at Hartford, Connecticut. Led by Doby, the Eagles showed their intentions to repeat as champions. He slugged three home runs, and Irvin and Pearson added two each, in a 24–0 runaway.[36]

Two months later, as the first half of the Negro National League season ended on July 4, the Eagles had in fact repeated their performances of

1946. Their 27–15 record, a .642 percentage, enabled them to edge the New York Cubans at .625 and the Baltimore Elite Giants at .534 for the first half championship. The Homestead Grays, playing without the deceased Josh Gibson, finished just under .500, followed in the standings by the Philadelphia Stars and the Black Yankees.[37]

It was a triumphant first half for all the Eagles, and especially Doby. His 14 home runs and .458 batting average were the best statistics in the league. He also had 16 doubles, 36 runs scored, and 35 runs batted in, all in just 42 games.[38]

Doby now looks back on his years with the Eagles as some of the happiest of his life. He does not look upon the men who played Negro baseball as "pathetic figures of history." "We were playing a game we loved. We had good times on our bus, fans in every town. When you come down to it, all the major leagues offered was more money, women, bars, more opportunities."

NOTES

1. Leland Stanford MacPhail to Albert B. Chandler, April 27, 1945. Chandler Papers, University of Kentucky.

2. J. G. Taylor Spink to Albert B. Chandler, May 5, 1945. Chandler Papers.

3. "No Good from Raising Race Issue," Editorial, *The Sporting News*, August 6, 1942.

4. Joe Bostic, "The Scoreboard," *People's Voice* (New York), May 5, 1945.

5. Thomas H. Richardson to Albert B. Chandler, October 24, 1945. Chandler Papers.

6. *New Jersey Afro-American*, January 26, 1946.

7. Ibid.

8. Ibid., February 2, 1946.

9. Ibid., March 20, 1946.

10. *Evening News*, April 2, 1946.

11. *New Jersey Afro-American*, April 20, 1946.

12. *Evening News*, May 3, 1946.

13. *Evening News*, May 6, 1946.

14. Amiri Baraka, *Autobiography* (New York: Freundlich Books, 1984), pp. 33–36.

15. *New Jersey Afro-American* and the *Evening News*, May 6 through July 6, 1946.

16. *New Jersey Afro-American*, July 20, 1946.

17. Ibid., July 6, 1946.

18. Personal interview with Helyn C. Doby, June 12, 1980.

19. Helyn C. Doby, loc. cit.

20. *New Jersey Afro-American*, August 24, 1946.

21. Ibid., September 7, 1946.

22. Ibid.

23. *Amsterdam News*, September 14, 1946.

24. *New Jersey Afro-American*, September 14, 1946.

25. *Evening News*, September 20, 1946; *Star-Ledger* (Newark), September 20, 1946.

26. The author is indebted to Merl F. Kleinknecht of Galion, Ohio, for these statistics.

27. *Evening News*, September 28, 1946; *Courier*, October 5, 1946.

28. Dan Burley, "Confidentially Yours," *Amsterdam News*, October 5, 1946.

29. *Defender* (Chicago), October 12 and 19, 1946; *Courier*, October 12, 1946; *New Jersey Afro-American*, October 19, 1946.

30. John Holway, *Voices from the Great Black Baseball Leagues* (New York: Dodd Mead, 1975), pp. 7, 10.

31. *New Jersey Afro-American*, December 28, 1946.

32. Ibid., January 11, 1947.

33. Ibid., February 22, 1947.

34. Ibid., April 5, 1947.

35. Ibid., May 10, 1947.

36. Ibid.

37. Ibid., July 12, 1947.

38. *The Sporting News*, July 9, 1947.

6

Pioneer

In January or February of 1946, Bill Veeck hired one Louis Jones "to prepare the black segment of Cleveland for the arrival of a black ball player, unnamed."[1]

Veeck had long intended to integrate baseball. The idea had been planted in his mind by his father, William Veeck, Sr., when his father ran the Chicago Cubs. It germinated in the winter of 1941–42, when Veeck told Abe Saperstein, famed as the promoter of the Harlem Globetrotters, to prepare a list of promising black baseball players. And it blossomed briefly late in the 1942 season, when Veeck's plan to buy and integrate the Philadelphia Phillies fell victim to Commissioner Landis.

Now, in 1947, Veeck sat as president of the ball club on the shores of Lake Erie. First, he hired Jones, a "self-determined PR guy," who made his living as a public relations man for the American Federation of Labor. Later in his life, Jones became an agent in show business. He also had been the first husband of Lena Horne.

To hire Jones "to prepare the black segment of Cleveland," Veeck admitted, "was presumptuous on my part, but I didn't have any idea of what would happen, since this was what looked like a comparatively major step. I would have done the same in Philadelphia."

For Phase Two of his plan, Veeck called upon "Reindeer Bill" Killefer to "casually scout" for black talent. Veeck had known Killefer most of his life, going back to Veeck's boyhood with his father and the Cubs, when Killefer was the team's catcher and manager. Later, Killefer worked for Veeck, Jr., as the manager of the minor league Milwaukee Brewers. Veeck knew that Killefer could do his scouting "casually" because Veeck knew that games in the black leagues attracted white fans.

Working with an updated version of the list Saperstein had prepared for him in 1942, Veeck instructed Killefer not to identify an "aging star, but one in whom there is some future." As the 1947 season began, Veeck watched intently as Jackie Robinson made his debut in the National League with the Brooklyn Dodgers, and quickly narrowed his list. Although he had not yet consulted with the player-manager of the Indians, Lou Boudreau, he did talk with sportswriter Wendell Smith of the black weekly newspaper, the Pittsburgh *Courier*.

According to Veeck, Smith, more than anyone else, "influenced Rickey to take Jack Robinson, for which he's never completely gotten credit. I had known Wendell since '42. So Wendell and Abe and I met a couple of times and we arrived at Larry Doby as the best young player in the [Negro] league."

During this phase of Veeck's plan, personality and character did not figure in the judgments they made. Then Smith "checked" on Doby the person, Veeck recalled. "We had the transcript of his grades and we knew he had been to college for one semester. We knew what there was to know about him second or third hand. This played a part. This was going to be a rather ticklish situation."

Veeck, one of the most perceptive of men, offered no comment that his personality and character checks imposed a double standard on Doby. He thought that they were fully justified.

With their search now focused on Doby, Killefer and Bill Norman, a minor league manager at Wilkes-Barre, Pennsylvania, who had had a two-year stint as a player with the Chicago White Sox in the early 1930's, followed the Eagles to validate their impressions.

By late June 1947, Cleveland Jackson told his black readers in the Cleveland *Call and Post* that he had "discovered" that the Indians were scouting Doby, at that time the leading hitter for power and average in black baseball. Jackson confronted Veeck, who confirmed the discovery. Jackson then gave his readers a restrained report, perhaps the result of Veeck's continuing strategy of requesting restraint, in the June 28 edition of his paper. "The news break coming directly from colorful Bill Veeck, Cleveland Indians president, revealed that the veteran baseball scout, Bill Killefer, had scouted Larry Doby in Brooklyn and had wired in a very good report on the sepia keystone star."[2]

On the following Monday, June 30, Louis Jones, who had been dispatched to make further character checks on Doby, filed a positive report: Doby did not smoke, drink, or swear. He did not even drink coffee!

On Tuesday, July 1, Veeck decided to act. He telephoned Effa and Abe Manley, owners of the Eagles, and offered Mrs. Manley $10,000 for Doby, with $5,000 more to be paid "if we keep him." Mrs. Manley agreed to the transaction, and then made Veeck a stunning offer of her own. She urged Veeck to buy Monte Irvin, her other great star, "for a $1,000 look, and then pay me what you think he's worth," as Veeck recalled it.

By making the offer, Effa Manley demonstrated beyond any doubt that not all the owners of the teams in the Negro Leagues would stand in the way of opportunity for their players, as some white major league officials had asserted. Her offer of Irvin to Veeck probably has few parallels in the annals of commercial sport.

But Veeck refused the offer, and lost a player whose plaque now hangs in the Hall of Fame at Cooperstown. "I said, and this shows how bright I am—," Veeck remembered, " 'Effa, I think I'm going to have enough trouble bringing in one black. I'm afraid two may be not twice as complicated, but would become, instead of arithmetical, geometric. So I'm stumped.' I didn't think at the time, nor do I think in retrospect—I felt that this was the best way to handle it, individually to start with."

Following their telephone conversation, Veeck confirmed his offer to the Manleys with a telegram. They had agreed that before leaving the Eagles, Doby would complete the first half of the Negro National League schedule in the doubleheader slated for July Fourth. Then he would travel quietly to Cleveland, to be introduced there when the Indians began a home stand after the three-day break for the major league All-Star game.

But on Tuesday evening, July 2, one of the wire services informed its client editors of a rumor that the Indians were going to sign a black player, still unnamed. One editor, Bob Whiting at the *Morning Call* in Paterson, read the rumor and suspected that the unnamed player was the hometown hero, Doby. Whiting immediately got on the telephone, sensing that he had the story of his life.

Effa Manley refused to confirm or deny the rumor. "I have nothing to say at this time," she told Whiting. "If Cleveland has signed a Negro second baseman, then it will make the announcement. That is not for me to do." Given that response, Whiting's suspicions increased.

Helyn Doby had little to add but hope when Whiting called her. "Larry has been watched by several major league clubs, and one of them may have purchased his contract," she said. "I'll have to wait until he gets home to find out."

Doby himself could not be reached for comment. That night, the Eagles opposed the Philadelphia Stars at Wilmington, Delaware, in a league game. Afterwards, sportswriters there asked if he had reached agreement with Cleveland. "I don't know," he replied. "It could be. I will have to wait until I return to Newark to find out. I am under contract to the Newark Eagles and I cannot sign myself. Cleveland would have to purchase my contract from Mrs. Manley."[3]

Doby could not deny the rumor. As he told Whiting the next day, "The first inkling I had that Cleveland even knew I was playing baseball came about two weeks ago. One day while Cleveland was in New York I was introduced to Louis Jones of the Cleveland Public Relations Department.

He took me to the ball game, and to dinner afterwards. He told me then that Cleveland had scouted me for two months, and that the reports had been favorable.

"When he left me he said, 'You will probably be in our organization in two or three weeks,' but I thought he was kidding."[4] The veteran players on the Eagles had apparently taught him well: a black man should not get his hopes up.

On the basis of the comments from Effa Manley, and the wire service reports of Doby's reply to the reporters in Wilmington, Whiting, after midnight, completed the call he had placed to the Indians. Without identifying his source, he then wrote his scoop for page one of Wednesday's *Morning Call*:

Larry Doby, brilliant former Eastside High School all-around athlete, today became the first Negro player in the history of the American League. The Cleveland Indians early this morning confirmed the report that reached The Call earlier in the evening that they had signed the star second baseman of the Newark Eagles of the Negro National League.[5]

While Whiting wrote and the *Call* went to press, Doby slept in the Eagles' bus during the long ride back to Newark from Wilmington. He then drove his Ford convertible home to Paterson, arriving at 5:30 A.M., and went to bed. At 7, Mrs. Manley telephoned to inform her star that she had sold his contract to Veeck.[6]

After the *Call* hit the streets that July 3, reporters descended on the Doby apartment on Hamilton Avenue. Later in the morning, the Indians themselves announced that they had signed Doby. At 1:30 in the afternoon, still not having had breakfast, Doby received a call from Louis Jones in Cleveland further informing him that the Indians had, indeed, made him the first black man on the roster of an American League team.[7]

The announcement by the Indians that morning came just a few hours after Veeck had tried to inform Lou Boudreau, his player-manager. But Boudreau, up early, had already heard a radio report out of Paterson, based on Whiting's exclusive story.[8] Boudreau, Veeck said, reacted "extremely well." Veeck, Boudreau says, advised him that Doby could play first and second base, but at the time Boudreau told reporters that Doby could play second base and shortstop. Boudreau also says that Veeck, who claimed that he never interfered with his manager's decisions, also told him "to have Doby play, to break in."[9]

By the time the sports reporters reached Boudreau in the Del Prado Hotel in Chicago, the manager had a written statement in hand:

The acquisition of Larry Doby, an infielder formerly with the Newark Eagles team, is a routine baseball purchase in my mind.

Creed, race or color are not factors in baseball success, whether it be in the major or minor leagues. Ability and character are the only factors.

Doby will be given every chance, as will any other deserving recruit, to prove that he has the ability to make good with us.

The reports we have received on his ability are outstanding. I hope that he can succeed with us as he has with other teams.[10]

The statement, with an opening paragraph that is more political than true, reads as if Boudreau may have had some help from Marshall Samuels, the team's publicity director. Nevertheless, Boudreau pulled a Veeck chestnut out of the fire by placing his signature on the typewritten statement. He made it seem that the Cleveland president and field manager were a coordinated team. Veeck the tactician could not have succeeded without Boudreau's cooperation on that hectic morning in Chicago, yet Boudreau has never been accorded, nor has he sought, recognition for this and many later contributions to the integration of the American League.

In the afternoon phone call from Jones, Doby learned that he would become the property of the Indians after the July Fourth doubleheader the next afternoon at Ruppert Stadium in Newark. He also learned that Jones would come to Newark to meet him, and then accompany him back to Cleveland.

"We have already clinched the first half championship," he told Whiting, "and Mrs. Manley may permit me to leave with Mr. Jones shortly after I meet him in the morning. I'd like to finish out the first half schedule, but I'm so excited about the prospect of playing with Cleveland maybe I'd be better to skip these games. It's all up to Mrs. Manley, however."[11]

On July Fourth, as Jones and Mrs. Manley agreed on the final details of the purchase, Doby finally came to believe the news. He played only in the first game that afternoon, belting a home run in his farewell at bat. Before the second game, in a ceremony at home plate, his teammates presented him with a traveling bag and a shaving kit, and the Old Timers Athletic Association of Paterson gave him $50. Doby expressed his thanks, hurried to the dressing room to shower and change, and, accompanied by Jones, rushed to catch The Admiral out of Newark's Pennsylvania Station for the overnight train trip to the midwest.[12]

Doby's departure from Newark excited black Americans, even as it sounded the death knell for black baseball. In the 11 weeks that Jackie Robinson had been playing for Brooklyn, his presence there seemed experimental. But with the signing of Doby in the other league, the integration of white baseball had suddenly become as certain as the consequent death of the black leagues. Amiri Baraka, in his *Autobiography*, memorialized them:

The Negro league's like a light somewhere. Back over your shoulder. As you go away. A warmth still, connected to laughter and self-love. The collective black aura that can only be duplicated with black conversation or *music*.[13]

At some point on July 3 or 4, Veeck decided to change Doby's desti-
nation from Cleveland to Chicago, where the Indians were playing the
White Sox. "Once the story was in the papers," he explained, "I didn't
want a period of speculation. I figured this would have made Larry more
distraught, put increased pressure on him. We had a whole series at Chicago, and I felt it would be an interminable and very difficult time for
him."

Veeck also figured that a delay might allow opposition to Doby by
Cleveland players to "solidify," and that some would "react badly, as [some
players did]. To give them enough time to do some proselytizing would
be a grave mistake. So I figured, 'We'll do it now.' " Veeck, often accused
by his critics of being a bit reckless in his innovations, certainly proved
himself to be a master tactician once his strategy to introduce Doby in
Cleveland, after the All-Star game, failed.

As Doby listened to his new mentor, Jones, on the overnight train to
Chicago, other morning newspapers caught up with Bob Whiting's scoop
of July 3 in their Fourth of July editions. The *New York Times* carried a
United Press story which quoted Veeck as saying:

Robinson has proved to be a real big leaguer. So I wanted to get the best of the
available Negro boys while the grabbing was good. Why wait? Within ten years
Negro players will be in regular service with big league teams, for there are many
colored players with sufficient capabilities to make the majors. [No] man should
be barred from the majors on account of his color. The entrance of Negroes into
the majors is not only inevitable—it is here.[14]

Larry MacPhail, president of the Yankees, refused to comment on Doby's signing. Branch Rickey, on the other hand, said, "If Doby is a good
player, and I understand that he is, the Cleveland club is showing signs
that it wants to win." In Washington, Clark Griffith, owner of the Senators, told the United Press that "the gate has always been open to the
Negro player. If anybody wants to sign a Negro player, that's fine and
dandy. I wish the player and the club good luck. If he turns out to be a
credit to the game, more power to him."[15]

The *New York Times* also carried an Associated Press story quoting Doby
as saying that he was not sure whether he was "more surprised than excited, or more excited than surprised."[16]

At the other political extreme from the *New York Times*, *The Daily
Worker*, the organ of the Communist Party in the United States, congrat-
ulated everybody—the city of Cleveland, Veeck, "who lost a foot fighting
for democracy on Bouganville and seems to know what he was fighting
for," Rickey, Communist sportswriters who had campaigned for the integration of baseball, and Doby himself.[17]

In Cleveland, the morning *Plain Dealer* told its readers in an optimistic editorial that Boudreau's citation of "ability and character" as the only factors to be used in judging Doby "expressed the sentiments of Cleveland fans," who would be "pulling for Larry Doby to make good."[18] At the conclusion of a "man in the street" story, the consensus, said the *Plain Dealer*, was that Doby would "meet with the approval of Tribal fans— provided he maintains his current high batting average."[19] The *Plain Dealer* seems not to have known that when Doby left Newark he was hitting .458.

The next morning, July 5, Louis Jones and Doby arrived in Chicago on The Admiral at 10:45. They first picked up Veeck at the Congress Hotel in their cab, then headed for a press conference in the Bard's Room at Comiskey Park. In the back seat of the cab, Veeck introduced himself to the black man he had selected, out of approximately four million black men in America, to join Robinson as a racial pioneer. Veeck and Doby at once formed a relationship that would endure, that Doby characterized as "father-son," that Veeck cherished until the time of his death in 1986 as one of the most important of his life.

Veeck had already spoken to Boudreau about Doby's arrival. "I wanted to acquaint the players with some ground rules that I had pointed out: I expected the players to react favorably, and not make it any more difficult. I did know that a couple of them were going to be upset. I knew my athletes pretty well."

When rumors about Doby reached the Indians players, some of them began to make threatening statements. Inevitably, such talk got back to Veeck, who called a rare meeting in the clubhouse in Comiskey Park the previous day, July Fourth, with a group comprised mainly of players from the southern states. Veeck told them, "I understand that some of you players said that 'if a nigger joins the club' you're leaving. Well, you can leave right now because this guy [Doby] is going to be a bigger star than any guy in this room."

One player continued to object, causing Veeck to call him to a private meeting. In retrospect, Veeck thought, "I had only one that I thought was going to be a problem—who, doesn't matter, really. I managed to mention to him [on the morning of July 5] that this was something I had thought about, that it was going to be good for my future and our future. He may or may not decide that he was going to be part of it, but if he didn't to say so now and I would find out how far I could send him. He decided to cooperate. He wasn't friendly, but at least he wasn't too outspoken."

Veeck, once again displaying his mastery of tactics if not of strategy, had decided that there was "nothing to be gained by a formal introduction to the team." And so he arranged that Boudreau would talk to the players in the clubhouse while Veeck introduced Doby to the press in the Bard's Room. Before a battery of photographers, Doby ceremonially signed his contract in an office adjoining that of Leslie O'Connor, general manager of the obliging White Sox.

Facing the reporters, Doby admitted to feeling nervous, but guessed that he'd get over it. "Just remember," the ever-quotable Veeck told him as the reporters listened, "that they play with a little white ball and a stick of wood up here just like they did in your league."[20]

While the press conference took place upstairs, Boudreau held his meeting with the players downstairs in the clubhouse. As he remembered it, he informed them that Doby was about to become a "part of our team. He'll be wearing the same uniform as we are, so we'll fight for him as well as you'd fight for me or anybody else." Boudreau then pointed to several players and said, "Just as you fellas have to earn your job, he's going to be treated the same way. He's going to have to earn his spurs. He realizes that."

Boudreau also claims that in the meeting he mentioned Jackie Robinson in the National League, and told his Indians, "We should be honored by having the first black ball player joining us."[21]

These were wise and courageous words for Boudreau. He could not know what reactions his players would have, but he knew his own, and they served him well. He had grown up in West Harvey, Illinois, just south of Chicago, and had come to know and respect black athletes in his high school days there. Boudreau stands even taller when one realizes that he never knew of Veeck's plans until about 27 hours prior to the club-house meeting. Nor did Boudreau know that Louis Jones had been working behind the scenes to prepare Cleveland's black community for integration, a phase Veeck left out when informing his manager about Doby. Boudreau learned about Jones's work when he came to Shea Stadium in Flushing Meadow, New York, to broadcast a Chicago Cubs–New York Mets game in September of 1980.[22]

When the simultaneous press conference/team meeting ended, Jones, publicity director Samuels, and traveling secretary Harold A. "Spud" Goldstein escorted Doby to the clubhouse to introduce him to Boudreau. The manager greeted his black rookie with a smile, saying, "Hi ya, Larry, I am very happy to meet you." Doby replied, "Thank you, Mr. Boudreau. I am very glad to meet you."[23]

Accounts differ as to what happened next. With testimony from Goldstein, Boudreau, *Plain Dealer* sportswriter Gordon Cobbledick, *Call and Post* sportswriter Cleveland Jackson, and Chicago *Defender* sportswriter Fay Young, and of course from Doby himself, the sequence seems to have been that Doby, escorted by Samuels and Jones, went from his introduction to Boudreau to his locker next to that of Dale Mitchell, another rookie up from Oklahoma City in the Texas League. Doby kept his eyes straight ahead. The players followed with their eyes. No one spoke. After donning a uniform with the number 31 on its back,[24] Doby went to Boudreau's office, where the manager informed his newest player what might happen when Doby met his new teammates. Boudreau's advice: "shrug it off." Boudreau also explained the hit-and-run, bunt, and steal signals, then said, "You are now a member of the Cleveland Indians baseball team. I shall use you when I need you and the opportunity presents itself."[25]

Doby said little, causing Jones to comment later to Cobbledick, "I don't think we'll ever have to worry about his getting in bad by talking too much or saying the wrong thing. He doesn't speak a half dozen words an hour."[26]

Doby now stood more or less prepared for the next step, meeting his teammates. To prepare him for possible hostile reactions from them seems an obvious precaution. But to have him dressed in the uniform of the Indians was either a master stroke, or a provocation. In uniform he was, without need of a word, visibly equal to all the other players. But he might also be, in the minds of some, an uppity Negro who needed a lesson in deference to his white superiors.

As Doby thinks about it now, he understands the importance of being in uniform. But, in keeping with his preference for making statements without using words, he thinks that, "If I had been in street clothes, it would have been the first time that most of the players had seen a black man who was well-dressed."

In any case, Doby's preparation for the personal trials of major league baseball lasted about one and one-half *years* less than Jackie Robinson's. Robinson had a whole winter, followed by a full season in the International League at Montreal, followed by another whole winter, to prepare to integrate the National League. He had sessions with Branch Rickey and with friends to plan and even practice strategies for personal and professional survival. Most of all, he had time—time to talk with his wife Rachel, and with wise and respected black and white friends, time to think, time to allow his feelings to move and change him.

Even if Veeck's plan to sign Doby on July 3 but to introduce him at Cleveland on July 10 had not been spoiled by Bob Whiting's scoop, Robinson would still have had an enormous lead time advantage over Doby. Yet Doby, today, doesn't regret the brevity of his preparation for the rigors of life in the American League. "I look at myself as more fortunate than Jack," he says. "If I had gone through hell in the minors, then I'd have to go through it again in the majors. Once was enough!"

Ready or not, the time had come for Doby to meet his teammates. But many, if not most, had gone out on the field to warm up for the 1:30 P.M. game. As it was, they had remained in the clubhouse as long as they did not only because their manager wanted to introduce them to Doby, but because it had been raining in Chicago all morning. The groundskeepers had not yet removed the tarpaulin from the infield, and there had been no batting practice for either team.[27]

To those who were still in the clubhouse, Boudreau went to each in turn to introduce Doby. According to Boudreau, no one refused to shake Doby's hand, "but there might have been a few that gave him what we call a 'cold fish,' a limp hand. There were a few who didn't look up." [28]

According to Spud Goldstein, most of the players were still in the clubhouse. Doby, he says, looked "frightened" because it was "a whole new world" for him. Goldstein recalled no specific incidents, but said that among all the players there would be some who "wouldn't pay attention," some who "wouldn't care," and some who "resented it." He would not be more specific. [29]

It is simply not possible to determine how each player reacted to meeting Doby. The team's roster at the time included Jim Hegan of Massachusetts; Bob Feller, Mel Harder, Ken Keltner, Don Black, Hank Edwards, Ed Klieman, Steve Gromek, Hank Ruszkowski, and Hal Peck from the midwest; Joe Gordon, Bob Lemon, George Metkovich, Red Embree, and Bryan Stephens from the far west; and Al Lopez, Les Fleming, Dale Mitchell, Eddie Robinson, Pat Seerey, and Al Gettel from the south.

Cobbledick did not describe any introductions in the clubhouse. His story in the *Plain Dealer* reported that after Boudreau's meeting with Doby, Boudreau said, "Let's get out on the field, and don't stop to give any autographs." [30] They then went down the tunnel leading to the White Sox dugout and the field.

Doby, given the pressure on him, may be less reliable as a witness than any of the others. His recollection of the scene in the clubhouse involves a line of players, introductions by Boudreau to each person in the line, and handshakes. Two players rejected Doby's outstretched hand. They were, Doby heard later, Les Fleming and Eddie Robinson.

When asked about this in 1981, Robinson said he did not remember Doby's introduction to the team in Chicago. Of all the people who were there and were interviewed, 11 in all, only Robinson did not remember. [31] Fleming could not be interviewed. He died in 1980 when his tractor turned over on him while he worked on his land in Cleveland, Texas. [32]

Veeck, who said that he saw "nothing to be gained by a formal introduction to the team" for Doby, did not go to the clubhouse or to the Cleveland dugout. He had entrusted Doby to his lieutenants, and then waited for the consequences. At the time, Veeck, confident of his ability to handle tactical situations, had no contingency plan in mind if the Indians players were to rebel, or if Doby were unable to stand up to the pressure. He certainly could not send Doby to Oklahoma City or Baltimore, both in states where segregation was a way of life. In 1980 he thought it might have been Toronto in the International League, although Toronto had a working agreement with the Phillies, not the Indians. "If I had sent Larry anywhere," he said, "I probably would have sent him to Wilkes-Barre, Pennsylvania, where Bill Norman was." (Norman, it will be remembered, had assisted Killefer in scouting Doby.) As Veeck watched Doby emerge from the tunnel in the White Sox dugout and cross the Comiskey Park infield to the Cleveland side, he was a man without a plan.

Cobbledick, who had found a spot to note the reactions of players and spectators, wrote:

As Doby emerged and started across the field to the Cleveland bench a few spectators saw him and applauded. With each step the chorus swelled until, as he approached the first base dugout, it had attained the proportions of an ovation. An uncommonly large proportion of the spectators were colored, but it was noticed that Negroes and whites alike joined in the greeting.[33]

Cobbledick, whose account of the events on the field seems to be the most reliable, carefully described the final minutes before the game began:

Boudreau made no attempt at a mass introduction of Doby to his teammates. Lou himself warmed up with the newcomer on the sidelines before infield practice began. Then as they took the diamond for their pregame drill he introduced him to Joe Gordon, with whom he shared the second base duties in practice. Other introductions were made at intervals—just, said Boudreau, as they would be with any new player.[34]

Boudreau played catch with Doby during the warm-up period because he felt it his "duty" to do so, and because "I didn't want anything to happen the first few days that he was with us,"[35] thus making another contribution to the integration of the American League. Gordon's thoughts and feelings were never recorded before his death in 1978.

When the game started, Doby took a seat at the far end of the dugout from Boudreau, in the time-honored tradition of rookies in the major leagues. With the Indians trailing the White Sox by 5–1 in the seventh inning, Gordon worked starting pitcher Edgar Smith for a base on balls, chasing Smith to the showers in favor of relief pitcher Earl Harrist. Ken Keltner also walked, but was forced out at second base by pinch hitter Hank Edwards, batting for Al Lopez.

With relief pitcher Bryan Stephens scheduled to bat next, Boudreau beckoned for Doby.[36] According to Cleveland Jackson, the dialog went like this:

Boudreau: "Doby, pick out a bat."

Doby: "Yes sir."

Boudreau: "How does it feel?"

Doby: "Okay."

Boudreau: "Go in and pinch hit for Stephens."[37]

For all Americans, but especially for black Americans, Jackson may have expressed the significance of the moment best. "For Larry Doby," he wrote, "it took but a few short minutes to walk up to that plate. But for 13 million American Negroes that simple action was the successful climax of a long up-hill fight whose annals are like the saga of the [black] race."[38]

Two players felt the impact of Boudreau's decision immediately. Both were pitchers—Stephens of the Indians and Harrist of the White Sox.

Stephens, born in Arkansas, moved with his family to Colorado when he was three years old and on to California when he was 12. He had had little contact with black people prior to the arrival of Doby at Comiskey Park. For many years a plate maker in the production department of the Los Angeles *Times* after he retired from baseball, he does not remember having negative feelings when Boudreau removed him from the game for a black pinch hitter. "It didn't make any difference to me," he says. "No, it didn't bother me, not one bit."[39]

Elsewhere on the Cleveland bench, feelings were not quite so positive. Catcher Al Lopez, now a member of baseball's Hall of Fame, apparently didn't envy Stephens. "I'm glad," Lopez told his teammates in the dugout as Doby walked up to the plate, "that he didn't hit for me."[40] Lopez, as it turned out later, managed Doby for seven and one-half seasons, longer than any other manager in Doby's playing career.

Out on the mound, Harrist, born and raised in Louisiana, displayed the outward indifference that pitchers always show for batters. Inside, Harrist was thinking that Doby was "another ballplayer. If they thought that it was time for blacks to be in our game, that was fine with me."[41]

Doby, who had hit a home run in his last at bat with the Eagles just 24 hours earlier, received enthusiastic applause from the crowd of more than 18,000 fans as he dug in, "nervous and taut,"[42] at the plate. The Associated Press described what happened:

Doby, a left-handed batter, swung from his heels and missed Harrist's first pitch. He also went after the second pitch and connected for a scorching drive down the left-field line which was foul by inches. Doby let the next two pitches go by for balls, but on the fifth toss, a little wide, he swung again and missed for a strike-out. The Negro again was loudly applauded on the way back to the bench.[43]

Harrist, the deputy sheriff of Ruston, Louisiana, since he quit scouting for the Houston Astros and Indians in 1969, remembers quite well his confrontation with Doby. Reminded that Doby ripped a line drive just outside the left field foul line, he says, "That doesn't count. Just a foul ball."

"I still think of Larry quite often," Harrist said in 1981. "We all thought that he was going to be a helluva player. He was a polite boy who had been given a chance. A lot of people try to blow up a lot of stuff that

Larry—or black—was going to be fought against, that we were going to
knock him down and stick one in his ear, and all that was a bunch of
hoogosh. That's your sportswriters and people trying to blow up stuff.
There was nothing to that. One of the best friends that I ever had in this
world, in this whole world, was Satchel Paige, and he's just as black as
tar. There were many good black ballplayers that I was proud to have a
connection with.

"A lot of people never did realize, we boys down here, we used to play
ball with the black boys. We'd choose up and have black boys on the
white team and white players against the blacks. In other words, we weren't
as far back as a lot of people thought we were. We southerners got along
with black players a lot better than the guys up [north]."

After that first day in Chicago, Harrist faced Doby in other games.
"He'd hit me and I'd strike him out. Just like all other ballplayers. We'd
have our good days and our bad days. If we'd have been on the same team
we'd have been sure enough buddies. As it was, we were good friends. I
have nothing in the world to say against that boy."

Years later, Harrist requested a picture of Doby when they met at an
Old Timers Day game, but never got one. "Tell Larry I'm still waiting
for that picture," he said. "I still think of him quite often and it's pleasant
memories."[44] A few days later, Doby mailed Harrist an autographed picture.

Fourteen years after Doby's first at bat in the American League, Veeck
recalled his strikeout during an interview on a New York radio show:

I can remember Doby's first time at bat. . . . He swung at three pitches and
missed each of them by at least a foot. He walked back to the dugout with his
head down. He was so discouraged that he walked right by everyone on the bench
and sat in the corner, all alone, with his head in his hands. Joe Gordon was up
next and Gordon was having his best year and this particular left-hander was the
type that Joe usually *murdered*. Well, Joe missed each of three pitches by at least
two feet and came back to the bench and sat down next to Doby, and put his head
in his hands, too. I never asked Gordon then and I wouldn't ask him today if he
struck out deliberately. After that, every time that Doby went onto the field he
would pick up Gordon's glove and throw it to him. It's as nice a thing as I ever
saw or heard of in sports.[45]

Veeck's story, picked up by *Sports Illustrated*, subsequently surfaced in
newspaper and magazine articles about Doby over the years. Many other
baseball people, such as Bob Fishel, public relations director of the American League and a former associate of Veeck's, when asked to reminisce
about Doby, tell it.[46] Eventually even Veeck believed it. But Doby did hit
that foul line drive, and Joe Gordon was the runner on third base when
Doby came at bat![47]

The truth is that when Doby returned to the dugout, Boudreau spoke no more memorably than he did when he sent Doby into the game. According to Fay Young in the Chicago *Defender*, Boudreau said, "Well, now you know some of what it is all about. You are now a big leaguer."[48] According to Cleveland Jackson in the *Call and Post*, Boudreau said, "Well, Larry, that's over. You can relax now."[49] Both statements seem plausible. In any case, neither Doby nor Boudreau now remember what Boudreau said.

In the game, the fourth-place Indians lost to the sixth-place White Sox in a game that had little bearing on the 1947 pennant race. But in the year in which Winston Churchill alerted the Western nations about the "Iron Curtain" which had descended in Europe, and the United States Congress reduced the power of American labor unions by adopting the Taft-Hartley Act, Larry Doby had written a page of his own in American social history.

After the game, Doby quickly showered and dressed without incident in the Cleveland clubhouse. His escort, Louis Jones, then took him not to the Del Prado Hotel downtown, where the Indians players stayed, but to the black DuSable Hotel in Chicago's predominantly black South Side, near Comiskey Park.[50] The segregated arrangement established a pattern, on Doby's first day, that he would be compelled to follow, in spring training and during the regular season, in many cities, throughout his playing career.

The circumstances surrounding Doby's assignment to the DuSable are peculiar. When the Brooklyn Dodgers came to Chicago to play against the Cubs, Jackie Robinson stayed with his teammates at the downtown Stevens Hotel. So it was not city or state law or custom which separated Doby. Three explanations seem plausible. On the positive side, Spud Goldstein, the team's traveling secretary, may have thought, or been advised by Jones or someone else, that Doby would be more comfortable in all-black surroundings. On the negative side, Goldstein may have inquired at the Del Prado about housing a black guest and quietly agreed to the hotel's refusal. Or Goldstein may just have assumed that black men could not stay there and booked Doby and Jones into the DuSable. In any case, Doby says, "Nobody asked me."

Neither did anyone humiliate him. Although Cleveland Jackson reported that black Chicago was alive with rumors that Doby had been turned away from the Del Prado, Jackson told his readers that "the lad had not been subjected to any embarrassing actions.[51] Looking back, Doby says, "I began to wonder, when I got to the DuSable, why I was not with my teammates. After that, I wondered why they didn't take me to the Grand Hotel. In my trips to Chicago with the Eagles, and when I played in the East-West All-Star game in 1946, I stayed there. Satchel Paige's wife worked there."

That night, Jones followed Veeck's instructions by protecting Doby from autograph seekers and well-wishers. Doby and Jones had a quiet dinner at the Palm Tavern with Fay Young and Cleveland Jackson, then returned to the DuSable for a quiet night.

On Sunday, July 6, Doby reported to Comiskey Park for a double-header between the Indians and the White Sox. A large crowd began to gather well before the first game. White Sox officials reported that, as word about Doby spread through Chicago, all box seats for the double-header had been sold by the seventh inning on Saturday. On Sunday morning, many black churches in Chicago ended their worship services early so that their parishioners could get out to see Doby. In some cases, entire congregations went directly from church to the ball park.[52] A crowd of 31,566 fans turned out. About 30 percent, guessed Fay Young, were black.[53]

Many, if not most, of the fans were disappointed when Doby did not play in the first game. But between games, Boudreau surprised everybody by pencilling "Doby, 1b" on his lineup card. Doby, after all, had never played first base in the Negro National League. Boudreau had told some sportswriters the previous day that Doby could play second base and shortstop,[54] and told some others that Doby could play second base and first base,[55] which he had played from time to time in high school.

Having listed Doby at first, Boudreau now had a problem: Doby did not have a first baseman's mitt. Of Cleveland's two first basemen, Les Fleming threw left-handed, rookie Eddie Robinson right-handed. Doby threw with his right hand. Boudreau, whose role as player-manager already imposed many responsibilities, often depended on Spud Goldstein for help of all kinds. He also remembered Veeck's advice of the previous day that Goldstein would serve as the "in between man" in matters involving Doby. Thus the traveling secretary got the job of approaching Robinson.

"Would you lend your glove to Larry Doby?," Goldstein asked. "No," Robinson allegedly replied, "I won't lend my glove to no nigger."

Persisting, Goldstein is supposed to have asked, "Eddie, would you lend it to me?" With that, Robinson tossed his glove to Goldstein, saying, "Here, take the glove."[56]

Boudreau, in retrospect, and probably at the time, hesitates to judge Robinson negatively. "He was upset maybe not as much with Larry as with me in replacing him at first base. He thought that Larry was a second baseman and an outfielder."[57] To add to Robinson's confusion about Doby's position, Boudreau had Doby working out at shortstop during infield drill before the first game of the doubleheader.[58]

Robinson, as a rookie hoping to make it in the big leagues, knew that Doby was a threat to his job, the more so because first base on the Indians was the weakest position in one of baseball's best infields—"Flash" Gordon, future Hall of Famer Boudreau, and Keltner, famed as the third baseman who stopped Joe DiMaggio's 56-game hitting streak in 1941. At the same time, it should not be forgotten in judging Robinson's reaction to Doby that, just a year before, he did not deny kicking Jackie Robinson in the back when they were opponents in the International League.

Eddie Robinson, as executive vice-president in charge of baseball operations for the Texas Rangers in 1981, recalled his reactions to Doby. "I wasn't happy because he never had been a first baseman, and they wanted him to play first base. He never played first base, the way I heard it. I had just asked Boudreau—I wasn't doing anything great—I just asked him to leave me in the lineup. He said he would. And then the first thing I know Larry is coming in and they want him to play in my place. So that was the source of my disagreement. I didn't want to loan my glove. I was incensed. I was fighting for my position, just like anyone else."[59]

Furthermore, Robinson says, "I think Larry never played first base after that."[60] He's almost right. Doby didn't play first base again for 12 years, when he appeared there twice in the uniform of the White Sox in his final season as a major league player in 1959.

The "Eddie Robinson incident" is an unfortunate illustration of a facet of the dilemma of race in America. Many witnesses to the scene in the clubhouse heard Robinson refuse to lend his glove to Doby not only because Doby was a rival for Robinson's position, but because of Doby's race. Yet Robinson denies that race was a factor in his refusal. He says, "I had no animosity toward Larry Doby. I wanted to play first base. And that was it."[61]

The dilemma lies in the fact that no white men interviewed for this book ever admitted to prejudice toward Doby. Therefore they could not talk about how they had changed over the years, or how they had tried to change. If nobody was racially prejudiced, then there was no problem. And if there was no problem, why did Doby have to break a color line to play in the American League?

Looking back, Boudreau's decision to insert Doby into the lineup at first base, which probably originated in a "suggestion" from Veeck, was a gross blunder that could have set back the integration of the American League, and maybe all of baseball, for many years. Had Eddie Robinson been steadfast in his refusal to lend his glove, other members of the Indians sympathetic to him might have rallied around him. If that had happened, surely the owners of other teams who were watching Rickey and Veeck would have feared a player rebellion. Veeck could not have fired 30 or 40 percent of his ball club. A chain reaction of resistance to integration might have exploded in both leagues. Given that potential outcome, then, Eddie Robinson deserves a certain kind of credit. When he threw his glove to Spud Goldstein, he saved a whole lot more than the career of Larry Doby.

The incident also exposed some dynamics that Veeck never admitted anticipating, thus making him a genius, or lucky. By not clearly presenting Doby as a specialist at any one position, Veeck didn't threaten any one of his white players. None, therefore, made a major issue of Doby's presence. On the other hand, the confusion about Doby's position could have made everybody except the pitchers and catchers jumpy, causing a widespread rebellion. That no individual or group uprising took place suggests that in awarding accolades for integrating the American League, perhaps Bill Veeck has been awarded too much of the credit and his 1947 manager, coaches, players, and traveling secretary too little. They, including Eddie Robinson, had to make integration work, and somehow they did.

In the game, Doby overcame his nervousness to play well. Alex Zirin reported in the *Plain Dealer* that Doby accepted eight putouts at first base without an error, including one double play. In the ninth inning, with Cleveland ahead by a 5–1 score, he made a "fancy, one-handed leaping catch" of a throw by Gordon in a futile attempt to prevent an infield hit by Jack Wallaesa.

During the decisive third inning, with two out and runners on first and third, Doby got his only hit in four times at bat. He hit a high bouncer between second baseman Cass Michaels and first baseman Rudy York. Michaels fielded the ball and threw to pitcher Orval Grove, who had come over from the mound to cover first. But Doby's speed enabled him to beat the throw, and allowed Dale Mitchell to score from third base.[62]

In the ninth inning, according to an unsigned story in the Cleveland *Press*, two black Chicago plainclothesmen appeared on the field and entered the Cleveland dugout. It must have happened quickly, because only the *Press* reported it in its July 7 edition, and only Bill Veeck remembers it. Umpire Bill Summers stopped the game, approached the dugout, and learned that the men were there to escort Doby from the field.[63]

According to Veeck, the policemen were requested by Grace Comiskey, owner of the White Sox, who was "more upset about this than I." Veeck saw nothing unusual in her request. He claimed that for 25 years there was always a uniformed policeman in the dugout of his father's Cubs at Wrigley Field.[64]

Nonetheless, several aspects of the event are intriguing: the men were in plainclothes, not uniforms, and they were black, not white. No threatened incidents were reported, and no one seems to have asked if there were any. The appearance of two black men in the Cleveland dugout could not have endeared Doby to his white teammates. Yet today neither Doby nor his teammates who were interviewed remember what happened. The significance of Grace Comiskey's precautionary steps seems to lie more in her fear than in reality.

Thus, no Big Story arose from Doby's appearances on July 5 and 6. The Big Story was that there was no Big Story. Instead, at the conclusion of play that day, most of the players from all 16 major league teams simply looked forward to the break in the schedule for the fourteenth annual All-Star game, scheduled that year for Wrigley Field.

On Monday, July 7, the Indians were scheduled to play against their farm team at Wilkes-Barre, but rain forced cancellation of the game. The Indians returned home to Cleveland the next morning, to no fanfare. Veeck had persuaded black leaders not to stage any special ceremonies welcoming Doby to his new home city.[65] Football players Marion Motley and Bill Willis, who had integrated the Cleveland Browns and the All America Conference in 1946, quietly greeted Doby as he stepped from the train.

Louis Jones had arranged for Doby to stay at the Majestic Hotel in Cleveland, which catered to a black clientele. Among the guests that day were players from the Chicago American Giants of the Negro American League, in town to play the Buckeyes that night in Cleveland Stadium. At lunch, Jones hosted a private party for the publisher of the *Call and Post*, a prominent black attorney, Motley, Buckeyes manager Quincy Trouppe, and Candy Jim Taylor, manager of the American Giants and one of the greatest figures in the history of black baseball. After lunch, Doby talked with many of the Giants players.[66]

By then, the special mid-summer meetings of the major leagues had been concluded in Chicago. It was another case of "no news is good news," for although Doby became the focus of many conversations among owners and general managers, nothing of significance developed. In addition, although Dan Daniel had reported in the New York *World-Telegram* that an "outstanding American League player of Southern birth" talked to him about reviving an organization known as the "Players Fraternity," the Fraternity remained dead.[67]

Doby, now settled in the Majestic Hotel, made his first appearance before his hometown fans on Thursday, July 10, the date originally planned by Veeck. The Philadelphia Athletics had arrived to begin a series with a twi-night doubleheader. Doby, of course, had played in Cleveland before, when the Eagles opposed the Buckeyes at League Park in 1942 and Cleveland Stadium in 1946. He had also played in the Stadium in August 1944, when the black team from Camp Robert Smalls thrashed a team of local amateur all-stars, 14–0. "But it sure does look different now," Doby told Harry Jones of the *Plain Dealer*. "That fence looks a thousand miles away."

During a workout in the Stadium the day before, Doby found time to reflect on his hectic two days in Chicago:

When I first went to bat in Chicago I was so scared I didn't even know how many men were out and all I had to do was look at the scoreboard. I never did swing at a strike, I was so tense at the plate. It all seems like a dream now.

On Sunday I was beginning to feel a little better. Boudreau would tell me what to look for against Orval Grove and all the fellows on the team were encouraging. When I went to the plate, though, I was still trying a little too hard and swinging at bad balls. Hope I can get a few base hits Thursday night.[68]

Doby didn't. Sent up to pinch hit for pitcher Red Embree in the seventh inning, he hit a double play ground ball to Eddie Joost at shortstop. But Joost dropped the ball in his haste, allowing Ken Keltner to be safe at second and Doby at first. One out later, Joost fielded a ground ball by George Metkovich near second and touched the bag to force Doby for the third out. When the game ended, the Indians had lost, 4–2.

The people of Cleveland seemed unconcerned about Doby's presence on the Indians. Although they drew one and one-half million fans in 1947, only 2,932 paid their way into the stadium that night.[69] That day, the letters to the editor of the *Plain Dealer* did not deal with racial matters at all. They were about mysterious new objects in the Ohio sky called "flying saucers."[70]

After Thursday night's games in Cleveland, Veeck and Doby could breathe a little easier. No storm of protest or criticism had blown up in Cleveland. Doby may not have been universally accepted by the people of northern Ohio, but neither was he the victim of their scorn.

Such was not the case elsewhere. On Friday, July 11, Fred Russell of the Nashville, Tennessee, *Banner* criticized Veeck for "the cheapest kind of effort to lure a few more customers" by timing Doby's debut for Chicago's South Side, where many blacks lived. Russell also equated the Newark Eagles with Class B or Class C minor league teams, and concluded that Veeck "has proved an opportunist and exhibitionist never missing a trick."[71]

While Russell's readers were confined mainly to Tennessee, J. G. Taylor Spink enjoyed a nationwide audience in *The Sporting News*. In an editorial headed "Once Again, That Negro Question," Spink commented that "a vast percentage of the white players in the majors opposed integration." He went on to endorse the comments of an unnamed player, who had just appeared in the All-Star game in Chicago, elevating the "economic stability" of white players above those of black players, raising the red herring of opening up the black leagues to whites, and demeaning Doby's and Robinson's apprenticeships in black baseball.[72]

In Cleveland, meanwhile, Doby bathed in the warmth of the black community—a steady stream of well-wishers at his hotel, laudatory editorials in the *Call and Post*.[73]

During the following week, news about Doby centered around the question of where he could break into the Cleveland lineup. Sam Lacy of the *Afro-American* compared Robinson with Doby in that just as Robinson could not dislodge Eddie Stanky or Peewee Reese from second base and shortstop in the Brooklyn infield, neither could Doby replace Gordon and Boudreau at the same positions in Cleveland.[74] Ed McAuley's story in *The Sporting News* pointed out that rookie first baseman Eddie Robinson had recently improved his batting average and home run total, thereby intensifying the question.[75]

Boudreau and Veeck were even more acutely aware of this than the press. With the advice of coach "Deacon" Bill McKechnie, whose major league experience went back 40 years, and whose record as a manager won him election to the Hall of Fame, Boudreau and Veeck made a private decision: Doby would see spot duty for the rest of the 1947 season, and would be converted to the outfield in spring training in 1948. Actually, Veeck's plans to convert Doby to the outfield dated back to the month before Veeck bought Doby from Newark, after his scouts told him that they liked Doby more than any outfielder in the Negro leagues. Having affirmed his earlier decision, Veeck still did not tell Doby, who was left sitting on the bench, where he had never been before, wondering how he would ever replace Boudreau or Gordon.[76]

For public consumption, Boudreau and Veeck said that Doby "will have every chance to make good." Boudreau added, "I do not plan to rush him because that would be unfair to the player. He will be worked in gradually."[77] Boudreau acted on this plan on July 16. Doby pinch hit for pitcher Al Gettel and whistled a line drive into center field in a game against the Yankees.

Doby's unique status in the league ended abruptly on July 17, in the city that most observers regarded as likely to be the last to hire black players. The St. Louis Browns signed Henry Thompson and Willard Brown of the Kansas City Monarchs. Owner Richard Muckerman also announced that the Browns had obtained a 30-day option on Lorenzo "Piper" Davis of the Birmingham, Alabama, Black Barons. That night, manager Herold "Muddy" Ruel inserted Thompson into his lineup at second base for a game against the Philadelphia Athletics.

Thompson and Brown were signed, Muckerman explained, "to help lift the Browns out of the American League cellar."[78] Thereafter Thompson and Brown played frequently, while Doby continued to see only occasional action with the Indians. He knew, as he sat, that the statistics of black baseball showed that he was a better player than either Thompson or Brown. He also knew, though, that the Browns had Johnny Berardino, not Joe Gordon, at second base, and that their outfield of Al Zarilla, Paul Lehner, and Jeff Heath had a composite batting average of only about .250.

On the same night that Thompson played at St. Louis, Doby played a few innings in Cleveland. Boudreau, on his own thirtieth birthday, removed himself from the lineup in the fifth inning of the second game of a doubleheader against the Yankees. In his place, Doby went hitless in two times at bat. The first time, Joe DiMaggio robbed him of an extra base hit with a leaping one-handed catch near the center field fence. The second time, Tommy Henrich prevented a possible triple with a running catch of a line drive to right field. At shortstop, Doby handled three chances flawlessly.[79] (The Yankees won both games to stretch a winning streak to 19; they eventually won the pennant, 12 games ahead of the Detroit Tigers.)

Doby's real hometown newspaper, the weekly Camden, South Carolina, *Chronicle*, finally took notice of him on July 18. In an exception to its habit of mentioning black residents only when they committed a crime or went to jail, the *Chronicle* ran a two-column headline on the lower half of page 10. The seven paragraph story attributed Doby's baseball skills to Richard DuBose and to Doby's father. "This fellow Richard DuBose," the story said, "has been a leader in Camden Negro baseball for many years." It described David Doby as "one of the best first sackers in the colored baseball ranks of the state. David wanted Larry to be a good ball player and when the youngster was but seven years of age, David had him playing baseball."[80]

In contrast to Camden's tardy recognition of Doby, a delegation from the Old Timers Athletic Association of Paterson wanted to honor Doby on Cleveland's next trip east with a "Day" at Yankee Stadium, journeying to Cleveland to see Veeck, but he turned them down. "Let the lad prove that he is a major leaguer before you start having days for him," he told the proud Patersonians. "Mel Harder served twenty great years for the Indians before the public recently honored him with a day at the [Cleveland] Stadium."[81]

The Indians closed out the month of July with a road trip to the east coast, to stadiums in cities where Doby had played many times with the Eagles. Joined for the first time since July 4 by Helyn, he stayed in the same hotels with his teammates in Philadelphia (the Warrick), in Boston (the Kenmore), and even in Washington, D.C. (the Statler). In Washington, Doby's presence caused a demonstration by an organization called American Youth for Democracy. As fans entered Griffith Stadium, they received handbills asking Clark Griffith, president of the team, "Why Wait Senators?" Below sketches of Doby and Robinson, the handbill said: "Will Washington be less American? Let's follow the example of other cities on the roll of honor and boot loathsome discrimination out the window. Write or call Clark Griffith to get a Negro player."

Griffith would not comment on the handbill.[82] Neither did he hire a black player for many seasons to come.

For Doby, the highlight of the trip to Washington was a chance to see Mickey Vernon, the All-Star first baseman of the Senators who led the league in hitting the year before and who was Doby's companion on Mog-Mog during World War II. Vernon remembers that the Senators had "a lot of good black supporters" who were segregated in seats along the right field foul line. "When Larry came to bat as a pinch hitter," Vernon recalled, "he forced a man at second and beat the return throw to first. A big colored fan who was out there every day with a leather-lunged type of voice yelled out, 'Let him steal second! Let him steal third! But don't let him touch that rubber!' He didn't want Larry to score against the Senators."[83]

During the first 10 days of August, four news items brought Doby to public attention. The largest day crowd of the season, 62,537 fans, saw him make his debut in a Cleveland uniform at Yankee Stadium. He grounded out for Bob Feller in the thirteenth inning of the first game, and struck out for Al Gettel in the eighth inning of the second. The twin highlights of the day, though, occurred before each game, when "Bojangles" Bill Robinson, the famed black dancer, put hexes on the Cleveland dugout. Apparently his love for the Yankees outweighed whatever sentiment he had for Doby.[84]

When the Indians returned from the east, they did so without Doby. The *Plain Dealer* reported the incident, saying, "The colored boy missed the Tribe's train, he explained in a telegram to Manager Lou Boudreau, and departed at a later hour. He has made himself eligible for a fine."[85] But Boudreau forgave Doby without a fine.

Doby finally found his batting stroke during batting practice on August 5 in Detroit. He propelled two balls into the upper right field seats of Briggs Stadium, drawing Boudreau's notice. The next day, Doby started at second base in the second game of a doubleheader, but he went hitless in two times at bat and handled just one putout in the field.[86]

Three days later, on August 9, Doby and Henry Thompson of the Browns wrote another page into the history of major league baseball: for the first time, black players opposed each other on the diamond. During the second game of a doubleheader, with Thompson playing second base, Doby drew a walk as a pinch hitter for Al Lopez, and later scored a run in a 5–4 Cleveland victory.[87]

In the days prior to that game, Browns manager Muddy Ruel talked outfielder Paul Lehner out of quitting the team in protest against the signing of Thompson and Brown.[88] Thus, in each of three instances up to that time, at Brooklyn, Cleveland, and now St. Louis, Rickey, Veeck and now Ruel had to quell objections to integration.

Doby continued to make occasional appearances in the Cleveland lineup during August and September, causing much debate as to whether Veeck should have placed him in a minor league rather than with the Indians.

Scouts for the Dodgers, for example, said that Veeck should have followed Rickey's example of placing Jackie Robinson in the International League. Doby could not, they said, pull the ball to right field and did not know the strike zone. One said Doby was "two years away from the majors."[89]

But A. S. "Doc" Young, who replaced Cleveland Jackson as sports editor of the *Call and Post*, pointed out once again that Cleveland's top farm teams, at Oklahoma City and Baltimore, were "below that unrighteous line,"[90] the Mason-Dixon line which divided the North from the South.

In late August, the Browns, who had signed Thompson and Brown to 30-day contracts, dropped both players from their roster and dropped their option on Piper Davis as well. Thompson had a batting average of .265 and Brown .175 when they were released.[91] Also in late August, the Dodgers added black pitcher Dan Bankhead to their roster and assigned him to room with Jackie Robinson on road trips.[92]

Of more direct interest to Doby, Eddie Robinson fractured his ankle in late August. Doby, suddenly hopeful that Boudreau might revive the idea to play him at first base, then felt his hopes decline when Les Fleming took over at first and stayed there.[93]

On September 8, Doby's hopes slipped even further when the Indians called Al Rosen up from Oklahoma City. Rosen had been the All-Star third baseman in the Texas League, but he was not likely to replace Keltner at third for the Indians. Instead, he began to play right field and hit in the regular batting rotation.[94]

When the season ended, Doby had appeared in only 29 games, usually as a pinch hitter. He appeared in the field only six times—four times in relief of Gordon at second base, once in place of Boudreau at shortstop, and, of course, once in place of Robinson at first base. He had come to bat 32 times, connecting for four singles and a double and walking once for a final batting average of .156. He scored three runs, drove in two, and struck out 11 times. It was hardly an auspicious beginning for a man who later played in five All-Star games and was selected for a sixth.[95]

Before leaving Cleveland at the end of the season, Doby sat down for a talk with McKechnie, the wise old coach. He advised Doby to spend part of his winter reading a book about playing the outfield, because that's where the Indians planned to try him in spring training in 1948. It was the first time that Doby heard about a decision that had been made almost three months earlier.

In October, Sam Lacy reported in the *Afro-American* a rumor that Doby would be farmed out to Portland, Maine, in the Class C Canadian–American League in 1948.[96] Doby heard rumors that he would be sent, by special arrangement, to Toronto of the International League. But the rumors could not compete with a far more important story that month. Jackie Robinson, who had led the Dodgers to the National League pennant, became the first black man to appear in the World Series, which the Dodgers lost to the Yankees, four games to three.

After the Series, Veeck told Doc Young that Doby would remain in the Cleveland organization, but that it had not been decided whether he would be assigned to a minor league team. Veeck also said that Cleveland's managers and coaches had not changed their high opinions of Doby's potential, yet admitted that he should have handled Doby the way Rickey handled Robinson. "Rickey was smarter than I was on that," he said. "I tried to bring him along too fast."[97]

Veeck took full responsibility in his interview with Young. He placed none of the blame on Boudreau. Young, however, pointed out that after Doby's first few days with the Indians, his relationship with Boudreau "never extended beyond the 'Hello, Larry' stage; nor did the shortstop-manager detail any coaches to advise or help Doby improve his play."[98]

"That's right," Doby remembers. "I was on my own with the Indians in 1947. Nobody helped me until spring training in 1948."

During the final days of 1947, Doby barnstormed with a black all-star team organized by Jackie Robinson. They had joined Joe Louis and Jesse Owens as the most famous black athletes in America, and here was a chance to capitalize on their fame. They played about 30 games, from Newark in the north to Miami in the south, and drew large crowds everywhere. While he played among men who admired and accepted him, Doby began to relax and to ponder the sudden turn his life had taken.

In *The Souls of Black Folk*, written in 1903, black leader W.E.B. Du Bois wrote almost as if he knew the players on the Cleveland Indians. A few of them, notably Joe Gordon, Jim Hegan, Steve Gromek, and Bob Lemon, befriended Doby in the summer of 1947. At least one hated him, expressed his hatred openly, and was banished by Veeck to the minor leagues at the end of the season. Most were just passively indifferent, feeling no obligation either to protect him or to protest his forced segregation from them at night. Thus, as Du Bois observed, "despite much physical contact and daily intermingling, there [was] almost no community of intellectual life or points of transference where the thoughts and feelings of one race [could] come into direct contact and sympathy with the thoughts and feelings of the other."[99]

Du Bois also wrote as if he knew Doby:

In those sombre forests of his striving his own soul rose before him, and he saw himself,—darkly as through a veil; and yet he saw in himself some faint revelation of his power, of his mission. He began to have a dim feeling that, to attain his place in the world, he must be himself, and not another. For the first time he sought to analyze the burden he bore upon his back, that deadweight of social degradation partially masked behind a half-named Negro problem.[100]

What Du Bois did not, could not, see, was that baseball is at bottom a game of measurable merit. There, in its use of statistics, was Doby's opening, his highway to professional, if not personal, acceptance.

NOTES

1. The source for the material quoting Bill Veeck in this chapter is a personal interview with Veeck, conducted on April 23–24, 1980.

2. Cleveland Jackson, *Call and Post* (Cleveland), June 28, 1947.

3. *Morning Call* (Paterson), July 3, 1947.

4. Bob Whiting, "Time Out!" *Morning Call*, July 4, 1947.

5. *Morning Call*, July 3, 1947.

6. Ibid., July 4, 1947.

7. Ibid.

8. Personal interview with Lou Boudreau, September 13, 1980.

9. Ibid.

10. *New York Times*, July 4, 1947.

11. *Morning Call*, July 4, 1947.

12. *Plain Dealer* (Cleveland), July 5, 1947.

13. Amiri Baraka, *Autobiography* (New York: Freundlich Books, 1984), p. 37.

14. *New York Times*, July 4, 1947.

15. Ibid.

16. Ibid.

17. *The Daily Worker*, July 4, 1947.

18. *Plain Dealer*, Editorial, July 4, 1947.

19. Harold Sauerbrei, *Plain Dealer*, July 4, 1947.

20. Gordon Cobbledick, *Plain Dealer*, July 6, 1947.

21. Boudreau, loc. cit.

22. Ibid.

23. *Call and Post*, July 12, 1947.

24. According to Doby, his uniform that season bore the number 31. But accounts written by Cobbledick and Fay Young of the Chicago *Defender* at the time reported that Doby wore the number 14, the same number that he wore throughout his major league career.

25. Fay Young, "Through the Years," *Defender*, July 12, 1947.

26. Cobbledick, *Plain Dealer*, July 6, 1947.

27. Ibid.

28. Boudreau, loc. cit.

29. Telephone interview with Harold A. "Spud" Goldstein, October 25, 1980.

30. Cobbledick, *Plain Dealer*, July 6, 1947.

31. Telephone interview with Eddie Robinson, July 8, 1981.

32. *Enterprise* (Beaumont, Texas), March 8, 1980.

33. Cobbledick, *Plain Dealer*, July 6, 1947.

34. Ibid.

35. Boudreau, loc. cit.

36. Alex Zirin, *Plain Dealer*, July 6, 1947.

37. Cleveland Jackson, *Call and Post*, July 12, 1947.

38. Ibid.

39. Telephone interview with Bryan Stephens, June 22, 1981.

40. Ibid.

41. Telephone interview with Earl Harrist, June 22, 1981.

42. Jackson, *Call and Post*, July 12, 1947.

43. Associated Press, *New York Times*, July 6, 1947.

44. Harrist, loc. cit.

45. *Sports Illustrated*, December 4, 1961.

46. Personal interview with Bob Fishel, November 7, 1980.

47. Zirin, *Plain Dealer*, July 6, 1947.

48. Fay Young, *Defender*, July 12, 1947.

49. Jackson, *Call and Post*, July 12, 1947.

50. Ibid.

51. Ibid.

52. Ibid.

53. Fay Young, *Defender*, July 12, 1947.

54. Cobbledick, *Plain Dealer*, July 6, 1947.

55. United Press, *New York Times*, July 4, 1947.

56. This episode has been pieced together from a telephone interview with Goldstein and from accounts provided by witnesses who asked not to be identified. Goldstein was careful not to attribute to Robinson any statements impugning Doby on the grounds of race.

57. Boudreau, loc. cit.

58. *Call and Post*, July 12, 1947.

59. Eddie Robinson, loc. cit.

60. Ibid.

61. Ibid.

62. Zirin, *Plain Dealer*, July 7, 1947.

63. *Press* (Cleveland), July 7, 1947.

64. Veeck, loc. cit.

65. Ibid.

66. Jackson, *Call and Post*, July 12, 1947.

67. Dan Daniel, "Daniel's Dope," *World-Telegram* (New York), July 5, 1947.

68. Harry Jones, *Plain Dealer*, July 8, 1947.

69. Zirin, *Plain Dealer*, July 12, 1947.

70. *Plain Dealer*, Letters to the Editor, July 12, 1947.

71. Fred Russell, cited in the *Defender*, July 19, 1947.

72. J. G. Taylor Spink, Editorial, "Once Again, That Negro Question," *The Sporting News*, July 16, 1947.

73. Charles H. Loeb, *Call and Post*, July 12, 1947.

74. Sam Lacy, "Looking 'em Over," *New Jersey Afro-American*, July 12, 1947.

75. Ed McAuley, *The Sporting News*, July 16, 1947.

76. Veeck, loc. cit.

77. Lacy, "Looking 'em Over," *New Jersey Afro-American*, July 12, 1947.

78. *Plain Dealer*, July 18, 1947.

79. Ibid.

80. *Chronicle* (Camden, S.C.), July 18, 1947.

81. Jackson, *Call and Post*, July 19, 1947.

82. *Plain Dealer*, July 28, 1947.

83. Telephone interview with Mickey Vernon, April 25, 1981.

84. *Plain Dealer*, August 3, 1947.

85. Ibid., August 5, 1947.

86. Ibid., August 6 and 7, 1947.

87. Ibid., August 10, 1947.

88. *New Jersey Afro-American*, August 10, 1947.

89. Hal Lebovitz, *Plain Dealer*, August 15, 1947.

90. A. S. "Doc" Young, *Call and Post*, September 13, 1947.

91. *The Sporting News*, September 3, 1947.

92. Ibid.

93. Ibid.

94. *Plain Dealer*, September 9, 1947.

95. David S. Neft, Richard M. Cohen, and Jordan A. Deutsch, *The Sports Encyclopedia: Baseball* (New York: Grosset and Dunlap, 1981), p. 271.

96. Lacy, *New Jersey Afro-American*, October 11, 1947.

97. Doc Young, *Call and Post*, October 18, 1947.

98. Ibid.

99. W.E.B. Du Bois, *The Souls of Black Folk* (Millwood, N.Y.: Kraus-Thomson, 1973), p. 183.

100. Du Bois, *The Souls of Black Folk*, p. 8.

1. Doby, pen in hand, smiles in pleasure just after signing the contract which made him the first black player in the American League on July 5, 1947. Returning the smile is the president of the Cleveland Indians, Bill Veeck. The signing took place in the offices of the Chicago White Sox at Comiskey Park. (Photo courtesy of Wide World)

2. Doby, less than 24 hours after hitting a home run in his farewell appearance with the Newark Eagles of the Negro National League, poses in the dugout in Comiskey Park, Chicago, with Lou Boudreau, player-manager of the Cleveland Indians. Boudreau, still twelve days short of his thirtieth birthday, learned just two days earlier that he would be a key figure in the integration of the American League. (Photo courtesy of Wide World)

3. Doby and Satchel Paige, roommates, congratulate each other after a 1-0 victory over the Chicago White Sox in 1948. Paige pitched his second straight shutout, a three-hitter, and Doby singled in the only run of the game in the fourth inning. A record crowd for a night game, 78,382 fans, watched at Cleveland Stadium as the Indians continued their drive to the American League pennant.

4. Doby watches the flight of the baseball as he prepares to run the bases in a game at Cleveland Stadium in 1948. Doby batted .396 over the last 20 games of the season, highest on the team, to finish his first full season in the American League with a batting average of .301.

5. Four of the five black players in major league baseball participated in the All-Star game in 1949. Jackie Robinson (right) appeared first, to be followed innings later by Doby (second from left), Roy Campanella (left), and Don Newcombe (second from right), in that order, at Ebbets Field in Brooklyn. The fifth, Satchel Paige, was not named to the team by American League manager Lou Boudreau.

6. Doby, most noted as a slugger, poses in the clubhouse at Yankee Stadium in August 1955 after playing in his 158th straight game without an error to set a record for American League outfielders. His record reached 164 games, but has since been surpassed by Al Kaline of the Detroit Tigers, who played in 242 consecutive errorless games, the record for both major leagues.

7. On his first visit to Cleveland as manager of the Chicago White Sox, Doby hands his lineup card to umpire Dale Ford on August 18, 1978, as opposing manager Jeff Torborg of the Cleveland Indians looks on. Doby came within a weekend of becoming the first black manager in major league history with the Indians in 1974, then waited until Bill Veeck fired Bob Lemon and named Doby to manage the White Sox in July 1978.

8. Doby, at an Old Timers Day game dedicated to him, waves his cap to appreciative fans at Cleveland Stadium in August 1987. Doby's appearance reminded Cleveland fans of his heroic performances on their pennant-winning 1948 team, which went on to defeat the Boston Braves in the World Series, and of their 1954 team, which set an American League record by winning 110 games but then lost to the New York Giants in the World Series.

7

The Most Significant Player in the League

When Larry Doby arrived home in Paterson after the 1947 season ended, he followed Bill McKechnie's advice to read a book about playing the outfield, borrowing Tommy Henrich's *How to Play the Outfield* from the public library. Nevertheless, partly out of his uncertainty about what lay ahead, on New Year's Eve he signed a contract to play professional basketball for the Paterson Crescents of the American Basketball League, enabling owner Sam Bozza to claim that Doby had, for the second time in six months, integrated a professional sports league.[1]

As he had with Cleveland, Doby sat on the bench for two road games, inducing even greater uncertainty about his future. But when the team returned home for a game at the Paterson Armory on January 3, Coach Len Merson satisfied the 2,200 fans who turned out by putting Doby in the starting lineup. He played most of the first half, and for the final five minutes of the game, scoring three points on a set shot and a free throw. The Cresents won, defeating the Philadelphia SPHA's (the South Philadelphia Hebrew Association) by a score of 76–65.[2]

The Crescents were a competitive team, but not of championship caliber. Their most famous players were Doby and Kevin "Chuck" Connors, briefly a first baseman for the Brooklyn Dodgers and Chicago Cubs, later star of the television series "The Rifleman" and an actor in "Roots" and other films.

Doby played in just a few more games with the Crescents in 1948, then began to concentrate on preparing himself for the baseball season. In mid-January, he returned his signed contract to Cleveland, calling for a salary of $5,000, the same amount Effa Manley had persuaded Bill Veeck to pay Doby in 1947.[3] Jackie Robinson, whose reported salary for 1947 was $5,000, had been raised to an estimated $15,000 for 1948.[4]

By the end of the month, Veeck and his aides implied their judgment of Doby's chances of making the Indians as an outfielder by buying out-fielder Thurman Tucker from the White Sox. Previously, they had bought Walt Judnich, a first baseman–outfielder, from the St. Louis Browns, and traded pitcher Red Embree to the Yankees for outfielder Allie Clark. The holdovers from 1947 were Hank Edwards, Dale Mitchell, Hal Peck, and Pat Seerey. With Doby, eight outfielders would report to Tucson, Ari-zona, for spring training in March. Only five could make the team.[5] Gor-don Cobbledick, sports editor of the Plain Dealer, thought Doby the least likely to stick.[6]

In mid-February, Veeck dismissed Louis Jones from his post on the Cleveland public relations staff, in part for not fulfilling Veeck's expecta-tions of him as Doby's traveling companion. Veeck's action not only left Doby without a roommate, but also stripped major league baseball of its only black man in a front office position.[7]

The presence, or absence of Jones, made "no difference" to Doby. "Even when he was supposed to be with me, he wasn't," Doby remembers. "In 1947, we would usually eat together in our hotel, but then he'd be gone for the rest of the night. If we were staying in the same hotel as the team, I wasn't invited to go out by the other players. They might go to a place where I wouldn't be served, so they didn't do it. The veterans on the team all had their own friends, and they'd go out together. And I didn't drink in those days. There weren't many non-drinkers on the Indians. So Louis Jones or no Louis Jones, I would go upstairs to my room alone."

Jim Hegan, who was there when Doby arrived in 1947 and remained with Cleveland for 10 more years, expressed a view that is very close to Doby's. Speaking as one of his closest friends in baseball, Hegan said that it "was a stand-offish position, really. You didn't know how to react to the situation, since it was the first time this happened in the American League. For the fellas who lived in the north, it didn't make any differ-ence. But you didn't know if you were going to hurt the feelings of the fellas from the south, who were your friends at the time, if you went over and welcomed Larry too strongly. It was a little touchy. And players wouldn't invite Larry because they were afraid he'd be embarrassed when we got to where we were going."[8]

When Doby reported for spring training in Tucson on March 1, he came prepared by a winter of decompression from the pressures of 1947. Now 24 years of age, he had reached his physical peak through strenuous workouts and his usual habit of clean living: he still did not smoke, imbibe alcohol, or drink coffee.

Upon arrival in Tucson, however, he soon discovered that he would be segregated from his teammates. The operators of the Santa Rita Hotel had informed the traveling secretary, Spud Goldstein, that Doby would have to live elsewhere, claiming that Doby's presence would "hurt business." In need of help, Goldstein consulted the black foreman of the company that supplied the Santa Rita with its clean sheets and towels, Chester Willis. Willis had many contacts in Tucson's black community, and might find a black family that would take Doby in.[9]

Willis didn't have to look very far. After consulting with his wife, Lucille, the Willises decided to offer Doby a room in their own home. There, in the midst of the three Willis children, all under the age of five, Doby found the family atmosphere that he loved since his days with Aunt Alice and Uncle James Cooke in South Carolina.

Although Doby's friends soon dubbed his spring training home the "Doby Hacienda," a reference to a popular song of that time,[10] it was a bad arrangement. He told Charles Dexter, for a book by Jackie Robinson entitled *Baseball Has Done It*, that he missed "not having another player to communicate with, talk over the game with after it's over and start me thinking about the next game."[11]

Neither Veeck nor Goldstein reported putting any pressure on the operators of the Santa Rita. The Indians continued to train there until 1954, seven years later. When Helyn Doby accompanied her husband to spring training in 1949, they lived with the Willises. After they had their first child, they lived with Zelma and John Bennett, who had rooms vacated by their grown children. In the five years that followed, all the black players on the Indians lived with black families in the Tucson area.

Doby's segregation received scant notice in the Cleveland press. Of seeming greater importance was a complaint, in an unsigned story in the *Plain Dealer*, about the scarcity of hotel rooms for the wives of the white players.[12]

Notwithstanding his segregation, or perhaps angrily motivated by it, Doby began to impress everyone in camp almost immediately. On March 3, just two days after training began at Randolph Park, he hit a pitch by Ed Klieman 380 feet over the right center field fence, despite a desert wind blowing toward home plate described as "brisk."[13]

At the time, Boudreau had assigned Doby to the second string outfield on the "B" team.[14] Yet his assignment there did not restrict his access to the "Gray Eagle," Tris Speaker, who had been hired by Veeck to work with the outfielders. Speaker is one of baseball's legendary outfielders, one of the few men in the history of the sport who might have made the Hall of Fame on the strength of his defensive skills alone. But Speaker also had a lifetime batting average of .344, tied for seventh on the all-time list.

Speaker, a Texan, made Doby a special project. The two worked together in the outfield, Doby shagging flies and fielding ground balls while Speaker furnished knowledge he had accumulated in 2,789 major league games. "No man ever knew more," Veeck said a year later in the *Saturday Evening Post*.[15]

By the end of the first week of camp, Doby was the subject of a column by Cobbledick in the *Plain Dealer*:

Larry Doby has come a long way since that afternoon last July when, a badly frightened boy, he met Bill Veeck . . . at Comiskey Park. . . .

It isn't easy to tell in just what way he has progressed, but a difference in his attitude was sensed by everyone . . . and it has become the subject of an increasing volume of comment with the passing days.

Doby isn't afraid of whatever it was that scared him last summer. He has found no hostility among his teammates, but, on the contrary, has discovered that most of them are anxious to help him. . . .

The big difference between the Doby of 1948 and the Doby of a few months ago is found in the complete absence of the tension that made it impossible for him to display his talents to good advantage last season.

With the tension gone, he has earned new respect from the other Indians by showing what he never was able to show before—namely, that he is a richly gifted young athlete with a better than even chance to become a top flight big league star.[16]

The Indians left Tucson for their first "Cactus League" game at Phoenix against the New York Giants on March 7. Boudreau, having decided to put Doby to the test, placed him in the leadoff spot in the batting order, and in center field on defense. Doby, capitalizing on the opportunity, delivered two singles in seven times at bat and caught one fly ball as the Indians won, 13–8.[17]

Rapidly gaining the confidence that he always had with the Eagles, Doby continued to excel. On March 11, against the Los Angeles Angels of the Pacific Coast League, he ran 40 yards to catch a ball in the fourth inning, made a "diving somersault catch" in the sixth, and handled three routine chances. He capped his performance in the top of the ninth inning, hitting a 3–2 pitch over the right center field fence for the final run in a 5–2 Cleveland loss.[18]

Then came a one-week lull while Doby recovered from a "charley horse,"[19] an injury that would recur throughout his career. He came back with three hits in four at bats as the "B" team defeated U.C.L.A., 14–2, and played center field in a manner described as "spectacular."[20] Doby passed an even tougher test two days later against the New York Giants at Wrigley Field in Los Angeles. He singled and walked in two times at bat, made a "masterful throw" to catch a base runner at home plate, and "literally flew" from first base to third on a single.[21]

Promoted by Boudreau to the "A" team, Doby celebrated in a game against the St. Louis Browns with a single, a double, and a stolen base.[22] More significantly, when his spikes grazed shortstop Eddie Pellagrini in a play at second base, Pellagrini realized it was an accident and play continued without interruption.

Doby's achievements on the field stood in clear contrast to his shabby treatment off the field. Before Cleveland's stay in Los Angeles, then a minor league city, Veeck had told Doc Young of the *Call and Post* that Doby would stay with the Indians in the Biltmore Hotel. When the team arrived, however, traveling secretary Goldstein assigned him to an all-black hotel, the Watkins, instead. Queried about this discrimination by the publisher of the Los Angeles *Sentinel*, Leon H. Washington, Goldstein stated that the Biltmore refused to admit Doby. But when questioned by Washington, the hotel's manager stated that Doby was not on the list of reservations presented by Goldstein, and denied that the Biltmore had refused to house Doby. When Goldstein, and then Doby himself, declined to comment on the situation, Washington dug a little deeper. He discovered that, at the time, two black persons were already residing in the Biltmore, thus casting a cloud of doubt over Goldstein's behavior as an official of the Cleveland team.

Doc Young, long a resident of Los Angeles before going back east to Cleveland, told his readers that California civil rights laws prohibited this type of discrimination,[23] but Doby, nevertheless, continued to live at the Watkins, still unable to talk with and get to know his teammates.

Life there had its compensations, though. As Doby recalls, "I met a lot of nice people at the Watkins—Kenny Washington, the Mills Brothers [a popular singing group], Tom Bradley, now the mayor of Los Angeles, and other prominent black people."

Given Doby's performances on the field, Boudreau found him to be a main topic at a press conference on March 23. Asked whether Doby had made the squad or would be farmed out, the player-manager said, "I'll keep Doby only if I feel quite sure that he can play regularly. Right now, I don't think he can." At that point, Doby's batting average was .350, third best on the team. Only Thurman Tucker had played better in the outfield.[24]

A year later, in his autobiography *Player-Manager*, Boudreau elaborated on one of Doby's problems. "I was skeptical about his chances of staying with us all season because I felt his bad-ball hitting would not be likely to improve overnight and, with so much at stake in the pennant race, I dared not do any unjustified experimenting."[25] Flawed though he seemed to Boudreau, Doby continued his against-the-odds efforts to make the Indians. In four successive games he hit one home run, two triples, and three singles; stole one base; and threw out one base runner.[26]

As March drew to a close, a strange coincidence of events made Doby's efforts to succeed in baseball seem to be a mere aberration in the degraded status of black Americans. On the same day that Doby pinch hit a double to help the Indians defeat the Browns, the entertainment pages of the nation's press reported that the "Amos 'n' Andy" radio show would be adapted for a television series. Its comedy had depended on the conceit that Freeman Gosden and Charlie Correll, both white men, were stupid and lazy black men. Now the new but growing national television audience would actually see black men portraying the stereotyped roles which had to be imagined during "Amos 'n' Andy's" many years on the radio.[27]

As the Indians prepared to follow the warm weather gradually northward to start the 1948 season, Ed McAuley summarized Doby's spring for *The Sporting News*:

. . . the No. 1 story of the spring was the American League's only Negro, Larry Doby. Two weeks ago, Boudreau indicated that Larry would be farmed out for further experience unless he could win the starting job in center field from Walter Judnich—an unlikely turn of events. As the squad broke camp, Boudreau revealed that Doby was being considered for right field, as well as for center. On the spring record, Doby rated in all-around value ahead of every outfield competitor.[28]

In 1980, Boudreau expanded on the conclusion he reached in April 1948. In a statement that can be read as highly complimentary to Doby, and as evidence of a double standard in judging white and black players, he said, "Larry proved to them [the other players] that he was a major leaguer in handling himself in more ways than one—on the field and off the field."[29]

On the field, according to Franklin Lewis in the Cleveland *Press*, Doby was a "six hour ball player per day." Off the field, he was "an 18–hour Jim Crow personality the rest of the time." In a conversation with Lewis, Doby described himself as "lonely," living in segregated hotels as the Indians barnstormed east and north,[30] an echo of his four years in high school when he lived alone with a different family each year.

Loneliness was not Doby's only problem. At Lubbock, Texas, gate attendants at a local ball park would not admit him because, having been separated from the team the night before, he was not wearing his Cleveland uniform. He went from gate to gate, trying to explain his situation, before Spud Goldstein arrived to confirm that Doby was, indeed, a member of the Indians. The rest of the team, meanwhile, had put on uniforms at the hotel and swept through the players entrance to the admiring shouts of local fans.

At Texarkana, a city on both sides of the Texas–Arkansas border, Doby put on his uniform in the private home arranged by Goldstein through the minister of a local black church. In trying to get to the ball park for that day's exhibition game against the Giants, though, Doby found that he could ride only in Jim Crow taxi cabs, both of which were in service. With that, he set out on foot for the ball park, walking the streets in his baseball uniform, only to find once again that the gate keepers would not admit him despite the uniform. At length, after Doby stood in humiliation, Boudreau rescued his angry young player from the hostility of the white crowd which had gathered.

In the game, played before an overflow crowd restrained behind ropes around the outfield, Doby left his position in center field when a barrage of bottles and other objects came down around him in the fourth or fifth inning. Boudreau "solved" that problem by taking Doby out of the game, at once protecting him and allowing the racist fans of Texarkana to drive the object of their hatred from the field.[31]

Doby's triumphs and his problems continued as the Indians meandered toward Opening Day. At Buffalo Stadium in Houston, vicious racist insults assaulted Doby as he came to bat against Larry Jansen, ace right-handed pitcher for the Giants. Doby answered by smashing the longest home run ever seen there, longer than a blast by Jimmie Fox, according to local sportswriters. The ball may have traveled 500 feet before landing far beyond the fence in center field. As Doby circled the bases, and the enormity of his home run sank in, he received an ovation from most of his teammates. Even the fans, moments before so hostile, applauded him as he touched home plate. Their cheers, so soon after their jeers, did not mollify him. "In fact, I resented their cheers," he says.

With that home run, all doubts that Doby would make the 1948 Cleveland team vanished. From then on, virtually everyone considered him part of the team. They showed it, and Doby felt it, although he still had no direct assurances from Boudreau.[32]

The Indians finally arrived in Cleveland on April 17 for two more exhibition games against the Giants. Knowing full well that they were going to start one of the National League's toughest left-handed pitchers, Dave Koslo, in the first game, Boudreau decided to give Doby a final test.

In the first inning, down by a no balls, two strikes count, Doby took four straight balls for a walk to first base. The tense Doby of 1947 could not have done that, and so the base on balls, in its own way, was as impressive as his huge home run in Houston. Later in the game, he doubled, singled home a run, drove in another run with an infield out, and stole a base.

Doby's two hits in four times at bat raised his spring average to .358, second on the team. Now Boudreau had just one more exhibition game to decide if Doby would not only make the team, but if he deserved to be the starting right fielder. To do so, he replaced Doby with Pat Seerey, but Seerey went hitless, striking out twice. Doby had won out.[33] In seven intense weeks he had progressed from converted infielder destined for assignment to the minor leagues to a position as the first-string right fielder.

A major league record Opening Day crowd of 73,163 fans turned out in Cleveland on Tuesday, April 20, to see the start of one of the most dramatic pennant races in American League history. Eventually, more than 2,600,000 people, the league record for 32 years, would cheer the Indians at home. But that day, few of their cheers were directed at Larry Doby.

At bat, he went hitless in four tries. In right field, he looked shaky.

After the game, Boudreau tried to cheer up Doby, but he knew as he did so that Helyn Doby had told her husband about a miscarriage of the baby they had been expecting in August when she arrived from Paterson the previous Saturday.[34]

The Indians helped the Detroit Tigers open their home season on Friday, April 23. Before 45,233 fans, Doby beat out an infield single against starting pitcher Fred Hutchinson, but the Indians could not bring him around to score. On his next at bat, he took matters into his own hands by blasting a home run 385 feet into the upper deck in right field. With the help of another single by Doby, his third hit of the day, the Indians stopped the Tigers, 8–2.[35]

Doby continued to hit on Saturday, and added some fielding heroics as well. He tripled to left center field in the third inning and scored on Joe Gordon's single. He singled to left center in the eighth and scored on another single by Gordon. In right field, he looked uncertain while catching a sinking line drive, caught a fly ball with his back pressed against the right field wall, and made a nice catch after a long run.

Perhaps equally important, Doby was hit by a pitch from Art Houtteman, but after a brief inspection by trainer Lefty Weissman, Doby limped down to first base as no one raised an eyebrow.[36]

On Sunday, given Doby's five-for-eight performance in the first two games at Briggs Stadium, Boudreau decided to start him against Hal Newhouser, the best left-handed pitcher in the league. In three times at bat, Doby struck out every time. Then, against right-handed relief pitchers Virgil "Fire" Trucks and Rufus Gentry, Doby struck out twice more to tie a major league record held by eight other players at the time.

His dismal performance with the bat didn't seem to harm his fielding, though. He saved the game for the Indians in the sixth inning when he leaped high to make a one-handed catch near the right field wall to rob pinch hitter Fred Hutchinson of a probable triple, preserving a 6–4 Cleveland victory.[37]

The series at Detroit brought back memories of Lubbock and Texarkana to Doby. Because the Tigers restricted their black fans to the upper and lower stands in right field, the white fans felt safe enough to hurl loud racial insults at him. He also had to withstand racist remarks from Detroit's dugout, noticing especially coach Dick Bartell.

Doby's fortunes dropped sharply during the following week. His batting average slumped, and in one stretch of three games he made five errors in the outfield. Discouraged, Boudreau sent Hank Edwards to right field and sat Doby on the bench.[38] "I hadn't really learned how to keep my body under control," Doby remembers, but as he sat he saw an opposing outfielder pause before fielding a ground ball and making a throw. With that insight into the difference between playing second base and the outfield, Doby's fielding improved.

When Doby returned to action a couple of days later, he hit a home run in Griffith Stadium that stands as one of the longest, and strangest, in the history of baseball. With two runners on base and right-handed pitcher Sid Hudson ahead of Doby with a no balls, two strikes count, Doby smashed a towering line drive into a loud speaker 35 feet above the 408-foot sign on the center field fence. The ball bounced back to the playing field and, under the ground rules, was still in play, requiring Doby to sprint for home. Only after he slid, head first, across the plate did the 11,902 fans and reporters realize what Doby had done. In the history of Griffith Stadium, only Babe Ruth and Josh Gibson had matched Doby's shot. Observers estimated that had the ball not hit the loud speaker, it would have landed more than 500 feet from home plate. Yet, despite the fact that it was one of the longest clouts in history, it was an inside-the-park home run.[39]

The next day, continuing to establish himself as something more than a racial experiment, Doby connected again. During a doubleheader at Fenway Park in Boston, one of his two hits in 10 times at bat landed 430 feet from home plate in the center field seats. This time, though, he could trot around the bases and enjoy his fourth home run of the young season. At the end of the day, although his batting average stood at only .246, Doby had batted in 12 runs in 12 games on 14 hits.[40]

He raised his average fully 40 points the next day, however, with his best performance yet in the American League. He belted a pitch from Dave "Boo" Ferriss 440 feet into the right field stands, added three more singles, scored three runs, and batted in two.[41]

With daily coaching from Tris Speaker, Doby's fielding continued to improve. In a game against Chicago, he waited on a line drive in front of him, taming his tendency to charge in like an infielder. That play, as much as his .270 average, 17 runs scored, 15 runs batted in, and five home runs, helped to convince Boudreau to keep Doby past May 20, when all teams had to reduce their rosters from 40 to 25 players.[42]

In June, though, Boudreau benched Doby again, prompting a conference with team vice-president Hank Greenberg. Greenberg, a slugger whose career with the Detroit Tigers earned him a berth in the Hall of Fame, told Doby that he was "swinging at bad pitches." In response, Doby told Greenberg that he hadn't seen "anything up here that I can't hit," and assured Greenberg that if he could "play enough I'm sure I can hit .300." "That," concluded Greenberg, "sold me on Doby."[43]

As Doby thinks back upon Greenberg's comments that he was a "bad ball hitter," he feels able now to defend himself on grounds that he could not present to Greenberg in 1948—race. "Sometimes it was a case of umpiring, too," he says. "Some of them had no love for me. There was a big difference between what they called on Ted [Williams] and what they'd call on me. The umpire who gave me the hardest time was Ed Rommel.

But a couple of them were really fair in their calls. Guys like Bill Summers and Bill McKinley in the beginning, and Ed Runge later on." He also recalls, though, that Greenberg didn't merely criticize him. He worked with Doby in batting practice to learn the strike zone and to become a more "selective" hitter.

As Doby struggled toward mid-June, the Indians returned home at the top of the standings in the American League, inspiring a case of pennant fever among their followers. As a symptom of their fever, 82,781 fans, a record for a major league game, turned out for a doubleheader against the contending Philadelphia Athletics. Boudreau marked the occasion with a bold move, for the first time inserting Doby into the lineup in center field. Doby responded with a stunning performance, sending the huge crowd home rejoicing over Cleveland's three and one-half game lead over the hated Yankees.

In the first game, Doby singled to right field to drive in Hal Peck with the run that broke a 3–3 tie. In center field, he raced in to catch a short fly ball, and later ran to deep left center field to intercept a line drive. In the second game, he doubled and singled to drive in two runs and made five putouts to preserve a 10–0 shutout for pitcher Bob Lemon. By the end of the day, not only had he achieved a .267 batting average, but he seemed to have found his natural positon as well.[44]

A couple of weeks later, after Doby left the field on a stretcher with an ankle injury, his importance to his teammates, and his acceptance by them, became apparent in Lefty Weissman's training room. Outfielders Hal Peck and Hank Edwards checked on his condition and kidded him. Pitcher Sam Zoldak helped Weissman apply an ice pack. Rudie Schaffer, Veeck's business manager, dropped by to express his concern. Later, X-rays revealed only a sprain.[45]

Having seen his prized black player establish himself, Veeck now permitted Doby to make public appearances. Approximately 800 people showed up at the all-black Cory Methodist Church to help the Leaman Young Men's Club honor him. Veeck sent Greenberg with Doby.

Greenberg began his remarks by tacitly acknowledging how whites and blacks might perceive Doby differently. "Fans ask me," he said, " 'Why do you keep Doby in the lineup?' I suppose you [his black audience] wonder why we *don't* put Larry in the lineup. Well, we want to win ball games. When we think Doby can help us win games, we put him in the lineup; when we take him out, it is because we think someone else can do a better job. His ability as a ballplayer is the only thing that counts with us." Greenberg ended by asking his black audience to "be patient" until Doby became a regular player.

Then, after brief speeches by sportscaster Tom Manning, sportswriters Ed McAuley and Doc Young, and Judge Perry B. Jackson, Doby's friends were introduced: Marion Motley of the Cleveland Browns and his wife,

Eula, and Arthur and Doris Grant, whose home he lived in when the Indians were in Cleveland.

To conclude the program, the first of many to follow during Doby's long career in Cleveland, the young men's club presented him with a traveling bag and Helyn Doby with a necklace and flowers. Mayor Thomas A. Burke sent an emissary with a wooden "key to the city."

When Doby's turn came to speak, he briefly thanked everyone for their best wishes, and then presented new uniforms to a new junior team in the Class F Cleveland City baseball league, the "Dobys."[46]

A landmark event in the history of the integration of baseball marked Doby's slow recovery from his ankle sprain. On July 7, a year and two days after Doby's pioneering debut, the Indians signed a 42-year old rookie pitcher named Leroy "Satchel" Paige to a contract. Now Doby had a roommate, none other than the most famous, and possibly the greatest, player in the history of the black leagues.

Years later, Doby felt that Paige's arrival was a "big break." "I had a roomie at last," he told editor Charles Dexter, "—and what a roomie! Satch arrived with twenty suits of clothes, a big smile, and no advice except to keep in there playing ball. Satch didn't care what people said or did. All he thought about was baseball."[47]

Yet, according to Doc Young in a book published after Paige left the Indians, Paige was a new but not necessarily positive element in Doby's life:

On the road, Satch roomed with Doby. They represented a contrast: Satch was a fabulous name, he was confident, and he was a proven success, regardless of the record he was to make during the twilight of his career in the majors. Doby was young, ambitious, and was fighting, as much as his nature allowed, for a place in the sun. They called each other "Roomie." Sometimes, in the manner of college kids, Satch called Larry his "old lady." But they were never buddy-buddy.

Once Satch asked Larry why most major leaguers did not wear hats. The young player stung the veteran when he replied, "Do as we major leaguers do; don't ask questions!"

That kind of ribbing was new to the moundmaster from the far-away barnstorming hills. Another time Larry told a white reporter that Satch was carrying a gun, indicating that he [Doby] was afraid to room with him. It was a jest, but by neglecting to tell the writer that Satch, a collector of antiques, had picked up an ancient firearm, Doby had implied that Satch was a sort of Stepin Fetchit. Satch didn't like it—rightly.[48]

Paige, though, did carry a real gun in his suitcase. Doby never asked why, but it's likely that Paige began the habit in his barnstorming days, when he'd often leave town with hundreds or even thousands of dollars as his share of the gate of an exhibition game. He was, after all, one of the highest paid players in baseball, black or white, during much of his career. In 1946, Paige was the only player in the sport to have his own airplane, chartered by the Kansas City Monarchs, to fly him back and forth from what he called "special engagements."

Actually, catfish was the principal problem between Doby and Paige. In contradiction of his famous rule, "Don't eat fried foods. They angry up the blood," Paige had taken to frying catfish during his barnstorming days, and continued the practice with the Indians. He would set up his small electric stove in their hotel room, buy catfish from the nearest fish store, and fry it for dinner. His recipe called for a liberal sprinkling of Duff Gordon No. 28, an expensive sherry wine. As soon as Doby got his first whiff of Paige's dinner, he looked for company elsewhere. Long ago, in South Carolina, he had been taught to detest catfish, which "live in the mud, and eat anything."

Paige's arrival, and the addition of black catcher Roy Campanella to the lineup of the Brooklyn Dodgers, produced yet another step in the history of the integration of baseball in 1948. On July 21, an exhibition game between the Indians and Dodgers to benefit the Cleveland Baseball Federation brought together all four of the black men in the major leagues at that time: Doby and Paige of the Indians, and Robinson and Campanella of the Dodgers. A crowd of 64,877 fans showed up, about 40 percent of them black.

Only Campanella played the entire game. Robinson left after the second inning because he had previously pulled a muscle. Paige struck out the side on 13 pitches in the sixth inning and induced three pop-ups in the seventh before he retired for the night. And Doby, still recovering from his ankle sprain, played only four innings.[49]

The teams had met the previous month in Brooklyn for the benefit of the Milk Fund. Doby and Robinson were the only black men in the major leagues at that time, and the two provided the laugh of the night for the crowd at Ebbets Field. With Robinson playing first base and Doby the base runner there, the two engaged in conversation. At that point pitcher Rex Barney tried to pick Doby off first, but Robinson was so engrossed in talking that the ball hit him in the chest and bounded away. Robinson recovered before Doby could advance to second, then broke up laughing when he saw the grin on Doby's face.

After the game, Doby and Robinson talked at length about their lives in the two major leagues, a habit they usually practiced on the telephone.

Still learning to play the outfield in the midst of a hot pennant race, Doby went from one extreme to the other in late July and early August. Against Philadelphia, a fly ball lost in the sun bounced off the bill of his cap, allowing two decisive runs to score in a 4–3 defeat.[50] Against the Yankees, he made two catches that drew the ultimate accolade. He leaped high above the right center field fence to thwart George McQuinn's bid for a home run, and later ran almost 60 yards to deprive Joe DiMaggio of a triple "with one of the most sensational sprints seen in this town since Tris Speaker roamed the pasture."[51] With his bat already a factor in the pennant race, Doby had now added his glove. His two catches helped the Indians to defeat the Yankees in both games of a doubleheader, enabling Cleveland to remain in a virtual tie for first place with Philadelphia.[52]

At some point during the month of August, the sound of voices raised in song began to drift out of the Cleveland shower room. With Doby as lead, Jim Hegan as tenor, Eddie Robinson as baritone, and Satchel Paige as bass, this most interesting quartet sang "Down Among the Sheltering Pines," "Sweet Sue," and "Old Black Joe" in an expression of team unity that no one could have imagined on July 5, 1947.

There were other signs of unity, too. As Doby strengthened his position in the starting lineup, Gordon and Steve Gromek began needling him. If Doby had a bad day at bat, Gordon would tell him, "They never had pitchers like that in that bush league you came from." Gromek would call out, "Hey Larry, there's a phone call for you!" Doby, taking the bait, would ask, "Who is it?" And Gromek would reply, "Lena Horne!"

On the road, the Indians briefly lost their league lead to the Athletics, only to have roommates Doby and Paige restore it on August 12 at Comiskey Park. Sixty-six thousand fans showed up at the gates in response to Paige's advertised appearance on the pitching mound, 15,000 more than the old ball park could accommodate. They were not disappointed, as Paige limited the White Sox to five scattered singles. Meanwhile his roommate, Doby, tripled and scored in his first at bat, singled and scored the next time up, and drove in a run and stole two bases when the Indians scored three times in the last inning. The Sox were not the only casualty of the day, though: the crowd broke an entrance gate in its frenzy to see the game.[53]

Two days later, Doby's bat crushed the White Sox in both games of a doubleheader. He staked Bob Feller to all the runs Feller needed in the first inning of the first game by doubling with the bases loaded to drive in three runs, and singled to produce the only run Bob Lemon needed in a shutout victory in the second game.[54]

At St. Louis, Doby almost self-destructed in a rage of temper. Furious at a heckler who kept insulting him with racial obscenities, Doby grabbed a bat and started to climb the low fence behind the Cleveland dugout. In the uproar that followed, no one was quite sure whether it was Paige, Hal Peck, Thurman Tucker, or Bill McKechnie who restrained him.[55]

The incident seemed not to distract Doby, however. As the Indians went into a brief tailspin, falling four and one-half games behind the red-hot Boston Red Sox on Labor Day, he was in the midst of a 21-game hitting streak, raising his batting average to .282. He also played center field more aggressively as his confidence grew and his skills improved.[56]

After Labor Day, the Indians reversed their fortunes, winning 17 of 20 games. Rookie pitcher Gene Bearden reeled off five victories in a row, veteran Bob Feller won four times without losing, and Sam Zoldak won four out of five. But it was Doby, because his contributions were so unexpected in April, who loomed largest. Larger, even, than those of Gordon and Keltner. They, after all, had been expected to provide the punch in the Cleveland batting order, and they did, driving in 19 and 18 runs after Labor Day.[57]

Three times Doby's hits were game winners. On September 15 at Cleveland, he smashed a grand slam home run in the first inning to lead a 6–3 triumph over the Washington Senators.[58] On September 18, before a crowd of 75,382, his dramatic home run with one out and one on in the bottom of the ninth inning produced a 5–3 win over the Athletics.[59]

And on Saturday, October 2, with a victory over the Detroit Tigers assuring the Indians of at least a tie for the pennant, Doby had another sensational day. He singled, doubled, and scored a run; doubled in a run; and singled again to complete a four-for-four day and raise his average to .302.[60]

Now the season came down to its final day. The Indians, assured of at least a tie for the pennant, again took the field against the Tigers, while the Red Sox opposed the Yankees in Boston. But the Indians disappointed the 74,181 fans who came to their immense stadium prepared to celebrate. Detroit pitcher Hal Newhouser outpitched Bob Feller, stopping Doby without a hit and dropping his average to exactly .300. Meanwhile, in Boston, the Red Sox came through with a 10–5 victory on home runs by Dom DiMaggio and Vern Stephens and two doubles by Ted Williams. Only Joe DiMaggio carried a big bat for New York, with two doubles, two singles, and three runs batted in.

Thus the 1948 American League regular season ended in a tie, with both Cleveland and Boston showing records of 96 wins and 58 losses. It would take one more game, the first playoff in league history, to decide who would oppose the Boston Braves in the World Series.[61]

On a cold October Monday in Fenway Park, the Indians got off to a quick start when Boudreau homered over the left field wall in the first inning. After the Red Sox tied the score in the bottom of the inning, Doby tried to start a Cleveland rally in the second, but Dom DiMaggio made a fine running catch in center field to deprive him of a single.

Cleveland's veteran infielders took matters into their hands in the fourth inning. After Boudreau and Gordon singled, Keltner lofted a fly ball over the screen atop the wall in left field for three runs and a 4–1 Cleveland lead. Such a lead, though, could not be considered safe in Fenway Park. And with a trip to the World Series hanging in the balance, Doby's quest to bat at least .300 for the season seemed inconsequential when he followed Keltner's home run with a double off the wall in center field. Doby moved on to third on Bob Kennedy's sacrifice bunt, then scored on a

Indians' Stretch Drive (Last 20 Games, 1948 Season)[62]

Player	AB	H	2B	3B	HR	RBI	Pct.
Doby	48	19	0	1	3	10	.396
Keltner	77	27	2	0	4	18	.351
Mitchell	93	31	4	2	1	7	.333
Gordon	78	24	5	0	8	19	.308
Hegan	74	21	5	0	2	13	.284
Boudreau	74	20	2	0	2	10	.270
Clark	52	14	0	0	2	6	.269
Judnich	49	13	3	0	0	10	.265
Tucker	58	15	5	1	0	8	.259
Robinson	28	5	0	0	0	4	.179
Totals (plus Others)	722	206	26	4	22	109	.285

fielder's choice ground ball by Jim Hegan, making the score 5–1, Cleveland.

After Boudreau's second home run of the day, in the fifth inning with nobody on base, Boston's hopes stirred when Bobby Doerr hit a two-run shot in the sixth inning, making it a 6–3 game.

With such a tenuous lead, Doby's personal goal still seemed to matter little when he came to bat in the seventh inning. What the Indians needed were runs, and they envisioned more when Doby rapped yet another double to left center field. In a replay of the fourth inning, once again Kennedy bunted Doby over to third. But the Red Sox foiled a squeeze bunt when catcher Birdie Tebbetts called for a pitchout and picked Doby off third base.

When neither team could score after that, the dramatic struggle ended with the Indians in possession of their first pennant flag in 28 years. That night, in celebration, jubilant Bill Veeck threw a party for his team at the Kenmore Hotel in Boston. Despite the contents of his glass—milk—nobody there was happier than Larry Doby. Despite a ninth inning strikeout, he had stood the American League on its head with a .396 average since Labor Day and finished the season at .301.[63]

In mid-October, Boudreau divided the credit for Cleveland's success between Doby and the only other teetotaler at the party, Jim Hegan. "Hegan and Doby made this ball club," he told Sam Lacy. "It was the great improvement made by this pair that transformed what may have been a fourth-place club into a pennant winner."[64]

When the World Series between the Indians and the Boston Braves opened at Braves Field in Boston on October 6, the Indians failed despite a two-hit pitching performance by Feller. Johnny Sain of the Braves threw a four-hitter to win a 1–0 game. Doby got one of the hits, a single, and advanced to second on an infield out, but his teammates could not drive him home.[65]

The Indians drew even with the Braves the next day as Doby proved to be the difference between the two teams. In the fourth inning, with the score tied 1–1, he grounded a single to right to drive in what proved to be the winning run for his good friend, pitcher Bob Lemon. Cleveland went on to win the game, 4–1.[66]

After a day off to travel west to Ohio, the Indians moved ahead of the Braves by scoring a 2–0 victory in Game Three. This time, an infield error allowed the Indians to score the only run they needed, and it was Doby who helped to create the decisive situation. With runners on first and third and one out, he hit what might have been a double play ground ball, but shortstop Alvin Dark threw wildly to first, allowing Doby to be called safe and allowing pitcher Gene Bearden to score what proved to be the only run he needed to win. Under the rules of scoring, Doby could not receive credit for a run batted in.[67]

With the excitement building, the greatest crowd in World Series history, 81,897 fans, jammed the stadium on the shore of Lake Erie on Saturday, October 9. They cheered happily when the Indians took a 1–0 lead in the first inning on Boudreau's double to right, remained quiet in the second and third innings, then rose to a standing ovation in the fourth. After Gromek struck out and Mitchell grounded out, Doby hit the second pitch from Sain into a "jubilant, milling mob of standees behind the low outfield barrier in right field," some 420 feet from home plate.

As Doby planted his spiked shoe on home plate, Boudreau's handshake put a symbolic seal on one of baseball's greatest stories of 1948. Years later, Boudreau termed that handshake "my thanks to myself. I was playing, managing, and worrying about Larry."[68]

And when Doby's home run turned out to be the decisive blow in a 2–1 victory for the Indians,[69] more symbolism followed—the photograph of Gromek, the winning pitcher, and Doby, the slugger, in spontaneous embrace in the Cleveland clubhouse. Baseball became, for the first time in Doby's mind, an "All-American game."

With the prospect of clinching the world championship now clearly in view, an even bigger crowd of Cleveland partisans appeared for Game Five the next day. But the 86,288 fans went home disappointed. The Braves defeated the Indians by an 11–5 score to draw within 3–2 in games, and to force the Series back to Boston for Game Six. Doby grounded out twice, struck out twice, and flied to left. His wild throw on a close play at third base allowed the Braves to score one of their six runs in the seventh inning.[70]

In Game Six, Doby played well. He singled in the first inning, flied to the base of the left field wall in the third, walked in the fifth, and singled again in the seventh. Playing right field, he helped to limit Boston to one run in the eighth inning with his running catch of a low line drive, and by playing a ball perfectly as it caromed off the right field wall to hold Earl Torgeson to a double.

The final drama of the Series came, fittingly, in the bottom of the ninth inning. With Cleveland clinging to a 4–3 lead, Hegan made a lunging catch of a pop-up and doubled Eddie Stanky off first base. Then, Tommy Holmes, one of the National League's most dangerous hitters, hit a long fly ball toward the left field seats. But Kennedy, a defensive replacement for Mitchell, caught the ball near the wall for the final out, and Cleveland's world championship.[71]

That night the Indians staged one of the most riotous cross–country parties in the history of railroading. They drank, sang, and drank some more all the way back to Cleveland. A few brief fistfights punctuated the celebration, all of them harmless. By the time their train got to Union Terminal in Cleveland, Bill Veeck owed the Pennsylvania Railroad several thousands of dollars to repair badly damaged railroad cars.[72]

Despite their hangovers, the Indians loved every minute of their reception the next day. More than 200,000 people, the largest crowd in the city's history, lined the 10-mile parade route through the city's streets. Doby rode in an open convertible with Dale Mitchell.[73] It was a long way from Lubbock and Texarkana in the spring.

Larry Doby rested for a few days in Cleveland before he and Helyn packed their blue Ford convertible for the drive back home to Paterson. While preparing to leave, they learned that, because of the record crowds in Cleveland, Larry's World Series share would be the biggest in history. His check for $6,772.05 more than doubled his season's salary of $5,000.[74]

As the Dobys drove east, the proud people of Paterson began to plan ceremonies to honor him. The celebration began at City Hall, festooned for the occasion with a huge banner which read, "Welcome Home Larry Doby. Paterson Is Proud of You." A motorcade of dignitaries escorted the Dobys to Bauerle Field in front of Eastside High School, where the entire student body had been assembled. Hundreds of other well-wishers swelled the total crowd to about 3,000 people, who heard a succession of speakers, including Mayor Michael U. DeVita, Effa Manley, and Charlie Jamieson.[75]

Jamieson, in the coincidence which nobody could anticipate when he watched Larry Doby play stickball in the playground across the street from his house, had played outfield for the Indians in their championship season in 1920. He batted .319 during the regular season, and .333 while helping to defeat the Brooklyn Dodgers in the World Series. Predicting that Doby would be "one of the greatest players in the game because you have speed in your legs and power in your bat,"[76] Jamieson quietly enabled the city of Paterson to bridge the racial gap which barred black men from the game in 1920, but accepted them, however grudgingly, in 1948.

When the line of speakers finally ran out, Doby took the microphone to a great ovation. "I'm not good at making speeches," he said, "but I want to thank Mayor DeVita for all the kind things he said about me today.

"I'd like to thank as a group the people who have made this day possible. To the teachers at Eastside, especially Mr. [Al] Livingstone [Doby's baseball coach], I want to say that I'm grateful for the sportsmanship and clean play which they taught me. I particularly want to express my gratitude to Pat Wilson, who gave me my first uniform.

"I know I'm not a perfect gentleman, but I always try to be one."

As Doby finished, the crowd rose in approval of the most prominent black man in their city's history. Doby's mother, Mrs. Etta Walker, and his mother-in-law, Mrs. Emily Curvy, alternately smiled and cried as the applause died down.[77]

In November, Doby began coaching the freshman basketball team at Eastside, which gave him immense pleasure. Sometimes, at the invitation of two of his old coaches, Henry Rumana and Bob Dimond, Doby spoke to the students in gym classes, telling them how his Eastside coaches had been a good influence on his life. As he did so, he could not help but notice that the number of black students at Eastside had increased since his graduation some six years and one world war earlier.

Doby felt especially honored to be asked to speak to the students. "I felt that Rumana and Dimond respected me because I was a successful person, not just a famous athlete. I preferred it that way. Fame is just a myth, but being a person is real," he says.

NOTES

1. Associated Press, *Plain Dealer*, December 31, 1947.
2. *Evening News*, January 5, 1948.
3. *The Sporting News*, January 21, 1948.
4. Ibid., February 18, 1948.
5. Gordon Cobbledick, "Plain Dealing," *Plain Dealer*, January 29, 1948.
6. Ibid.
7. *Call and Post*, February 14, 1948.

8. Personal interview with Jim Hegan, July 23, 1980.

9. Telephone interview with Harold A. "Spud" Goldstein, October 25, 1980.

10. Personal interview with Harry Jones, January 11, 1981.

11. Jackie Robinson with Charles Dexter, *Baseball Has Done It* (Philadelphia: J. B. Lippincott, 1964), p. 61.

12. *Plain Dealer*, March 2, 1948.

13. Harry Jones, *Plain Dealer*, March 4, 1948.

14. Ibid., March 5, 1948.

15. Veeck, *Saturday Evening Post*, March 23, 1949.

16. Cobbledick, "Plain Dealing," *Plain Dealer*, March 7, 1948.

17. *Plain Dealer*, March 8, 1948.

18. Ibid., March 12, 1948.

19. Ibid., March 18, 1948.

20. Ibid., March 19, 1948.

21. Jones, *Plain Dealer*, March 21, 1948.

22. Ibid., March 23, 1948.

23. A. S. "Doc" Young, *Call and Post*, March 27, 1948.

24. *Plain Dealer*, March 24, 1948.

25. Lou Boudreau, *Player-Manager* (Boston: Little, Brown and Co., 1949), p. 109.

26. *Plain Dealer*, March 26, 28, 29, and 30, 1948.

27. Ibid., April 1, 1948.

28. Ed McAuley, *The Sporting News*, April 14, 1948.

29. Personal interview with Lou Boudreau, September 13, 1980.

30. Franklin Lewis, *Press*, April 14, 1948.

31. This account of the events at Lubbock and Texarkana is based on a telephone interview with Harold A. "Spud" Goldstein, October 25, 1980; a personal interview with Harry Jones, January 11, 1981; and an interview with Doby.

32. Ibid.

33. *Call and Post*, April 24, 1948.

34. Doc Young, *Call and Post*, April 24, 1948.

35. Ibid., May 1, 1948.

36. Ibid.

37. Ibid.

38. Doc Young, *Call and Post*, May 8, 1948.

39. *Call and Post*, May 15, 1948.

40. Ibid.

41. Ibid.

42. Doc Young, *Call and Post*, May 22, 1948.

43. Art King, "He's Learned to Laugh," in *Baseball Stars of 1955*, ed. Bruce Jacobs (New York: Lion Books, 1955), p. 40.

44. Jones, *Plain Dealer*, June 21, 1948.

45. *Call and Post*, July 3, 1948.

46. Ibid.

47. Robinson and Dexter, *Baseball Has Done It*, p. 61.

48. Doc Young, *Great Negro Baseball Stars and How They Made the Major Leagues* (New York: A. S. Barnes and Co., 1953), p. 80.

49. Doc Young, *Call and Post*, July 24, 1948.

50. Charles Heaton, *Plain Dealer*, July 29, 1948.

51. Ed McAuley, *News* (Cleveland), August 9, 1948.

52. Cobbledick, *Plain Dealer*, August 9, 1948.

53. Jones, *Plain Dealer*, August 13, 1948.

54. *Call and Post*, August 21, 1948.

55. The many eyewitnesses to this event could not agree on who first restrained Doby.

56. *Call and Post*, September 11, 1948.

57. *The Sporting News*, October 5, 1948.

58. Associated Press, *New York Times*, September 17, 1948.

59. Ibid., September 20, 1948.

60. Ibid., October 3, 1948.

61. Ibid., October 4, 1948.

62. *Plain Dealer*, October 1, 1948.

63. *New York Times*, October 5, 1948.

64. *Afro-American* (National Edition), October 16, 1948.

65. *New York Times*, October 7, 1948.

66. Ibid., October 8, 1948.

67. Ibid., October 9, 1948.

68. Boudreau, loc. cit.

69. *New York Times*, October 10, 1948.

70. Ibid., October 11, 1948.

71. Ibid., October 12, 1948.

72. Jones, loc. cit.

73. *Plain Dealer*, October 13, 1948.

74. *Afro-American* (National Edition), October 16, 1948.

75. *Morning Call*, October 19, 1948.

76. Doc Goldstein, *Evening News* (Paterson), October 19, 1948.

77. Ibid.

8

Prime Time

The year 1949 began with Larry and Helyn Doby embroiled in a frustrating attempt to buy a house in the Eastside section of Paterson. With Larry's World Series check as down payment, they anticipated raising a family in a nicer neighborhood than the Hamilton Avenue location where they had been renting an apartment.

Hamilton Avenue was only two blocks away from the old Twelfth Avenue neighborhood which had welcomed Doby back in 1938. In the 11 years since then, World War II hastened the combination of black migration from the south and white flight to the suburbs, the classic pattern for America's cities. The old neighborhood was about to become a ghetto of the urban poor.

The Dobys, as Paterson's most famous black couple, did not foresee the tricks of the real estate brokers. Sellers suddenly decided they no longer wanted to sell. Buyers miraculously appeared just moments before the Dobys visited. Brokers steered them to undesirable houses and locations. These were the tactics which had become standard in the de facto segregation of America's housing. To the man who just a few months before had been paraded through an applauding city and praised by its mayor in front of 3,000 people, the tactics of "but not next door" were an outrage. In anger, Doby called a friend, who called Mayor DeVita, for help.

To his credit, DeVita responded. He twisted a few arms and bullied a few brokers and ward leaders. Soon the Dobys had a house they liked on East 27th Street in a quiet, well-kept middle-class neighborhood. They swallowed their bitterness and lived there as the family grew: Christina in 1949, Leslie in 1954, Larry, Jr., in 1957, and Kim in 1958.

Years later, when they needed a larger house after Kim's birth, and encountered the same discriminatory devices again, the Dobys moved, in 1960, to an integrated neighborhood in the more enlightened town of

Montclair, eight miles to the south. Susan, their last child, was born there in 1962.

When Doby left for spring training in late February, he did so as a 25-year-old homeowner and expectant father, a man of means and responsibility. These attributes were of little value in Tucson, though. Once again the Santa Rita Hotel refused to house or feed him, and he roomed once again with Chester and Lucille Willis and their children. Four other black men endured the same segregation that spring: Satchel Paige, Saturnino Orestes Armas "Minnie" Minoso, Artie Wilson, and Roy Welmaker.

Three events involving Doby marked Cleveland's spring training exhibition season. In late March, when the world champion Indians visited Los Angeles for a series of games, Doby refused to stay at the Biltmore Hotel, even though he could have done so. He remembered that, in 1948, he stayed at the Watkins when the team's traveling secretary, Spud Goldstein, did not try to billet him at the Biltmore. Doby liked the Watkins and its famous black clientele so much that he chose to stay there again. Paige, Wilson, Minoso, and Welmaker then decided to follow him.[1]

A week later, in Houston, before a record crowd of 13,998 fans at Buffalo Stadium, Doby drove a pitch from New York Giants right-hander Larry Jansen far beyond the 434-foot sign on the center field fence. The drive reminded local fans that the only other player to hit a ball in that vicinity was Hack Wilson of the Chicago Cubs in 1929.[2]

As the Indians moved across the deep south with the Giants, a less pleasant incident marred Doby's spring. Although Goldstein took great care to arrange Doby's segregated housing and transportation, not every step of Doby's path could be anticipated. One day, Doby, Al Rosen, and a third player whom neither can now remember entered a taxicab in a southern town that they also cannot remember. "The cab driver made a comment about the fact that Larry would have to get another cab," Rosen says. "And I got out myself. I can't remember who else was with us—Lemon or whomever. While I was a southerner born and bred [Spartanburg, South Carolina], and because I'm a Jew who had been victimized by pettiness and anti-Semitic feelings, I remember feeling very, very bad about the whole situation.

"I was a little pugnacious at the time, and I threatened to kick the cab driver's teeth in. I was pulled away on the basis of, 'Let's not have a problem.'

"As a southerner, I knew those were the customs, but I knew it was wrong. Whatever the customs are, that doesn't necessarily make it right. That's why I wanted to take on the cab driver."[3]

Rosen stands, then, as one of the few teammates to stand up for Doby in a public situation. When the team bus picked up or dropped off Doby at his segregated hotel, none of them rose in protest. Nor did they express their sympathies for him when they saw him, often in uniform, standing on the street in front of his hotel waiting for their bus.

When the regular season opened, Doby alternately slumped at the plate
and hit prodigious home runs. Benched by Boudreau for two days in May
for not hitting, Doby came back with a home run beyond the 435-foot
sign in center field at Yankee Stadium. He connected with a low fast ball
by Bob Porterfield and deposited it in a spot not reached since a shot by
Lou Gehrig off Grover Cleveland Alexander in the 1928 World Series.
Not even Babe Ruth had ever hit one there.[4]

Doby hit the longest home run of his career one week later, on May
25, 1949, in Washington, D.C. He drove a pitch thrown by right-handed
pitcher Sid Hudson, his "baseball cousin," over a sign on top of the scoreboard beyond the right center field fence in spacious Griffith Stadium.
Witnesses estimated that the ball traveled well over 500 feet.[5] A few years
later, people compared it with a shot actually measured at 565 feet off the
bat of Mickey Mantle of the Yankees.

Doby's power that night may have been motivated by rage. He remembers that his teammates watched "Amos 'n' Andy" on television in the
clubhouse before the game. The players laughed often at the black actors
and actresses portraying dumb or shiftless or sly black men and women.
·In horror and rage, Doby fled to the dugout to be alone.

But after his titanic home run, feeling more relaxed, Doby told the
baseball writers, "I know I hit that ball further than any in my life." Then,
alluding to his tremendous inside-the-park home run off Hudson in Griffith Stadium the year before, he added, "Better than the one here last
year."[6]

As the mid-season All-Star break approached, American League manager Boudreau evaluated the statistics of the league's outfielders and named
Doby to the team for the first time. While Doby's .285 batting average
did not rank him among the leaders, his 13 home runs and 47 runs batted
in did. So did his defensive skills.

In the game, played on July 12 at Brooklyn's Ebbets Field, Jackie Robinson once again blazed the trail ahead of Doby. Robinson became the
first black man to appear in an All-Star game, to be followed innings later
by Doby, Campanella, and Don Newcombe. Doby played right field and
center field, failed to hit in one time at bat, and made two putouts as the
American League stars posted an 11–7 victory over the National League.[7]

The fact that four out of the five black men in the major leagues made
the All-Star game, Doby now observes, is "proof that for a black man to
play in the majors he had to be much better than a white player. In most
cases, that's still true." Boudreau, who won the honor of managing the
American League team by virtue of his having managed the pennant winner in 1948, did not name the fifth black player, his own Satchel Paige, to
the team.

Doby embarrassed himself in late July at Cleveland Stadium. With the
bases loaded in the eighth inning and nobody out, and with the Indians
trailing the Yankees by 7–4, Doby took a big lead off third base. When

he thought that Yankees catcher Yogi Berra had left home plate unguarded between pitches by lefty Joe Page, Doby suddenly dashed for home. But Berra yelled to Page, who threw home in time to catch the sliding Doby.

Later, Boudreau brought Doby into his office to tell him the obvious—his attempted steal of home was "a mistake." After it, the Indians failed to score, and lost the game. Although reports were published that Boudreau levied a fine against Doby, they were not true. "I didn't want to take that aggressiveness away from Larry because he was a good base runner," Boudreau observed.[8]

"It was all my idea," Doby admitted later, exonerating third base coach Steve O'Neill, who had been booed by the crowd. The next day, Doby quieted his critics with a home run in the ninth inning to defeat those same Yankees.

The incident followed Doby. When the Indians arrived in Philadelphia to play the Athletics, a professional heckler named Pete Adelis, paid by the A's and given a prominent seat in the deck just above the visiting team's dugout, went into his act. Wearing a steel German war helmet and equipped with a billy club, Adelis waited for Doby to come to bat. Simultaneously banging on his helmet and yelling in a loud voice, Adelis screamed, "Hey! Dopey! Hey! Dopey!"

Relieved to get away from Adelis when the series with Philadelphia ended, Doby looked forward to a visit with friends in New Jersey during a series against the Yankees in New York. To his disbelief, as he came to bat for the first time against the Yankees, he heard Adelis again—"Hey! Dopey!" accompanied by the clang of billy club against steel helmet. The Athletics had paid Adelis to follow the Indians to New York.

Later that season, in another game against the Yankees, this time in New York, Doby stole home successfully. "I wanted to prove a point," he says. "So when Vic Raschi went into his windup, I went without a sign from [coach] Steve O'Neill. I was safe by so much, there wasn't even a play at the plate. When I came back to the bench, I yelled, 'Now write that!' which was probably not a good thing to say. Nobody said anything at the time. Not O'Neill, not Boudreau, nobody.

"About a year later, I met Pete Adelis outside the ball park in Philadelphia. He said to me, 'You know, you're a good sport.' Then he decided to get off me and get on Luke Easter."

Doby's failure and success in stealing home had little relevance on the fortunes of the defending champion Indians in 1949. They had already fallen behind the Yankees by five and one-half games by mid-season, and ended up in third place, eight games back.

A Hollywood movie, though, may have been a factor. That spring and early summer, Republic Pictures tried to cash in on the fame of the Indians by using them in a film entitled "The Kid from Cleveland." As described by Bosley Crowther in his review in the New York Times, "The Kid" was a "labored tale of the generous attempts of a sports announcer [played by veteran actor George Brent] to help a wayward youth [Rusty Tamblyn]. And in these benevolent endeavors, he recruits not only Bill Veeck . . . but apparently the whole team. In fact, Mr. Veeck and the Indians pay so much attention to this pursuit that one perceives (since the time is the present) why the Indians are in third place."[9]

The film opened in Cleveland in August of that summer and did well at the box office for three weeks. But it died everywhere else. Surprisingly, the plot hinges on Larry Doby and Joe Gordon, which may be another reason why "The Kid from Cleveland" was a box office bust. Most Americans did not like to see black performers in other than servile positions in the movies until the 1960's. That's why Hollywood lightened Lena Horne's skin, and shot her films in such a way that her scenes were clipped out entirely before distribution in southern states.

Doby appears briefly in one scene about midway through the film, showing Rusty Tamblyn and other kids in a reform school how to swing a bat. Near the end, in a final effort to persuade "The Kid" to go straight, Veeck narrates a flashback, repeating his story about how, after Doby struck out in his first at bat in the big leagues, Gordon deliberately struck out so that Doby wouldn't feel bad. The scene shows Doby striking out and slumping back to the bench, head lowered, to take a seat at the far end of the dugout. Then Gordon strikes out, follows in Doby's footsteps and sits down beside him, head bowed equally low. Without dialog for either man, since Veeck is narrating, Doby sees the parallel between the rookie and the great star and manages a stagey smile. How this is supposed to make "The Kid" change from delinquent to upstanding citizen is not at all clear.

Although Doby may not have been an asset in the film, he was an asset to the Indians in 1949. His batting average dropped from .301 to .280, yet he led the team in home runs with 24, runs batted in with 85, runs scored with 106, bases on balls with 91, and in slugging percentage with .468. Unfortunately, he also led in strikeouts with 90.

A breakdown of his average showed that he hit .264 at home and .304 on the road, including .417 at Yankee Stadium. Batting with runners in scoring position, he averaged .468, one of the top figures in the American League.

In his second season as an outfielder, Doby improved his fielding average from .963 to .987.

He shared the league lead in just one category: he and Eddie Robinson were each hit seven times by pitches.[10]

The 1950 season proved to be one of Doby's greatest in the American League. It started out on a low note, however, with the by now usual discrimination by the Santa Rita Hotel in Tucson, except that this time Helyn Doby and their infant daughter were also its objects.

One day, when Helyn brought baby Christina to meet her father after the day's workouts, Christina began to cough, and seemed in need of a drink. Upon the suggestion of Aldona Jones, wife of *Plain Dealer* sportswriter Harry Jones, the trio went into the lobby of the Santa Rita and headed for the water fountain, to be intercepted there by a vigilant member of the hotel staff. Despite Mrs. Jones's explanation that the baby needed a drink, they were instructed to leave the hotel.

On another occasion, Helyn and Christina, and Aldona and her two children, took a day trip to Nogales on the Mexican border. Denied food and drink in a restaurant, they ended up eating sandwiches and drinking soda, purchased by Mrs. Jones, in a nearby park.[11]

Doby, who had always tried to bank the fires of his anger at racial discrimination directed at him and Helyn, now had to contend with discrimination directed at the next generation—their own baby.

When the 1950 season opened, first baseman Luke Easter had replaced Satchel Paige as the second black player on the Indians. In fact, with the release of Paige (after Bill Veeck sold his interest in the team during the winter of 1949–50), Doby and Easter were the only black players in the entire American League, four seasons after Doby's debut.

Easter, like Paige, did little to provide round-the-clock companionship for Doby. They were as different from each other as Doby and Paige had been. While Doby was totally serious on the field, Easter relaxed and enjoyed his new status, at the age of 35, as a big leaguer. Pitcher Mike Garcia remembers Easter as "a real likeable guy."[12] Harrison Dillard, who won the Olympic gold medal in the 100-meter dash at London in 1948 and who had replaced Louis Jones on the Cleveland public relations staff, describes Easter as "always bubbling."[13] Al Rosen rolled all the descriptions into one big one. "Luke was a great big, easy going, devil-may-care, jolly, hail fellow well met kind of guy who took a ribbing and dished it out. Larry, maybe inside, I think he may have looked at Luke like an Uncle Tom type."[14]

Easter could not help but be aware of Doby's attitude toward him. Once, catching Doby in a particularly serious mood, he advised, "Look, Larry, you fight just half the world and leave the other half to me."[15]

Easter apparently understood Doby's quiet and private crusade for racial justice, which Doby calls "a responsibility that called for all the dignity and diplomacy that had to be used, because I was involved in a historical and pioneering life. I could probably have been like an Easter or a Paige, but that wasn't my role. I think that I have gained some dignity and respect from those who have looked at me differently from what they were taught to expect from a black man, or different from what they were used to. It wasn't a matter of choice, though. That was the natural me."

Dillard thinks that Easter's presence provided a real benefit, but not one that white observers would have seen. He says, "When Doby and Easter were off together, or when they were among other blacks, I think then you could see the benefit of having an Easter-type personality around Larry.

You could see Larry relax and smile and joke and play and laugh under those circumstances. In mixed company, [Easter's presence] didn't appear to make any difference [in Doby's behavior]. I don't think Larry was ever comfortable when a black was acting up or having fun in mixed company. He wanted you to be a gentleman and be like other people, you might say."[16]

The white Cleveland players, although they could not see the private relationship between Easter and Doby, could see how different the two men were. According to Rosen, "It was often said in our clubhouse that if you could have put Larry Doby's talent with Luke Easter's outlook, you'd have the greatest player on two legs."[17]

But in 1950, whether helped by Easter or not, Doby was one of the great players in baseball. He batted .326, slugged 25 home runs, drove in 102 runs, scored 110 times, collected 164 hits, and drew 98 bases on balls. Three of his home runs came in consecutive times at bat, a rarity in baseball.

Doby's figures did not lead the league in any category. In fact, he led the Indians only in hits and runs, but that's partly because Easter and Rosen, both in their first full seasons, had such outstanding years. In home runs, Rosen had 37 and Easter 28. In runs batted in, Rosen had 110 and Easter 107.

In the outfield, Doby compiled a percentage of .987, 10 points behind the American League leader, Walter "Hoot" Evers of Detroit.[18]

Doby displayed his talent in the mid-season All-Star game at Comiskey Park, where he broke in as a frightened pinch hitter almost exactly three years before. This time he played center field for 14 innings, an All-Star record, as the American League bowed to the National League, 4–3.

In the field, he made nine putouts. At bat, he stroked two hits in six times up and scored one run. His speed on the base paths contributed to one of the key plays of the game in the fifth inning. After Bob Lemon walked and Phil Rizzuto struck out, Doby smashed what appeared to be a single off Jackie Robinson's glove behind second base. With a burst, Doby rounded first and slid into second with one of the shortest doubles in All-Star game history. Lemon moved to third on the play, from where he scored on a sacrifice fly by George Kell. Doby scored himself when the next batter, Ted Williams, singled.

During the game, American League manager Casey Stengel replaced Williams with Dom DiMaggio in left field and replaced Evers with Joe DiMaggio in right. That Stengel kept Doby in center field, flanked by two great center fielders, both named DiMaggio, revealed Stengel's regard for Doby as a ball hawk. Even though Stengel was protecting the ailing and aging Joe DiMaggio by stationing him in right, the tribute to Doby could not be missed. By reason of his stature alone, the "Yankee Clipper" had an almost divine right to center field.

The game went into extra innings when Ralph Kiner homered to tie the score in the top of the ninth inning. Larry Jansen, ace of the Giants, then blanked the American Leaguers over the last five innings, allowing only one hit, a single by Doby in the tenth. Finally, in the fourteenth, Red Schoendienst hit a home run for the National League to snap the 3–3 tie.[19]

During Cleveland's regular season, a fourth–place finish behind the Yankees became almost a certainty after the Indians lost four straight games to the St. Louis Browns in September. A surprising fistfight between Doby and Rosen provided more excitement than the pennant race.

The fight occurred in the visiting team's clubhouse at Yankee Stadium between games of a doubleheader. It was brief, but when teammates pulled the combatants apart, Doby could not play in the second game.

"I recall that it was my fault," says Rosen. "Larry was injured, and he was lying on the [trainer's] table. I started to needle him—'Come on, big man, we need you'—the kind of repartee that you have and everybody laughs about it. In this case, Larry was obviously feeling very badly about his injury. And I just over-stepped the boundaries. . . .

"I do think that at the outset there may have been some inner antagonisms toward me because I came on the scene as a rookie and was having a great year. Larry had been there and attention was being directed to me and not to Larry. Remember, you're dealing at that time with very young people. We had been in first place. We had just blown two games in Boston, and we came in to play a big series with the Yankees."[20]

In Doby's mind, he did not feel jealous of Rosen. Rather, he did not like Rosen's placing the burden of the team's success on him. Neither did Doby like what he considered Rosen's lack of respect for him as an established player. "In later years," he says, "we had that respect between us," a feeling which Rosen shares.[21]

The fight didn't prevent Cleveland sports writers from unanimously choosing Doby as "Man of the Year" in baseball that winter. On January 22, 1951, before an audience of 700 that included pitching immortal Denton True "Cy" Young and American League president Will Harridge, Doby made the longest, and most graceful, speech of his life up to that time.

As recorded in the Hollenden Hotel and printed in the Cleveland *Press*, Doby said:

Gentlemen, this is indeed a great honor. I'm so happy I just don't know what to say. You know I have been selected as "Man of the Year" and I'm proud of it.

However, I stand before you tonight as Larry Doby. There are quite a few men that I would like to mention as responsible for my being here.

I first want to thank the Lord above that He gave me the ability He did in order that I might earn my living playing baseball. I want to thank the speakers at the table for the wonderful tributes they paid me and I want to pay tribute to a great number of people.

First, a man who gave me my first contract, Bill Veeck. The next is a man I admire and appreciate very much, Lou Boudreau, who had confidence in me and gave me the chance to be the "Man of the Year" tonight.

Doby went on to express his appreciation of Bill Mckechnie, Mel Harder, Hank Greenberg, Tris Speaker, Muddy Ruel, his teammates, the fans, his family, the baseball writers, and even the park policemen and grounds-keepers.[22]

The glow of post-season honors quickly turned to ashes in 1951. Al-though he batted .295 and made the All-Star team for the third consecu-tive year, a late-season slump provoked one of the most destructive arti-cles ever to vilify a professional American athlete.

The baseball year began in its usual fashion in Tucson, where the "Man of the Year" in Cleveland was still just a nigger to the managers of the Santa Rita Hotel. But the racial dilemma took a new twist as the Indians barnstormed north. For the first time, four black players, two more than usual, proved worthy of making the roster: Doby, Easter, Minoso, and Harry "Suitcase" Simpson.

Although new manager Al Lopez now denies the existence of a quota of black players,[23] Doby and the others became convinced that either Simpson or Minoso would be traded. "We heard," Doby says, "that Greenberg had to make a choice. . . . He kept Simpson because he was a long ball hitter, which fit into Greenberg's pattern of thinking. Until then, the black players never talked about the quota. We just thought how strong we were going to be with the four of us, and how happy we were going to be with four of us together."

All four black players remained with Cleveland until April 30, when Cleveland, Chicago, and Philadelphia completed a complicated trade. Chi-cago got Minoso from Cleveland and outfielder Paul Lehner from Phila-delphia. Cleveland got pitcher Lou Brissie from Philadelphia. Philadelphia got outfielders Gus Zernial and Dave Philley from Chicago, and pitcher Sam Zoldak and catcher Ray Murray from Cleveland.

After the deal had been completed, Greenberg mystified everyone, and proved himself a prophet, when he predicted that Minoso would become "one of the really good players of our time."[24] Minoso, who broke down and cried when told to pack, dried his tears in time to hit .324 and lead the league in triples with 14 and stolen bases with 31. He eventually be-came, in 1980, one of only two men ever to appear in a major league game in five different decades (the other being Nick Altrock), and has been promised by Eddie Einhorn, the president of the White Sox, a chance to come to bat again in 1990.[25] Simpson, who remained with Cleveland, batted only .229 and drove in 24 runs in 1951.[26]

Trying to ignore the racial prejudice that the sale of Minoso represented, Doby began the 1951 season just as he had finished in 1950. He battered

American League pitchers from Opening Day on, prompting his admirers from Paterson to ask permission to honor him with a "day" at Yankee Stadium. Bill Veeck had refused such a request in 1947, but this time Greenberg consented.

Organized by baseball scout Ben Marmo, who had encouraged Doby's career back in his Eastside High School days, an estimated crowd of 1,200 Patersonians, including Mayor DeVita, appeared at the rainy stadium on Saturday, June 23. Their contributions of $1,500 enabled Marmo's committee to burn the mortgage on Doby's house in a ceremony at home plate. Prominent merchants added their gifts of clothing, luggage, jewelry, a desk lamp, and flowers for Helyn and for Doby's mother.[27]

In the game against the Yankees, Doby suffered a drop in his .313 batting average. He bounced into a double play in the first inning, walked in the second and scored on Rosen's grand slam home run, and popped out to Johnny Mize in the fourth. In the fifth inning, manager Al Lopez sat Doby down to rest a nagging groin injury.

The game didn't help the Indians, either. They lost 7–6 when the Yanks staged a three-run rally in the bottom of the ninth inning.[28]

Doby raised his average to .330 in the period following his "day," however, to qualify for another appearance in the All-Star game on July 10 at Briggs Stadium in Detroit. He pinch hit for pitcher Eddie Lopat in the fourth inning and popped out, but did not play in the field, as the American League lost by a score of 8–3.[29]

As the season moved on, the Indians failed for the third straight year to catch the Yankees, losing 10 out of 11 games against them in New York. Four games out of first place in mid-July, Cleveland finished five games back, in second place, in September.

Although many of the Cleveland players failed to produce in September, Franklin "Whitey" Lewis of the *Press* blamed Doby when Lewis evaluated the season in October. He passed over Doby's .295 batting average, .512 slugging average, 101 bases on balls (five of them in one game), and 84 runs scored to focus on Doby's puny total of only four runs batted in during the final weeks of the season. "This 26 year old [actually, Doby was 27] young man," Lewis told his readers on October 12, "is sensitive, mildly neurotic. He is equipped with the weapons of his trade to such a saturation you cannot conceive of him portraying any except the greatest of athletes in all fields, including baseball."

As a result of Doby's end-of-season slump, Lewis wrote, "You could hear the shudders all the way into the Tribe front office and there were mouthings everywhere that Larry Doby cost the pennant." Having vaguely quoted the "front office," Lewis moved on to comments of his own:

He [Doby] heard . . . [trade rumors]. Already wearing the shield of the Negro on his nameplate, he [then] withdrew further into his mental dungeon.

Larry Doby, impassionable as to his color, was a thousand-fold pierced by the awful thought that his co-workers might not accept him ever competitively. He had been hurt physically. Now he was wounded in his mind.

Relentlessly, Lewis went on to say that the Indians could trade Doby only to the St. Louis Browns or the Chicago White Sox because no other teams would want a black player. And St. Louis, under the direction of Bill Veeck since July, had little to offer Cleveland in a trade. No other owners, he concluded, would swap their prized "kewpie dolls" and "put a Negro statue in their place. You can get only bums in exchange."[30]

The vitriolic character of Lewis's racist language, printed in a major American daily newspaper in 1951, provides a prism through which to view the status of black Americans during this final year of the Truman administration, and four years before Dr. Martin Luther King, Jr., became the leader of the bus boycott in Montgomery, Alabama.

Lewis's language cannot be explained by the fact that Doby's average did drop 35 points in August and September, and his runs batted in total fell from 102 in 1950 to 69 in 1951. After all, Ted Williams of the Boston Red Sox, for all his gifts as a batsman, never was regarded as a player who produced when his team most needed him, and openly feuded with newspaper reporters, yet never suffered so vicious an attack as Lewis's assault on Doby. Williams was idolized as the "Splendid Splinter," his idiosyncrasies and aloofness became part of his legend, and his obscene gestures at booing fans only added to his mystique.

The intent here is not to equate Doby with Williams as a player. Rather, it is to say that while Williams and Doby could be equally difficult to get close to, only one of them would be deemed "mildly neurotic" and "wounded in his mind." Too, other Cleveland players also slumped late in 1951, but no one attributed their lapses to neuroses or mental injuries.

Before spring training in 1952, Gordon Cobbledick of the *Plain Dealer* picked up where Lewis left off. Cobbledick informed a nationwide readership in *Sport* magazine in February that Doby's statistics in 1951,

For a guy named Joe . . . would have been a fair enough performance. For a candidate for immortality, [they] left much to be desired.

A succession of crippling injuries in the form of pulled leg muscles explained Doby's decline in part, but only in part. Behind and beyond his physical troubles, increasing evidence of mental and emotional confusion was noted by those close to him.

"Larry's a mixed-up guy—a badly mixed-up guy," was a frequently-heard observation in Cleveland.

Cobbledick went on at length to picture Doby as a friendless loner, "presided over by his attractive wife, Helyn," and "dominated" by his two-year old daughter. When Helyn had to return to Paterson because of the illness of her mother, Cobbledick wrote, Doby "was left pitifully and almost tragically alone in Cleveland."[31]

To some extent, Cobbledick's judgments were correct. Doby was not a gregarious man in 1951. He did not play cards or drink, two of the major pastimes of his teammates. He preferred instead the company of Helyn, and of Arthur and Doris Grant and their children, whom the Dobys lived with, and other friends not associated with baseball.

Furthermore, Doby rejects Cobbledick's description of him as a loner. He says, "I think the word 'loner' is an unfair word to describe anybody. I needed my privacy to deal with some of the insults that were directed at me because of my race. That's how I handled the insults, in private. If I had stayed in the clubhouse, and spoken about my feelings, I think the writers would have called me a 'militant.' I feel that they had me in a no-win situation."

During the month of February 1952, while Cobbledick's article circulated, Doby began the conditioning exercises which he and Harrison Dillard had devised during the final weeks of the 1951 season. Many observers, including Dillard, attributed Doby's muscle pulls to his personal intensity, but thought they could be avoided with appropriate exercises.[32]

Doby feels, though, that he "had to play with intensity. If I didn't, I wouldn't have been in the big leagues. I don't think that was the real problem, though. I think it was the conditions I had to live with away from the ball park. They burned me up inside. If you're an introvert, which I probably am, your feelings stay inside, and that could create problems for my muscles.

"Now I can say that. But I didn't know that back in 1951. If somebody told me, it probably wouldn't have helped anyway, because to understand yourself is partly a matter of maturity."

One of Doby's stormiest, and most productive, seasons in the major leagues was the 1952 season. Muscle pulls and disputes with Lopez prompted Lopez to bench him in May.[33] Yet, by July, his hitting and fielding caused Yankees manager Casey Stengel to name Doby to the American League All-Star team for the fourth straight year. He stood third in the league in runs batted in with 47 and fifth in home runs with 13.

In the All-Star game, shortened by rain to five innings, Doby replaced Dom DiMaggio in center field in the fourth inning and remained there for the fifth. He handled no chances, and did not come to bat, as the National League won, 3–2.[34]

In August, Lopez benched Doby again, charging that Doby did not hustle from first to third base on an infield single.[35] Two games later, urged to apologize by Hank Greenberg, Doby refused. The next day, Lopez restored him to the lineup.

Despite these interruptions, Doby amassed impressive statistics in 1952. He clubbed 32 home runs, tops in the American League, and compiled a slugging percentage of .541, tops in the major leagues. He also drove in 104 runs and led the league in runs scored with the same number, 104. Doby struck out a lot, as usual, tying Mickey Mantle for the league lead with 111. Power hitters usually do strike out a lot, but Doby was unusual among them in that he also drew a lot of bases on balls. That year he walked 90 times, the fourth highest total in the league. He also "hit for the cycle"—a single, double, triple, and home run in one game in May.

With numbers like these, no one talked about Doby's batting average. It fell to .276, the lowest figure in his six-year career up to that time.[36] Nor did anyone lay blame for Cleveland's second place finish, two games behind the Yankees, on Doby. This time it was Bob Feller's turn. "Rapid Robert" won only nine and lost 13. No one, however, psychoanalyzed Feller.

With the home run and slugging titles to his credit, Doby had silenced his critics as the 1953 season approached. For a while, though, it looked as if the season would start without him.

In keeping with his new status as the home run king, Doby held out for more money, but soon settled for $28,000. "It's the best contract I ever got," he told Frank Gibbons of the *Press*. The contract made Doby "the highest paid Indian, exclusive of pitchers," Gibbons commented. The Indians, after all, had a pitcher named Feller on the payroll.[37]

Shortly after the 1953 season opened, Doby again became the subject of trade talk. Greenberg, rumor had it, had offered Doby to the Washington Senators in exchange for outfielder Jackie Jensen.

"I told Hank that I did not want to talk trade," Washington owner Clark Griffith said of a conversation with Greenberg. "Remember this. I would be delighted to have an outfielder like Larry Doby. Insinuations that the Washington club really is opposed to playing Negros on its team are lies.

"If I could find another Doby, or Minoso, I would make a place on the Senators for him. But nobody is going to stampede me into signing Negro players merely for the sake of satisfying certain pressure groups.

"The Washington club would benefit financially from Negro representation on the field.

"My attitude toward Negro players is indicated by the presence of four of them in our farm system. Perhaps one or two of these men will develop sufficiently in the next two years, and make the Senators."[38]

As the trade talk died down, Doby's hitting picked up. By mid-summer his average lagged, but his 16 home runs kept pace with his 32 of the previous season.

With the All-Star team now selected by the votes of the fans, Doby learned for the first time how popular or famous he had become. He collected only 461,155 votes, not enough to make the starting team. Mantle of the Yankees led the center fielders with 1,413,938, followed by Jim Busby of the Senators with 544,399.[39]

Despite Doby's low total, Casey Stengel named him to the team as a reserve player, the fifth straight time he had made it. In the game, played at Crosley Field in Cincinnati, Doby failed to hit in his only time at bat, had one putout, and threw out one base runner.[40]

The Indians, in their annual pursuit of the Yankees, didn't even make the pennant race exciting in 1953. Only Al Rosen's Most Valuable Player performance, highlighted by 43 home runs and 145 runs batted in, kept them as close as eight and one-half games behind New York in the final standings.

Doby had a solid if unspectacular year. His batting average sank a little lower, to .263, but his home run production stayed almost level at 29 and he drove in 102 runs. On the negative side, he set an American League record for strikeouts, his total of 121 approaching the major league record of 134 set by Vince DiMaggio with the Boston Braves in 1938.[41]

After the season ended, trade talk circulated again. This time Art Ehlers, general manager of the new Baltimore Orioles (formerly the St. Louis Browns) offered to exchange infielder Vic Wertz for Doby. But Hank Greenberg refused.[42]

A turning point and a climax in the playing career of Larry Doby came in 1954. The turning point came early, in March. The Santa Rita Hotel in Tucson, with a deceitful push from Spud Goldstein, allowed Cleveland's black players to live there during spring training. First Goldstein told the hotel manager that only three or four black players would register, when in fact there were six or seven. The manager agreed, on three conditions: the players would have to accept rooms on the mezzanine level, they could not use the elevator, and they could not sit in the lobby. Goldstein agreed, but neglected to pass along these restrictions to Doby and the other black players.[43] If he had, Doby says, "I would have ignored them, or gone back to live with Zelma and John Bennett."

The restrictions revealed the deep-seated psychological nature of racial prejudice in America in 1954: it was not merely petty or superficial, but was, instead, pathological and deep-seated. When the Supreme Court issued its unanimous opinion in the case of *Brown v. Board of Education of Topeka* in that very same year of 1954, striking down the "separate but equal" doctrine which permitted segregation and ordering integration of public schools "with all deliberate speed," the conditions imposed by the manager of the Santa Rita made it clear that the struggle for racial equality still had a long way to go.

After Doby registered at the Santa Rita, with a signature which re-

corded yet another quiet moment in the history of the civil rights movement, another signature, historically less significant but nevertheless important, had to be recorded. For once again Doby had decided to hold out
for more money, refusing Greenberg's salary cut from $28,000 to $25,000
because he had "slumped" from 32 to 29 home runs and from 104 to 102
RBIs in 1953.[44] When a face-to-face confrontation between Doby and
Greenberg in Tucson did not produce that signature, Doby boldly threatened to go home. Shortly thereafter, Goldstein, ever the all-purpose man,
conveyed an offer from Greenberg of $30,000, and Doby signed.[45]

With Doby in camp, the total number of black players in spring training
with major league teams rose in 1954 to 40. Among the many conclusions
that can be drawn from these figures, the one that most pertains to Doby
is that the presence of black players in the Cleveland organization no longer
depended on Bill Veeck. After Veeck sold his interest in the team in the
winter of 1949–50, Hank Greenberg carried forward Veeck's interest in
black players as his own interest.

Greenberg had given indications of his attitude toward blacks in baseball
seven years earlier, in 1947, when he played for the Pittsburgh Pirates and
the Brooklyn Dodgers had Jackie Robinson on their roster. According to
Ralph Kiner, also a Pirate, "The one guy on our team who befriended
[Robinson] was Hank Greenberg. He was near the end of his career, and
he had gone through the Jewish thing in the 1930's. He'd heard all the
tough words, too. Hank went out of his way to encourage him."[46]

Yet, under Greenberg, the number of black players on the in-season
Indians, while sometimes rising to four, remained basically three. In 1954
the three were Doby, Al Smith, and Dave Pope, all outfielders. Luke Easter,
who broke his foot in 1953, was gone, and so was right-handed pitcher
Dave Hoskins, who had compiled a 9–3 record that year.[47]

About a month into the regular season, amid signs that the 1954 Indians
might become a pennant-winning ball club, Harry Jones of the *Plain Dealer*

Black Players in Spring Training, 1954[48]

American League (18)		National League (22)	
Cleveland:	7	Brooklyn:	6
Chicago:	3	New York:	5
Washington:	3	Milwaukee:	4
Baltimore:	2	Chicago:	3
Philadelphia:	2	Cincinnati:	2
New York:	1	St. Louis:	1
Boston:	0	Pittsburgh:	1
Detroit:	0	Philadelphia:	0

sought to explain Cleveland's success. His attention focused on Doby. "Somewhere between his home in Paterson, N.J., and the Indians Tucson training headquarters he discarded the chip he had carried on his shoulder." Jones further observed that hitless days were not depressing Doby, as they had in previous seasons. "He is not the same Doby who would sulk and brood and sit alone and snap at people and give the impression that the whole world was against him."[49]

Doby, in trying to recall his thoughts and feelings in the early part of the season, says, "I don't remember feeling any different in 1954. As for Jones's comments, they don't make any sense to me. Did I have a chip on my shoulder in 49, 51 and 53, which were not my best years, but no chip in 48, 50, 52 and 54 when I had outstanding years?"

As the season progressed, the Indians continued to impress the Yankees that New York's five-year stranglehold on the American League flag could not be taken for granted. By the All-Star break the Indians held a wafer-thin one-half game edge over New York but at least they were in first place.

Certainly Doby was one of the keys to Cleveland's success. By mid-season his 61 runs batted in trailed only Minoso (68), Berra (65), and Mantle (64) for the league lead. His 15 home runs were second only to Mantle's 18.[50]

In the All-Star game, played before 68,751 fans at Cleveland, two of the American League's most powerful sluggers, Doby and Rosen, and one of its lightest hitters, Nellie Fox of the White Sox, helped the American League to an 11–9 triumph. Rosen hit two home runs early in the game. Doby, pinch hitting in the bottom of the eighth inning with the American League trailing by a 9–8 score, smashed a home run off Milwaukee Braves right-hander Gene Conley for a 9–9 tie. Mantle and Berra followed with singles and Rosen walked to load the bases. After Brooklyn righty Carl Erskine struck out Mickey Vernon, Fox connected for a bloop single to chase Mantle and Berra home for the final 11–9 score.[51]

Doby next hit the headlines on the last day of July. In the third inning of a game against the Washington Senators at Cleveland, with the Indians ahead by 5–3, he made a catch in center field that may be among the greatest ever made. Playing shallow against Tom Umphlett, Doby raced back into left center in pursuit of Umphlett's unexpected long drive. At the five-foot fence, Doby leaped high, placed his bare hand on the top of the fence, pushed himself still higher, caught the ball, fell against the awning over the bullpen bench, and bounced back on the field with the ball still clutched in his glove.

Left fielder Al Smith snatched the ball from Doby and, as umpire John Flaherty threw up his right hand to signal Umphlett out, almost threw out base runner Jim Busby retreating back to first base.

"That," declared broadcaster Dizzy Dean to sportswriter Hal Lebovitz, "was the greatest catch I ever saw, as a player or as a broadcaster. It was the greatest catch I ever saw in my whole life. I saw Terry Moore and Lloyd Waner make some great ones. But they was routine compared to this one."

"If I was the pitcher," said Dean, "I'd go up to Doby and say, 'Podner, here's half my month's salary. You deserve it.' "

Pitcher Art Houtteman didn't go quite that far, but he did wait for Doby in the dugout after the game. "I wanted to talk to you alone," he told Doby. "I wanted to thank you for that catch. As long as I live I'll never forget the greatness of that play."

Doby's old mentor, Tris Speaker, listening to the game while confined to a bed in Lakeside Hospital with a heart condition, reached for the telephone and called the stadium press box. "Tell Larry," Speaker said, "he gave this old man a great big lift."

After the catch, Doby got an ovation from the 17,504 fans every time he came to bat. He responded to their cheers in the sixth inning by belting his twenty-first home run of the season.[52]

Yet Doby's catch did not take the eyes of the baseball world off an even more significant story. The Indians had taken a two and one-half game lead over the second-place Yankees, and were on their way to the winningest record in the history of American League baseball. On September 18 at Detroit, needing a victory to clinch the flag, the Indians faced their old teammate, Steve Gromek, who shut them out over the first six innings before Dale Mitchell pinch hit a two-run home run in the seventh inning. With a 3–2 Cleveland lead and the championship hanging in the balance, Ray Narleski came on in relief of starter Early Wynn to pitch airtight relief ball, and the Indians had done it.[53]

That night, though, in comparison with 1948, they celebrated with restraint at the Book-Cadillac Hotel. One of the few surprises was that Doby sprayed Hank Greenberg with champagne, and then actually drank a little himself. Later, Doby and Jim Hegan joined in singing with a three-piece band hired for the occasion. One teammate, not identified by writer Art King, watched Doby and commented, "It's taken seven long years for Larry to join the team. What a doggone shame."[54]

Shocked by reading this observation, Doby asks, "I wonder how they thought of Jim Hegan? Jim didn't drink champagne even in 1954, but they always considered him part of the team. There's an example of the double standard, if anyone still needs one!"

As the Indians prepared for the World Series against the National League champion New York Giants, Doby's contributions to Cleveland's record total of 111 victories were evident. Once again he captured the home run title with a total of 32, three more than Ted Williams. For the first time he led his league in runs batted in, with 126, one more than Yogi Berra. He also led the Indians in games played, at bats, and, alas, strikeouts. He batted .272, nine points higher than in 1953.

On defense, a facet of baseball so often overlooked for sluggers, Doby racked up the best fielding average of any full-time center fielder in the league. He made just two errors in 427 chances for an average of .995.[55]

When asked to evaluate the importance of his players at season's end by Art King, manager Al Lopez pointed toward Doby. "There's the guy who makes the difference," Lopez said. "Without him. . . . " As his voice trailed off, Lopez gestured downward with his thumb.[56]

The 1954 World Series developed into an anticlimax for Larry Doby and the Cleveland Indians. They seemed to have spent all their energy in defeating the Yankees, hitting weakly, running the bases ineptly, fielding erratically. As a result, the Giants swept to victory in four straight games.

The greatest catch in World Series history, and what may have been the shortest home run, cost the Indians a 5–2 defeat in the opening game at the Polo Grounds in New York. With the score tied 2–2 in the eighth inning, Doby on second and Rosen on first with no outs, center fielder Willie Mays caught up to a towering drive by Vic Wertz 460 feet from home plate, wheeled, and with a powerful throw, prevented Doby from advancing to third base after the catch. In the tenth inning, with two runners on base, Dusty Rhodes hit a 270-foot fly ball down the right field line for a home run and the New York victory.[57]

The next day Rhodes defeated Cleveland again. He singled in front of Doby to drive in Mays in the fifth inning, and homered for an insurance run in the seventh as New York won by a 3–1 score.[58]

In the third game of the Series, played in Cleveland, the Giants won by 6–2. Doby connected for an early single off starting pitcher Ruben Gomez, but with two on and one out in the eighth, he could only nick a knuckleball thrown by relief pitcher Hoyt Wilhelm and grounded out easily to first baseman Whitey Lockman. The New Yorkers scored the winning run early in the game, again with a timely two-run single by Rhodes, followed by an RBI bunt by Davey Williams that confounded the Cleveland infield.[59]

The visiting Giants clinched the world championship by a 7–4 score the next day, only this time Doby's old teammate from his Newark Eagles days, Monte Irvin, replaced Rhodes as the batting hero. Irvin doubled home Hank Thompson in the second inning, and singled with the bases loaded for another run in the fifth.[60]

Doby did not hit in four times at bat, giving him a dreadful .125 average (2 for 16) for the Series. After the final game, he told George Lucas of the *Morning Call*, "We—I, just never got untracked. None of us hit except

Wertz." Taking a longer view, he added, "We've never looked this bad all year. We lost four straight to the White Sox, but didn't look this bad."[61]

A man who never played up his accomplishments, neither did Doby refer to an injury which hampered him through the World Series. On the last Friday of the regular season, he injured three discs near the top of his spinal column when he dove to catch a low line drive.[62]

Only his World Series check, for $6,457, soothed Doby's feelings in the winter that followed. After he got back to Paterson, he was able to make light of the disaster by giving a talk entitled, "How to Beat the Giants in Four Straight."

After the World Series, the Indians players looked forward to the announcement of the Most Valuable Player Award for the American League. Three of them were good bets to win: second baseman Bobby Avila, the batting champion with an average of .341; pitcher Bob Lemon, who ran up a 23–7 won-lost record; and Doby, the home run and RBI king. Their credentials were so good, however, that Berra of the Yankees won when the sports writers split their votes among the three Cleveland stars.

Berra got 230 points, Doby 210 and Avila 203 to finish one-two-three in the balloting. Minnie Minoso of the White Sox came in fourth with 186 points, followed by Lemon with 179.[63]

Although the truth may never be known, a feud with New York *Daily News* baseball writer Jim McCulley may have cost Doby the MVP award. A story circulated that, in retaliation for cancelling out of a dinner that Doby had agreed to attend, McCulley refused to cast his first place ballot, worth 14 points, for Doby. If, instead, McCulley voted for Berra, this 28-point shift cost Doby the award.

Nevertheless, when Doby celebrated his thirty-first birthday on December 23, he could look back on six seasons since the 1948 World Series as one of the premier performers in baseball. He had averaged 144 games played, 98 runs scored, 147 hits, 27 home runs, 98 runs batted in, and a batting average of .285. Not many players attain numbers like these in even a single season. In addition, he had been on the American League's All-Star team for six straight summers, compiling a batting average of .300.

NOTES

1. A. S. "Doc" Young, *Call and Post*, April 2, 1949.
2. *World-Telegram*, April 7, 1949.
3. Telephone interview with Al Rosen, July 14, 1981.
4. *World-Telegram*, May 20, 1949.
5. *Plain Dealer*, May 26, 1949.
6. Ibid., June 4, 1949.

7. *New York Times*, July 13, 1949.

8. Personal interview with Lou Boudreau, September 13, 1980.

9. Bosley Crowther, *New York Times*, September 5, 1949.

10. Cleveland Indians, *Sketch Book*, 1950.

11. Personal interview with Aldona Jones, January 11, 1981.

12. Personal interview with Mike Garcia, January 9, 1981.

13. Personal interview with Harrison Dillard, January 12, 1981.

14. Rosen, loc. cit.

15. Dillard, loc. cit.

16. Ibid.

17. Rosen, loc. cit.

18. Cleveland Indians, *Sketch Book*, 1951.

19. *New York Times*, July 12, 1950.

20. Rosen, loc. cit.

21. Ibid.

22. *Press*, January 23, 1951.

23. Personal interview with Al Lopez, August 2, 1980.

24. *New York Times*, May 1, 1951.

25. Robert McG. Thomas, Jr., and Thomas Rogers. *New York Times*, April 6, 1987.

26. David S. Neft, Richard M. Cohen, and Jordan A. Deutsch, *The Sports Encyclopedia: Baseball* (New York: Grosset and Dunlap, 1981), p. 286.

27. Personal interview with Ben Marmo, December 23, 1980.

28. *Morning Call*, June 25, 1951.

29. *New York Times*, July 11, 1951.

30. Franklin Lewis, *Press*, October 12, 1951.

31. Gordon Cobbledick, "Is Larry Doby a Bust?" *Sport*, February, 1952.

32. Dillard, loc. cit.

33. *Plain Dealer*, May 3 and May 6, 1952.

34. *New York Times*, July 9, 1952.

35. *World-Telegram and Sun*, August 18, 1952.

36. Neft, Cohen, and Deutsch, *Baseball*, pp. 290–91.

37. *Press*, March 7, 1953.

38. *World-Telegram and Sun*, April 17, 1953.

39. *New York Times*, July 6, 1953.

40. Ibid., July 13, 1953.

41. *World-Telegram and Sun*, October 26, 1953.

42. Ibid., December 10, 1953.

43. Telephone interview with Harold A. "Spud" Goldstein, October 25, 1980.

44. *Press*, January 13, 1954.

45. Goldstein, loc. cit.

46. Ralph Kiner, quoted in the *New York Times*, April 12, 1987.

47. Neft, Cohen, and Deutsch, *Baseball*, p. 294.

48. *Our World*, April 1954, pp. 40–43.

49. Harry Jones, *Plain Dealer*, May 9, 1954.

50. *New York Times*, July 13, 1954.

51. Ibid., July 14, 1954.

52. *Plain Dealer*, July 31, 1954.

53. *New York Times*, September 19, 1954.

54. Art King, "He's Learned to Laugh," in *Baseball Stars of 1955*, ed. Bruce Jacobs (New York: Lion Books, 1955), p. 40.

55. Cleveland Indians, *Yearbook*, 1955.

56. King, "He's Learned to Laugh," p. 37.

57. *Morning Call*, September 30, 1954.

58. Ibid., October 1, 1954.

59. Ibid., October 2, 1954.

60. Ibid., October 5, 1954.

61. Ibid.

62. *Herald-Tribune* (New York), October 6, 1954.

63. *World-Telegram and Sun*, December 10, 1954.

9

"A Load Off My Back"

In what was becoming a spring tradition, Larry Doby began the 1955 baseball season by holding out for more money. In the days before player agents and free agency, before collective bargaining between players and management, Doby personally asked for $35,000 for leading the league in home runs and runs batted in on a pennant-winning team. Greenberg offered $32,000 in direct response to Doby's request, and the two soon settled for $33,000. With little fuss, then, Doby became a member of the Cleveland Indians for the ninth straight season.[1]

As he prepared for spring training, Doby told Hal Lebovitz of the Cleveland *News* that he felt he had "matured" as a big leaguer, an assertion he affirmed in the summer. "Nothing bothers me any more," he declared in explaining a hot hitting and fielding streak. After missing 20 games with a bone chip in his right hand, he smashed eight home runs and drove in 12 runs in 15 games at the end of June and the beginning of July.[2]

As if to underline his point, Doby continued to excel despite the fact that American League manager Al Lopez named him, but did not use him, in the annual All-Star game. After that, on August 4, in a game at Yankee Stadium, he set an American League record for outfielders by playing in his 158th consecutive game without making an error. The string began on July 18, 1954, after Doby threw wildly past third base trying to stop a base runner. During it, he handled 421 chances flawlessly.[3]

He then set his sights on the major league record of 187 errorless games in a row, set by Danny Litwhiler for the Philadelphia Phillies in the years 1941–43. But on August 13, nine days after setting the record, against the then-Kansas City Athletics, Doby proved he was human. After catching Hal Renna's fly ball in center field, he dropped the baseball while trying to throw out Hector Lopez, who tagged second base and sprinted to third after the catch. Lopez continued around third and crossed home plate be-fore right fielder Al Smith or left fielder Gene Woodling could retrieve the ball.[4]

Thus Doby's streak, which had reached 164 games without an error, ended. Seventeen years later, Al Kaline of the Detroit Tigers improved Doby's mark, and the major league record for an outfielder as well, by playing in 242 consecutive errorless games. Doby's error mattered little to his team that day, however. The Indians defeated Kansas City by a score of 5–3, improving their temporary lead over the Yankees to two games.[5]

But Cleveland could not sustain that pace. The Indians had lost Vic Wertz's powerful bat to polio in late August, their pitching faltered in September, and the Yankees forged ahead to win their sixth pennant in seven years by a three-game margin. "As usual," Doby says in trying to explain his team's fourth second-place finish behind the Yankees in five years, "they had more depth on the bench and in the bullpen."

Doby, whose batting average rose as high as .295 in mid-September, dipped slightly to a final level of .291. His 26 home runs and .505 slugging average led his team, but he was far behind Mickey Mantle's league-lead-ing totals of 37 home runs and .611 slugging average.

In one offensive category, runs batted in, Doby dropped dramatically. In so doing, he demonstrated his importance to the Cleveland attack. From his league-leading total of 126 RBIs in 1954, he fell to 75 in 1955. The difference, 51 runs, almost equalled the team's total decrease of 57 RBIs below its 1954 level.[6]

Despite his relatively good statistics in 1955, Doby's long-standing dif-ficulties with manager Al Lopez, in a sense going back to Lopez's com-ments from the bench on the day Doby first came to bat in 1947, came to a climax after the season ended. On October 25, the Indians traded Doby to the White Sox in exchange for shortstop Chico Carrasquel and center fielder Jim Busby.[7]

The next day, sportswriter Franklin Lewis published another of his crit-icisms of Doby in the Cleveland *Press*. "Larry Doby," he began, "whose opportunities for immortality in baseball ended where his complexes be-gan—at the neckline—was in a new green pasture today. . . . " Evaluat-ing the trade, he continued, "the Indians got the worst of the bargain, though this does not mean that I consider the departure of Doby a calam-ity to baseball in Cleveland. He has been a controversial athlete. Highly gifted, he was frequently morose, sullen and, upon occasion, downright surly to his teammates and his public."

After citing Doby's contributions to the Indians over nine years, Lewis decided that they

did not add up to the potential established for him by Bill Veeck in 1947 when Doby became the first Negro player in the American League.

That probably was part of the load Doby carried ever since. He thought of himself, at the beginning, as the symbol of the Negro in his league. In later years he overcame this singular complex to a degree, because he beat back his temper and quit throwing bats and giving other visible evidences of his failures in his profession.[8]

Doby rejects Lewis's charge that he saw himself as a symbol, saying instead that, "I was looked on as a black man, not as a human being, a gentleman who carried himself in a way that people would respect. I did feel a responsibility to the black players who came after me, but that was a responsibility, basically, to people, not just to black people. I never thought of myself as a symbol. Lewis never asked me if I thought of myself as a symbol. He just wrote that!"

As he tries to remember how he felt about being traded away from the team he had served for nine years, Doby recalls that "I was disappointed. I had made friends. I had become acquainted with the community. I had been loyal to the organization, although of course they paid me. It might be different now, when the money is the big thing. At that time there was a closer type of community thing with players.

"After I got to Chicago, I was treated very, very well. I met good people in the community there, and that changed the disappointment I had felt as I left Cleveland. I had teammates that were great—Sherm Lollar, Nellie Fox, Dick Donovan, Jim Rivera, Luis Aparicio, Walt Dropo, and Minoso.

"And there was Marty Marion. I thought he could have been a good manager, if given the opportunity. He might have been ahead of his time in dealing with individuals as individuals and as human beings. I don't think a lot of people were ready for that. Playing for Marty Marion was a great relief."

The civil rights revolution which Jackie Robinson initiated in the minor leagues in 1946, and which he and Doby spread to the major leagues in 1947, simmered just below the surface of American life until 1954, when the Supreme Court of the United States issued its momentous decision requiring the integration of schools. Thereafter, White Citizens' Councils in many southern states began to threaten the proponents of desegregation, thereby serving notice that the doctrine of white supremacy was alive and well. This was the social setting, then, when Larry Doby learned of his trade from Cleveland to Chicago.

Then, just five weeks later, on December 1, 1955, the black population of Montgomery, Alabama, under a new leader, Dr. Martin Luther King, Jr., began to boycott the city's buses after a black woman, Rosa Parks, refused to relinquish her seat to a white man. The boycott abruptly broadened the struggle for black rights far beyond baseball and the other sports which had, more quietly, integrated black players into their all-white ranks.

Thus, as Doby reported for spring training in 1956, southern white supremacists had begun to redouble their efforts to resist integration in all aspects of life. For Doby, that meant segregation again, after just two springs of integration at the Santa Rita Hotel in Tucson. When he arrived at the White Sox camp in Tampa, Florida, he found, once again, that he could not live in the team hotel.

"All the White Sox players got meal money during spring training," Doby remembers, "and we had to go out to restaurants on our own. That's when I'd see the Jim Crow signs. The black players lived in private homes in Tampa. Not many people realize this, but I was segregated in spring training for 10 out of 13 years, right through the spring of 1959. Now do you see what I mean when I say that there were constant reminders that I was black? Was I imagining things when I was segregated? Does anyone think that the prejudice which caused segregation in the south didn't exist in the north?"

Had Doby remained with the Indians, he might have had integrated housing, but he would have encountered racism in another form. During that spring of 1956, while he played with the White Sox in Florida, the Indians and the New York Giants were forced to cancel an exhibition game scheduled for April 10 in Meridian, Mississippi. "Too close to Alabama," a spokesman for the Giants said in indirect reference to the bus boycott in Montgomery, but without reference to two equally important factors: Mississippi was a hot bed of the White Citizens' Councils, and both the Indians and the Giants had black players on their rosters.[9]

On the same day that the Indians and Giants made their announcement, other developments further poisoned the atmosphere in which Doby and other black players prepared for the baseball season. A disc jockey from Oxford, Mississippi, dropped 20,000 paper Confederate flags on Chicago, 30 southern Democratic congressmen urged President Eisenhower to deny the use of a government auditorium for a conference of civil rights leaders in Washington, D.C., and former Secretary of State James F. Byrnes of South Carolina warned that southern leaders might create another States Rights Party, as they had done in 1948.[10]

Ignoring these ominous developments, and his own segregation, Doby had an excellent spring in 1956. He batted .425 in 22 exhibition games before a skin infection forced him to miss the last four games before the season's opening game against, of all teams, the Cleveland Indians.[11]

Doby didn't have the pleasure of beating his old team on Opening Day, but the next day his sacrifice fly drove in the only run of the game to defeat Cleveland lefty Herb Score by 1–0.[12] "I should have had a home run," Doby remembers. "The wind held that ball up."

Doby gave the White Sox all they expected of him in 1956. In 140 games, he led the team in runs batted in with 102 and home runs with 24. But without a Rosen or an Easter hitting behind him in the batting order, Doby learned that rival teams could weaken the Chicago attack by pitching "around" him. That is, pitchers gave Doby few good pitches to swing at. They'd rather walk him, and pitch instead to Walt Dropo. Thus Doby drew 102 walks, the highest total of his major league career.

Doby's statistics disproved the expectations of his old manager at Cleveland, Al Lopez. Lopez had predicted in the spring that his new players, Busby and Carrasquel, would outhit Doby. At season's end, however, Busby and Carrasquel had a total of just 19 homers and 98 RBIs.[13]

Even with such solid statistics from their new center fielder, the White Sox, and no other team for that matter, could keep pace with the Yankees in 1956. The New Yorkers won their seventh championship in eight years by nine games over second-place Cleveland and 12 over third-place Chicago.

In the World Series, the Yankees went on to triumph over the Brooklyn Dodgers, four games to three, in Jackie Robinson's final appearance in a major league uniform. After the season ended he announced his retirement rather than accept a trade to the New York Giants, thus leaving Doby as the surviving member of a pair of civil rights pioneers.

Larry Doby wrote the big story of his 1957 season in Chicago not with his bat or his glove, but with his left fist. He began a new chapter in the integration of baseball with a punch described by *Ebony* magazine as a "symbolic left hook."

Not that he needed to replace his bat and glove with his fist. For the tenth straight season he demonstrated his value as a player with statistics that included a .288 batting average and steady play in the outfield.[14]

The "symbolic left hook" landed flush on the jaw of Yankees pitcher Art Ditmar, and triggered a 30-minute interruption of a game on June 13 at Comiskey Park with a fight that New York outfielder Enos Slaughter described as the best he had seen in 20 years of baseball.

In the first inning, Doby went sprawling in the dirt to dodge a fastball thrown by Ditmar. Instantly he rose, ran to the mound, and knocked Ditmar flat with that left hook. That aroused players from both dugouts to a mass fistfight in the infield. After the umpires thought they had restored order, Yankees second baseman Billy Martin challenged Doby and a second major fight broke out. When this one ended, Chicago police escorted Martin from the field, and the umpires ejected Slaughter and Sox first baseman Dropo from the game.[15]

League president Will Harridge, after reading a report from the umpires, termed the incident "a regrettable brawl." He imposed a $150 fine against Doby because "he threw the initial punch which started the trouble." Slaughter, who "was not in the lineup, but came off the bench and engaged in a fight with Dropo," drew a similar fine. So did Martin. "After the umpires had gotten the situation well in hand, he attempted to start a fresh fight with Doby and caused a new disturbance." Fines of $100 were also levied against Dropo and Ditmar.[16]

Two weeks later, sportswriter Shirley Povich put the fight in perspective in *The Sporting News*:

Ninety four and one-half years after Abe Lincoln delivered his Emancipation Proclamation, baseball the other day witnessed the complete emancipation of the American Negro in America's national game.

Larry Doby, a colored player of the White Sox, dared to take a punch at Art Ditmar, a white pitcher of the Yankees, and history was being made. Never before in the 11 years since the bars were dropped and colored players admitted, albeit gingerly, to the major leagues, had a Negro thrown the first punch in a player argument.

There is no intent here to condone what Doby did; merely to point out that the consequences fell far short of Civil War, or secession, or a violent sense of outrage except among Ditmar's Yankee teammates who dashed to his assistance, but in no more anger than if his attacker had been a white player. . . .

Now this was no white pitcher dusting off a Negro batter simply because of the difference in pigmentation. . . . But the Doby-Ditmar episode had special significance because for the first time a Negro player was daring to get as assertive as the white man whose special province Organized Ball had been for nearly a hundred years.

In conclusion, Povich wrote, "the Negro player can now shout for his rights. Doby demonstrated that even a punch doesn't necessarily carry racial connotations. A new understanding seems to have come to baseball. They don't print the box score in color."[17]

In September, *Ebony*, a monthly magazine for black readers, reviewed the history of restraint imposed by white owners on black players. It cited Branch Rickey's instructions to Jackie Robinson to have "the guts not to fight back." But, *Ebony* declared, "Negro players now had reached the position where they could assert themselves on an equal, man-to-man basis with white men in the game. The Doby-Ditmar brawl proved that Negroes now are accepted in the 'National Pastime' as players, first and foremost, that race, if of any importance on the diamond, is secondary."

Ebony, which had for years given maximum coverage to Robinson while virtually ignoring the less charismatic Doby, then demonstrated that its writers knew the differences between the two men: "Possessing neither Jackie's temper nor his leadership qualities, Doby was one of the Negro players least expected to start a brawl. For Jackie to have started a fight would have been only another case of the expected. When Doby did it, he performed the unexpected. The unexpected proved to be the best test yet of baseball's democracy."[18]

Ditmar himself put a lid on the discussion at the time. He brushed off writers who tried to question him by saying, "So we had a fight—so what? Why don't you quit trying to build it up?"[19]

Informed that his fight with Ditmar was the first interracial fight in major league baseball, Doby laughs and says, "Good. I like *that* first, because my reason for the fight had nothing to do with color."

Although Doby demonstrated his punching power in June, he could not marshal his batting power in July and August. Rather than becoming depressed, however, he became reflective. During a visit to Cleveland, he acknowledged his ups and downs during his Cleveland years to Franklin Lewis and reported that racial insults hurled at him had diminished over the years. Asked by Lewis about his "failure to attain even greater stardom," Doby answered, "I know that some people were disappointed in me. I certainly didn't know how to make myself even better a player, or I would have tried. Doesn't that make sense? . . . I may not have been a great player, but I've been a good one."[20]

These reflections traversed Doby's mind despite the fact that his manager in 1957 would no longer be Marty Marion, but his old nemesis, Al Lopez, who had replaced Marion the day before the season began. In April and May, Lopez kept Doby in the lineup despite a succession of minor injuries. But when Doby was in excellent physical condition in September, Lopez benched him, except for occasional pinch hitting.

At one point, Lopez told a New York sportswriter that he used light-hitting Fred Hatfield instead of Doby as a pinch hitter because Doby was "in a slump." The next day, Hatfield laughingly brought Doby a clipping from the writer's column. "Doby may be in a slump," it said, "but Hatfield has been in a slump all his life."[21]

As the result of his injuries and Lopez's decision to bench him, Doby appeared in only 119 games in 1957, his lowest total since his dismal half-season in 1947. He maintained his consistency at the plate by batting .288. His RBI production of 79 kept pace with his usual figure of about 100 RBIs in 150 games. But his home run total dropped all the way down to 14.[22]

After the White Sox finished in second place, eight games behind New York, Doby packed his bags to go home to Paterson for the winter. He felt certain that Lopez would trade him away, for the second time, before spring training in 1958.

He didn't have to wait long. At 7:00 A.M. on December 5, his daughter Christina, then eight years old and getting ready to go to school, awakened him with a report she had heard on the radio that morning. "Daddy, you've been traded to Baltimore," she said. Twelve hours later, neither Chuck Comiskey, the owner of the White Sox, nor Paul Richards, his new boss with the Orioles, had had the courtesy to call him.[23]

Now out from under Lopez for the second time, Doby evaluated him in an interview in *Jet* magazine two weeks later. "I can't have any respect for a man who lacks regard for a man because he's in a minority [group] and acts as if we're always wrong and they're always right," Doby commented. "I just don't care to play for him."[24]

The baseball year in 1958 began amid optimistic declarations by Paul Richards about Doby's bright future with the Orioles and contrary rumors, not denied by Richards, that Doby would be traded before the season began. In spring training, he found himself back in Arizona, after two years in Florida, segregated from his teammates in Scottsdale.

Told to work out in right field, Doby knew that Richards believed that Doby had "lost a step," as athletes say when their speed declines. Meanwhile, Richards continued to state that "Doby is my center fielder"[25] until the end of March, when he announced that Baltimore had traded Doby and pitcher Don Ferrarese to Cleveland in return for outfielder Gene Woodling, utility player Dick Williams, and pitcher Bud Daley.[26]

The trade reunited Doby with the team and the city where he had played so well during his first nine years in the major leagues. Yet he concealed his excitement from the sportswriters and from his new manager, Bobby Bragan, because he also remembered incidents which gave him sleepless nights during those nine years.

After Opening Day, Doby found that he could not play every day because of an injured shoulder. Feeling "useless" on the bench, he asked Bragan to use him despite the injury, asked the team's infielders to come out to meet his weak throws from center field, and informed Bragan that he expected "to come out in the late innings of close games or games in which we're ahead."[27]

Bragan did use Doby as requested in the weeks that followed, shifting young outfielders Rocco Colavito and Roger Maris to center field from time to time. When Cleveland stumbled through June with a 31–36 record, general manager Frank Lane replaced Bragan with Doby's first friend in white baseball, Joe Gordon.[28]

"I felt I had a new lease on life," Doby said in 1981. "I really wanted to play for Joe, but I ran into bad cases of injuries. I couldn't throw, but I really wanted to play." Gordon, sympathetic to Doby's problems, asked Doby to work out at first base before each game. There, Doby found an even older friend, Mickey Vernon. At age 40, recalling their long conversations on Mog-Mog atoll during World War II, Vernon tried to teach another aging veteran the intricacies of playing first base.

Gordon, however, had no immediate plans for Doby except pinch hitting. He never played at first base, appeared in the outfield just 68 times, and made 21 appearances as a pinch hitter that season. Yet he hit the ball often enough to bat .283, and he still had power. In 1958, Doby hit 13 balls, including his last, out of American League parks in just 247 at bats.[29]

With numbers like that, there is no reason to wonder why Doby now regrets that the league did not have the Designated Hitter rule then. "I think I would have been as good a DH as Tommy Davis, and with power."

Larry Doby played for four baseball teams, one of them in the minor leagues, in 1959. No other statement so succinctly describes the complex process by which managers tell a ballplayer that he has come to the end of his career.

The curtain began to fall as early as January of that year. Harry Jones reported in the *Plain Dealer* that the Indians wanted to make a drastic cut in Doby's salary, but Doby stood firm.[30] He was about to move Helyn and their four children to an expensive new home in Montclair, New Jersey, away from the de facto segregation of the real estate market in Paterson.

Leaving Helyn to manage the complications of moving, Doby headed for spring training in Tucson in late February, for more instruction from Mickey Vernon about playing first base. Soon after he arrived, though, Cleveland announced that it had traded Doby to the Detroit Tigers for 25-year-old outfielder Tito Francona in a straight swap.[31]

Deeply unhappy, reminded of his various changes of name and address in his youth, Doby didn't seek out Gordon or Vernon before he left camp. "I just packed and left Tucson," he says. "Those who were there when I was leaving, I said good-bye to."

Doby traveled from the integrated camp of the Indians to Lakeland, Florida, where the Detroit Tigers were in training. Upon reaching Lakeland, "There was that thing, segregation, again. Maury Wills was there. Detroit had bought his contract from the Dodger farm club in Spokane. We lived together. But they released him when spring training ended. Then the only other minority group player on the team was Ossie Alvarez, who was Spanish."

In a way, then, 1959 was like 1947 and the first half of 1948: Doby was segregated, and the only black American on a team in the American League.

Doby's new manager, Bill Norman, who might have been Doby's minor league manager in 1947 if Bill Veeck had decided to farm Doby out to Wilkes-Barre, Pennsylvania, announced that "Doby is my left fielder as of now."[32] And so he was, however briefly.

Doby opened the season in a Detroit uniform, appearing in 18 games during the first month. He batted .218, hit no home runs, and drove in three runs in 55 times at bat. Then, on May 13, the Tigers sold Doby to his third team in a month, the Chicago White Sox, now under the direction of Bill Veeck, for a price reported at "more than $20,000." No other players were involved.[33]

This time, Doby knew about the trade in advance. "Bill had come to Detroit for a banquet of some kind," Doby remembers. "At the banquet, he told me, 'You'll be back with me soon.' So when the trade came, I felt joy. That was like going back to Cleveland in 1958. I felt a closeness, a very close relationship with this man. He had done nothing but prove his feelings for me over the years. And this is why I really wanted to do more than I was really capable of doing from the physical standpoint.

"I knew Bill's manager was Lopez, but it didn't bother me. I blocked him. I had blocked him out a long time ago. Veeck came across as the bright picture.

"I knew that Bill got me against Lopez's objections. But Bill felt that I could help him. Unfortunately, physically I couldn't do it. That gave Lopez a chance to bury me. When the statistics showed that I was not performing, then there was nothing that Bill could do but to go along with his manager."

From May 14, when he reported to the White Sox, until July 26, when he pinch hit, Doby appeared in 21 games for Chicago. He played in the outfield 12 times, at first base twice, and as a pinch hitter seven times. In a game at Fenway Park in Boston on June 20 he got his last major league hit, a single off pitcher Tom Brewer which drove in Jim Landis from second base. The run made little difference as the White Sox lost, 8–2. In more personal terms, the hit raised Doby's career total to 1,515 and his RBI total to 969.[34]

Doby failed in pinch hitting roles that night and again on June 24. Then he sat on the bench until July 26, when Lopez sent Doby to the plate in place of pitcher Ray Moore. With 35,207 fans hoping that the veteran slugger could spoil a shutout by 20-year-old right-hander Milt Pappas of the Baltimore Orioles, Doby ended his career in the big leagues as he had started it: he struck out in Comiskey Park.[35]

Thereafter, bothered by a back injury suffered earlier in the season by sliding into home while trying to score from second base on a base hit, Doby remained on the Chicago bench. It had become apparent that his bat would not be a factor in the pennant race, and that the "Go-Go Sox," as they came to be called, would rely on speed and pitching more than on power. Finally, Veeck called a meeting of team officials to bring Doby's status to a vote. When the votes were counted, Vice-President Chuck Comiskey, general manager Hank Greenberg, and Lopez had all voted against keeping him. Veeck, who took no votes when he decided to sign Doby to a Cleveland contract in 1947, voted yes. By a 3–1 vote, Doby's major league playing career had come to an end.[36]

Filled with regret, Veeck himself called Doby to the Bard's Room in Comiskey Park, the same room where Veeck introduced Doby to the press in 1947. Veeck told him, Doby says, "Lopez thought that it would be best that you go to San Diego in the Pacific Coast League for a month and then come back later in the season." Doby replied, "Well, I've always stayed with ball clubs when I've been hurt." And Veeck answered, "I understand, but I want you to do this for me." With that, there was no further hesitation on Doby's part. "There isn't anything Bill Veeck would ask me that I wouldn't have done for him."

After Doby left, Veeck told a reporter, "I hated to do it. I'm just as fond of him today as I was when he helped us win a pennant in Cleveland in 1948. He always had great talent and he's far from through. But he's had a bad back and playing out there will be like going through spring training for him."[37]

"When I got to San Diego," Doby said as he thought back, "Ralph Kiner was there as general manager. He made it clear to me, 'Anything you need, anything you want, just come to me.' He probably had been told by Bill to take care of me."

For three weeks, Doby worked out with San Diego under field manager George "Catfish" Metkovich. Wearing a brace to support his aching back, Doby played briefly in a road game at Seattle before the Padres moved on to play the Solons at Sacramento. There, on August 23, he hit a triple 400 feet to right center field, raising his batting average to .222 in nine games. He has a vivid memory of what happened after he hit the ball.

"I was wearing that brace on my back on that particular night. I was running good rounding second base, but when I got the 'Slide' sign from Metkovich coaching at third base, I just couldn't get my left leg in the right position because the brace came right down to my coccyx. I hit the bag hard, and it just threw me over, about five feet past the bag, in foul territory. I was in pain. My foot was turned almost around, backwards. I knew my ankle was broken right away. Then they took me to the hospital and they gave me a shot to ease the pain. The doctor turned my foot around the right way and put it in a cast."

During the next few days, Doby's pride made him try to avoid the indignities which are so often inflicted upon a fallen hero. He refused visitors and local reporters alike. When X-rays revealed that Doby had torn the ligaments in his ankle as well as suffering a fracture, hospital attendants prepared him for a trip to the Johns Hopkins Hospital in Baltimore.

The trip was agony. Doby flew from Sacramento to New York, changed planes for a flight to Washington, and then traveled the final 40 miles to Baltimore by private automobile. There, Dr. George Bennett, who had treated Doby before, came out to greet his famous patient.

Lifted into a wheelchair, Doby asked the photographers not to take his picture. With each slight movement, he winced in pain. As an attendant wheeled him through the lobby, a persistent photographer rushed up to snap a picture.

"I told you no pictures," Doby yelled in anger. 'I'll get even with you! I'll get you for this!" With that, he disappeared down the hall.[38] That night, the Associated Press flashed Doby's picture by wirephoto to its clients throughout the United States. The next day, many editors printed the photo on their sports pages.[39]

After about a week of convalescence, Helyn drove the family station wagon from Montclair to pick up her husband. He remained in a cast for about eight weeks, returned to Baltimore to have it removed, and then began a course of physical therapy at Mountainside Hospital in Montclair.

The White Sox, meanwhile, combined their speed and pitching to win the American League pennant, five games ahead of Cleveland and 15 games ahead of the Yankees. They didn't fare as well against the Los Angeles Dodgers in the World Series, losing in six games, but before the Series started they voted Doby a half-share of their winnings. It was a generous gesture toward a player who had appeared in only 21 games that season, but many of the Sox may have remembered Doby's play during the 1956 and 1957 seasons.

When his third, and last, World Series check arrived, Doby banked $3,637.59.

During the winter of 1959–60, a resolute Doby continued his therapy with the hope that he could continue his playing career. When he reported to Sarasota, Florida, he found, to his great pleasure, that he would be allowed to live with his White Sox teammates. It was only the third time in 13 spring training seasons, and the first time since 1955.

With a pin in his ankle severely limiting its flexibility, Doby could not make the roster of the White Sox. Yet he persisted. On April 22, he signed a contract to play with the Toronto Maple Leafs of the International League, and flew from Sarasota to Canada.

Even with Toronto, though, Doby could not break into the lineup during a road trip to Havana, Cuba. He worked out daily at first base and took batting practice, but his still impressive power with the bat could not compensate for his immobility in the infield. Nor could it ease the constant pain in his ankle, which caused him to have X-rays after the series against the Sugar Kings. They showed that the pin in the ankle had caused deterioration of the bone at the site of the fracture.

Finally, on May 7, Toronto general manager Danny Menendez issued to Doby an unconditional release from his contract. In making the announcement, Menendez revealed that Doby would reenter Johns Hopkins Hospital for further surgery and removal of the pin.[40]

His release by Toronto came as no surprise to Doby. He had already thought, on the night he broke his ankle in Sacramento, that his career was over. "I saw it happen to a great player, Monte Irvin. He tried to come back and it didn't work. When they first took my cast off, I knew. It was like a peg leg, almost."

En route from Toronto to Montclair, before going on to Baltimore,

Doby felt "lost as to what I was going to do." By the time he reached home, his foremost thought was "to stay in baseball in some capacity," with coaching the leading possibility. He shed no tears, though. "I don't have an ego of that kind that I would feel sorry for myself. Shedding tears, to me, just takes away the man, the man in you, the adversity that you have to face, the adversity that you have to gain strength from. So my thinking then was to make a living for four kids and a wife and a home."

After surgery later in May, Doby became a scout for Bill Veeck that summer. With Morris "Dutch" Deutsch, he searched the diamonds of New Jersey looking for talented young players, and continued on the White Sox payroll as a scout until Veeck sold his interest in the team.

Thus, Larry Doby ended his pioneering career as a major league player. In 11 full seasons and parts of two others, he had appeared in 1,533 games, batted .283, slugged 253 home runs, and drove in 969 runs. Playing mostly in center field, he made 3,627 putouts and compiled a lifetime fielding average of .983. For six straight years he had been named to the American League All-Star team. Twice he helped to lead the Cleveland Indians to the World Series.

In the Negro National League he had played in what amounted to two full seasons and had appeared in two All-Star games and one World Series. In the Pacific Coast League he played in just nine games. Although he tried, he never appeared in an International League game with Toronto.

When he stopped playing, Doby deserved to be called a survivor. Of all the men who played in the 1948 World Series, only seven were still active. Of the 11 American black men who played in the major leagues between 1947 and 1950, he was the last to hang up his spikes. Furthermore, he had played in many more games than any of them.[41]

Nearing the age of 37, retired as an active player, Doby felt somehow relieved. "I had a load off my back as far as prejudice is concerned. The years had taken their toll on me in terms of the mental situation, in terms of the persecution that I went through all those years. I didn't gain respect from everybody as a normal human being, just trying to play baseball. It never, never got to the point where it was real nice, real fine, just to be me. There was still that certain section of life where there were reminders, that you knew you were black."

But in 1960, Doby still had half a life yet to live. More achievements, and more prejudiced assaults on his pride, were yet to come.

NOTES

1. *Plain Dealer*, March 1, 1955.
2. *Press*, July 8, 1955.
3. *New York Times*, August 5, 1955.

4. *Plain Dealer*, August 14, 1955.

5. Ibid.

6. David S. Neft, Richard M. Cohen, and Jordan A. Deutsch, *The Sports Encyclopedia: Baseball* (New York: Grosset and Dunlap, 1981), p. 302.

7. *New York Times*, October 26, 1955.

8. Franklin Lewis, *Press*, October 26, 1955.

9. *New York Times*, March 3, 1956.

10. Ibid.

11. *World-Telegram and Sun*, May 5, 1956.

12. Personal interview with Herb Score, September 17, 1980.

13. *Press*, December 10, 1956.

14. Neft, Cohen, and Deutsch, *Baseball*, p. 310.

15. *World-Telegram and Sun*, June 13, 1957.

16. Ibid., June 14, 1957.

17. Shirley Povich, "This Morning . . . ," *The Sporting News*, June 26, 1957.

18. *Ebony*, September 1957, p. 53.

19. Ibid., p. 51.

20. Franklin Lewis, *Press*, August 14, 1957.

21. A. S. "Doc" Young, "Inside Sports," *Jet*, December 19, 1957.

22. Neft, Cohen, and Deutsch, *Baseball*, p. 310.

23. *Herald-Tribune*, December 5, 1957.

24. Doc Young, "Inside Sports," *Jet*, December 19, 1957.

25. Gordon Cobbledick, "Plain Dealing," *Plain Dealer*, March 21, 1958.

26. *World-Telegram and Sun*, April 1, 1958.

27. *Press*, April 1, 1958.

28. *Plain Dealer*, June 30, 1958.

29. Neft, Cohen, and Deutsch, *Baseball*, p. 315.

30. *Plain Dealer*, January 22, 1959.

31. Ibid., March 22, 1959.

32. *Press*, March 27, 1959.

33. *Herald-Tribune*, May 14, 1959.

34. Neft, Cohen, and Deutsch, *Baseball*, p. 327.

35. *Herald-Tribune*, July 27, 1959.

36. *World-Telegram and Sun*, August 3, 1959.

37. Ibid.

38. *Herald-Tribune*, August 27, 1959.

39. Ibid.

40. *New York Times*, February 8, 1960.

41. Neft, Cohen, and Deutsch, *Baseball*, passim.

10

"Gaijin"

In the first days of his retirement as a player, and in his new position as a scout for the Chicago White Sox, Larry Doby began to hobble to amateur baseball games on his damaged ankle in the summer and early fall of 1960. That winter, he went to work for the Board of Recreation in Paterson.

When neither job proved challenging or lucrative, he and Helyn decided, in 1962, to invest their money in a bar and liquor store in Newark, where he was well known and where the large black population provided potential customers. Having done so, Doby then received a call from old and good friend Don Newcombe, also retired as an active player, inviting Doby to join him on the Chunichi Dragons of Nagoya in the Japanese baseball league for the 1962 season.

Because the deal on the tavern was still pending, and because his signature was needed on various legal documents, Doby delayed his departure for Japan for 10 days, arriving there on June 29, 1962. After he left, Helyn, brother George Curvy, and brother-in-law Ralph Brown began to operate the establishment, named the Center Field Lounge.

Newcombe explained the arrangements which led to their playing in Japan. "As I recall," he said, "two men came with an interpreter to my nightclub in Newark in 1962. They asked me if I wanted to play in Japan. When I agreed to go, and when the publicity came out on it, I got a call from Pierre Salinger, who was President Kennedy's press secretary.

"I knew Salinger because we played golf together the year before, when I pitched for Spokane in the Pacific Coast League. He asked me to come to the White House for an interview.

"When I got to the White House, Salinger told me that, in effect, I would be representing President Kennedy and the United States. He said we had established pretty good relationships with the Japanese people, and through baseball, we could establish further relationships and even open up the possibility of other American players going to Japan. There were no direct duties that I was expected to perform, but I was expected to comport myself in a certain way.

"After I signed to play with the Dragons, I talked them into contacting Larry. He didn't want to play because of his ankle, and he didn't think he could get in shape. I told him, 'Larry, here's a chance to make some money, and you won't have to work hard. It seems to me to be easy baseball to play. If you can get in any kind of shape, you can hit the ball.' "[1]

With a contract for $30,000, plus traveling and living expenses, offered by the Dragons, Doby quickly completed the purchase of his new bar and liquor store and followed Newcombe to Japan. He did not know, as he flew across the Pacific Ocean, that they would be the first former major league players to play in regular season baseball there.

Nor did Doby know that four Americans had played in the Japanese league before World War II, and that Wally Yonamine, soon to be one of his interpreters, was the first American to play in Japan after World War II. Yonamine, born in Hawaii of Japanese immigrant parents, had once been the property of the San Francisco Seals of the Pacific Coast League and had played Class C baseball in Salt Lake City.[2]

In Nagoya, Doby lived alone in a hotel downtown while Newcombe, who had brought along his wife and young son, lived in a house in the suburbs. Together, they were always conspicuous among the much smaller Japanese people. It was easy to see, given their color and size, that they were "gaijins"—foreigners.

With the help of Yonamine and Carl Honda, another Hawaiian who spoke Japanese, Doby and Newcombe gradually asserted themselves in Japan's Central League. Neither man started out well. In Doby's first game, against the Hiroshima Carps, he failed to hit in three times at bat, striking out twice. Newcombe, with a 10-day head start on Doby, also failed to hit in that game. But the Dragons won anyway, 2–0.[3]

Thereafter, although they didn't hit the ball often, they hit it far. While batting only .201 on 54 hits in 268 at bats, Doby slugged 10 home runs, nine doubles, and a triple, and drove in 35 runs. Newcombe had 73 hits in 279 at bats for a .261 average. His hits included 12 home runs and 23 doubles, and he drove in 43 runs.[4]

In his book, *40 Years of Chunichi Dragons*, published 13 years later, baseball writer Kiyoshi Nakagawa remembered Doby: "Even today, there are still quite a few fans who remember the sound of Doby's bat cutting the air and his special swing." The Japanese fans, Nakagawa wrote, noted the power in Doby's upper body and his legs. And well they might. One day he hit a 500-foot home run, one of the longest in the history of Japanese baseball, into the teeth of a typhoon wind.[5]

Another baseball writer, Toshio Tamakoshi, in his book *The Dragon's Story*, compared the two famous American visitors: "Thirty-nine year old

Doby [actually, he was 38], unlike Newcombe, who was a relaxed and easy-going type, was quite different. He was an athlete who gave one a feeling of great strength. When he hit, most of his hits were liners. Before the crowd could let out a gasp, the ball was up in the stands."

Tamakoshi noted that Doby's batting average was lower than Newcombe's. But, he wrote, "in terms of his spirit, Doby surpassed Newcombe."[6]

With Doby playing first base or the outfield and batting third, and Newcombe playing left field and batting fourth, the Dragons moved from last place to second place by the time the season ended.[7]

Neither Doby nor Newcombe had much to do with their manager, Takada Kazuo, because he didn't speak English. Through Yonamine and Honda, Doby and Newcombe offered batting, fielding, and pitching tips to their teammates. They also conducted clinics for kids where Doby, Newcombe says, was "very good at explaining some of the mistakes they made."

Away from baseball, Doby and Newcombe had few official duties. On one occasion, they were invited to meet Prime Minister Hayato Ikeda at his mansion in Tokyo, and were accompanied by the American ambassador, William O. Reischauer. On a few other occasions, Doby and Newcombe were guests at informal receptions.[8]

As Doby looks back on his experience in Japan, he says, "The first month or so it was tough, just getting into shape. But I enjoyed it there. I felt relaxed. I had Newk's friendship. The Japanese people treated us with a lot of respect and fine hospitality. I knew I was at the end of my career, so I took the games one at a time. It reminded me of when I was a kid, going out into the street to play. If it was raining, it didn't matter. You'd play tomorrow.

"After I played in Japan, I got letters from three of the guys on the team for many years after. I wanted to go back in 1963, because I felt I could be productive. It was easier to play there. The season was only 130 games and you had every Monday off. I gave no thought to making it back to the major leagues."

Neither man returned to Japan for the 1963 season, however. The Dragons never contacted them to do so, although, according to Nakagawa, Doby and Newcombe ignited a "foreigner boom" in Japanese baseball circles, just as they had ignited a "black boom" in baseball in the United States in the late 1940's.

Upon his return from Japan in early October, Doby began to work in the Center Field Lounge and its adjacent liquor store. For a man who never drank until he was 30 years old, and who still drank only occasionally, the liquor business seemed a strange choice. Yet it was an obvious choice. His good friends Newcombe and Roy Campanella owned taverns and liquor stores in Newark and Harlem, and were doing quite well. Monte

Irvin had become a public relations man for Rheingold Breweries. Buying a tavern did not require a major financial investment, an important consideration for a man who was well off but hardly wealthy. It did not require extensive or highly specialized knowledge or training. It was a field open to a black entrepreneur, as many fields of business were not. And it insulated Doby, by reason of its location, from the white world where he had grown weary of coping with open and subtle racial prejudice. In the Center Field Lounge, he might feel as comfortable as he did when he played in the Negro National League.

The liquor business seemed a strange choice for Doby in yet another respect, though. To cash in on his fame, he would have to promote himself, to expand the myths with which people endow their heroes. But despite the honors and adulation Doby had received during his long career in baseball, he did not come to see himself in mythic terms. Nor did he permit others to impose their myths upon him. "I always wanted to deal in truth and facts," he says. "As I have said many times, I just wanted to be plain me."

Neither did Doby like having to make payments to fire inspectors who had the power to close him down for alleged safety violations, and policemen who harrassed him for petty graft.

When business began to decline in 1965, Larry and Helyn decided to sell. In a sense, that decision resembled Doby's retirement from baseball: he was going away from something more than toward something. He was a "gaijin," a foreigner, in his own country. He was a man without a position in life.

Soon after the sale of the Center Field Lounge, at a net loss he estimates at $40,000, the Essex County Board of Freeholders, at the urging of prosecutor and future governor Brendan Byrne, appointed Doby to the position of Director of Bicycle Safety. Then, in the summer of 1967, when angry black residents of Newark expressed their feelings in an outburst of rioting, Doby set aside his regular work to meet with groups of teenagers, black and white, at Barringer High School. There, for the first time, Doby gave verbal expression to his belief in the "American system." He had not become, as a result of his experiences in the Navy and in professional baseball, an embittered social radical.

While he owned the tavern, and while he worked for Essex County, Doby wrote letters to the men who ran major league baseball teams in the 1960's. He felt he deserved a chance as a coach, because he had been one of the two pioneers who opened baseball to black players. He knew baseball and had a lot to teach. He had lived a life free of personal scandal and had never criticized baseball or the American way of life, as it had become fashionable to do in the United States during the era of the Vietnam war.

And he had been tested by racial prejudice and yet had survived as a whole man.

Ultimately, the outsider looking in got back into baseball not because baseball wanted him. Baseball *had* to take him. The nonviolent civil rights movement of the late 1950's and early 1960's, under Dr. Martin Luther King, Jr., had just turned violent, and the sheer number of black players in baseball made the lack of black coaches and managers ever more obvious.

Two tragic events brought matters to a climax. Newark, Detroit, and other major cities went up in flames in 1967, and the apostle of nonviolence, Dr. King himself, fell to an assassin's bullet in 1968. A number of American institutions, including baseball, found themselves embarrassed in their passivity. Soon the commissioner of baseball, Bowie Kuhn, let it be known to the owners that they'd better integrate their coaching staffs and their front offices. Kuhn was light years distant from one of his predecessors, Judge Landis, who had done so much to thwart black progress until his death in 1944.

As the number of black and Latin players on major league teams increased throughout the 1960's, so did the need for black and Latin coaches. In the years from 1947 through 1960, white players accounted for 88 percent of all at bats in the major leagues, while black players accounted for 7.6 percent and Latin players 4.6 percent. For the years from 1961 to 1968, the comparable figures are 64, 22, and 14 percent. Among pitchers, although the increase in innings pitched is not as dramatic, there is still an increase.[9]

The increase did not occur because white baseball owners wanted to encourage black players. Rather, the blacks rode in on the same highway traveled by Doby: objective statistics. In a game obsessed by numbers, and the desire to win, baseball owners could not exclude someone on the grounds of race.

But the increase of the number of black players did not, by itself, lead to the addition of black coaches. One essential ingredient was still missing. The black players would have to be more militant than their predecessors. They would have to act on the popular slogans which black leaders tried to teach black Americans in the 1960's: "Black Is Beautiful," "Burn, Baby, Burn," "Learn, Baby, Learn," "Violence is as American as cherry pie," and, perhaps most of all, "Black Power."

As Doby explains it, "A white coach may have had some problems after the riots of 1967 because now you're facing a different kind of black player. When I was playing, whites still felt superior to you, they still put you in the same category that you were put in during the time of slavery—not intelligent, slow to learn. All of a sudden, you've got a thing that surprised everybody when you had the riots. Now you're dealing with a totally different kind of black. And that, to me, is the real reason why white owners hired black coaches.

"I think that the black players opened the door for black coaches, not the other way around. I don't know that the owners looked at it from a positive, objective standpoint, though. My thinking is that if the owners looked at it from a positive standpoint, why is it that no black coaches later got the chance to move to third base? Why do the blacks only coach first base?"

Doby, and later the vice-president of the Los Angeles Dodgers, Al Campanis, answered these questions. Doby said, "The third base coach has to be more capable than the first base coach. He relays the signs from the manager, he controls the base runners. The black coaches are not considered to be intelligent enough to coach third.

"The black coaches are kept at first base for another reason. In baseball, you move from third base coach to manager. And not too many owners and general managers want their managers to be black."

Campanis's answer to Doby's questions serves to support Doby. He told Ted Koppel, on network television in 1987, that blacks "may not have some of the necessities to be, let's say, a field manager or perhaps a general manager."[10] Ironically, Campanis was a teammate of Jackie Robinson in 1946 at Montreal, and barnstormed with Robinson in postseason play when Robinson could not get enough good black players to meet his needs.

Baseball needed black coaches after the civil rights uprisings for another reason. As the temperament of black players changed, so did their behavior. They felt more free to be themselves, to behave as they wished. Doby explains this in concrete terms. "There's such a thing as 'jive talk,' " he says, "the hand slapping and all that kind of stuff. White folks just couldn't talk jive talk. I could, and other black coaches could. And I found it helpful with kids who came out of ghettos and could just talk that one type of language. If you could not talk jive, the black players would look at you a little differently. Or they put you in a different category, uppity or whatever. I made it a point of talking jive to black players who naturally talked that way, but not around a lot of whites. If there was a white kid who wanted to talk jive talk, I would. But he would be like me trying to speak English to the English people!"

Early in 1968, having been through Newark's holocaust, Larry Doby said in the pages of a national magazine that he thought baseball would "probably wait until we burn down a few ball parks before it decided to hire a black coach or manager." Apparently the article came to the attention of Commissioner Kuhn and John McHale, Kuhn's assistant at the time.

About a month later, McHale arranged to meet with Doby and another former black star, Monte Irvin, for dinner in Toots Shor's restaurant in New York City. McHale told his guests that there were two positions about to open in baseball. If they agreed, one would go to Irvin as special assistant to Kuhn. The other would go to Doby as a scout for the Montreal Expos, where McHale would soon become president of the National League's latest expansion team.

In explaining the offer from McHale, Doby says, "I don't know whether he respected my knowledge of baseball or whether he thought that since I had been a part of baseball from a pioneering standpoint, and since I had said a few [negative] things in the article, that it didn't look good for baseball to have me on the outside. McHale did not mention the magazine article at the dinner."

After a four-week, 10-city tour in the summer by Doby for presidential candidate Hubert Humphrey, which included induction into the Cleveland Indians Hall of Fame as part of the itinerary, McHale fulfilled his promises to Doby and Irvin. Irvin joined the staff of the commissioner's office; Doby became part of the Expos organization at a salary of $1,000 per month the following February.

The Expos eventually found that they had hired much more than a token black after Doby got a chance to work with young players. To his knowledge of baseball gained during 15 years as a professional player he had added eight years of watching baseball on television.

Thus, the "personal value of watching TV was that it gave me that motivation to put what I had learned into practice. It was hard sitting there watching game after game all those years and not being able to put that into practice. Television, during the eight years I was out of baseball, was a blessing in disguise. It was something I never thought too much of when I first left baseball."

It was almost as if Doby's separation from the game, painful though it may have been, was a necessary phase of his life. It enabled him, as a coach during the 1970's, to find gratification from baseball which he never thought possible when he was a player.

NOTES

1. Personal interview with Don Newcombe, September 10, 1981.

2. Robert Whiting, *The Chrysanthemum and the Bat: Baseball Samurai Style* (New York: Dodd, Mead, 1977), p. 142.

3. *Plain Dealer*, July 1, 1962.

4. Kiyoshi Nakagawa, *40 Years of Chunichi Dragons* (Nagoya: Chunichi Newspaper Press, 1975), p. 290. (The author is indebted to Professor Masaru Ikei of the Faculty of Law at Keio University for his assistance in finding information pertaining to Newcombe and Doby.)

5. Nakagawa, *Chunichi Dragons*, p. 295.

6. Toshio Tamakoshi, *The Dragons' Story* (Tokyo: Gendai Kikakushu, 1978), p. 205.

7. Newcombe, loc. cit.

8. Newcombe, loc. cit.

9. David S. Neft, Richard M. Cohen, and Jordan A. Deutsch, *The New Sports Encyclopedia: Baseball* (New York: Grosset and Dunlap, 1974), pp. 477–78.

10. *New York Times*, April 9, 1987.

11

Another Robinson

In the spring of 1969, the Montreal Expos, in the midst of preparations for their first season in the National League, assigned Larry Doby to work with the young hitters on the team's Class A farm team at West Palm Beach, with a rookie club at Bradenton, and with an instructional team at St. Petersburg. As they learned of Doby's success with John Mayberry and many other young players in Florida, they decided to take greater advantage of his talents, promoting him to the position of "Batting Instructor and Special Assignment Representative" in February of 1970. During spring training he tutored the hitters on their major league team, and spent the summer visiting their top farm teams in Memphis (Class AAA), Quebec City (AA), and West Palm Beach (A).

Since Doby had played so briefly in the minor leagues at the end of his playing career, these nomadic experiences filled in a gap in his overall knowledge of organized baseball. As his successes grew and his reputation flourished, so too did his aspirations. His vague dream of managing a major league team steadily became more focused. It became even clearer in 1971, when the Expos promoted Doby for the third straight year. In a press release, then vice-president Jim Fanning announced that Doby would be "a full-time major league hitting coach," but added, ambiguously, that Doby would also "retain some of his batting instruction responsibilities with the organization's farm teams."[1]

Ambiguity aside, Doby described the announcement as one of his greatest thrills. "Yes, this ranks right along with the thrills of personal performances and World Series victories," he exulted.[2]

Expos manager Gene Mauch, asked by baseball writer Ian McDonald to comment on Doby's promotion, observed that "There are few great hitters who can communicate. You'd be amazed how many great hitters don't even really know what they are doing that is right. It just comes naturally to them.

"Doby has sound theories and he can get the message across to the players. He is articulate and can communicate."[3]

The promotion caused Doby to comment on his prospects of becoming a major league manager. "I believe we are past that stage now where color will have anything to do with it," he told McDonald more hopefully than realistically. "It's just what a man can do that counts. If you're a stupid black man, you're stupid. If you're a stupid white man, you're stupid."[4]

Mauch, perhaps more than anyone in the Montreal organization, had a strong sense of perspective about his new black coach. As a young player in the farm system of the Brooklyn Dodgers during and after World War II, he had personally "witnessed the terrible things that Jackie Robinson went through," he remembered in 1980. "It had subsided some by 1949, due to the fact that both Jackie and Larry were so productive as players. Even some of the guys who didn't want to accept them had no choice because [Doby and Robinson] were good ballplayers.

"You have to be some kind of special person to go through what Larry and Jackie went through. They both are. I'm not too sure there's a player in the game today that could handle it."

As Mauch and Doby worked together over the next three seasons (1971–73), Mauch's estimation of Doby's ability grew. "I respect Larry Doby's ability to teach hitting. I think he's one of the few guys that have a real, true contribution to make as a hitting instructor. I thought Harry Walker was one, Joe Gordon was one, Wally Moses, and Larry. Larry had the ability to analyze hitting and make suggestions that would be helpful to that hitter. He knew a way to approach each hitter with what that hitter had to work with. Some other people who profess to be batting instructors, if the subject doesn't conform to the instructor's particular style, then they can't help. Larry had a very simple way of making the hitter come into his own, to narrow down the strike zone. And I think he learned from teaching, as many people do. He's a bright man."[5]

Doby had already helped John Mayberry, then with the Houston Astros, in the Florida Instructional League in 1969, early in Mayberry's long career in the major leagues. He provided a role model for Mayberry as well. "My father was a baseball fan for years," he said. "He was from Mississippi. He used to see the old Negro League teams years ago, and then he moved up to Detroit for four years. Doby went in there with Cleveland, and I guess he had a lot of black fans and supporters. He was such a good hitter. My father used to tell me about him all the time. He really praised Larry Doby because Larry was a gentleman."[6]

Now, at Montreal in 1972, two of Montreal's promising young players, acquired from the New York Mets, fell under Doby's influence. Mike Jorgensen, a white player, remembered that Doby "would work with the hitters all the time but he would not offer his opinion as much as some other hitting coaches would, unless a player would come to him." Jorgensen also appreciated Doby the man: "I thought Larry had a better sense of humor than people thought he did. I think he was most at ease and most comfortable when he was talking about hitting."[7]

Ken Singleton, a black man who grew up in Yonkers, New York, knew of Doby's significance in baseball history prior to meeting him in Montreal. Speaking as a star of the Baltimore Orioles in 1980, he remembered that Doby "told me about the old days—who were the nice guys, who were the guys who were really serious about him, helping the team and not worrying about race. He mentioned that some of his teammates were even against him. That's hard to fathom in this day and age because I know how this team [the Orioles] is, everybody pulling for each other to win. We realize that this is the only way we're going to win."

Summing up his feelings, Singleton said, "I just love the man. Every time I see him, I realize what he's done for me. He got me straightened out. He got my game together. I'm just thankful that he was around at the right time."[8]

Doby even helped at least one player who did not play for Montreal. Dusty Baker, a young outfielder with the Atlanta Braves in the early 1970's, used to "tag along" with his teammate and idol, Hank Aaron, when Aaron and Doby would visit each other after games. "I wanted to talk about hitting," Baker said. "But Larry wanted to talk more about mental preparation as far as baseball is concerned."

During his long talks with Doby and Aaron, Baker also figured out why Doby never became as well known as Jackie Robinson: "Larry's not very controversial. He doesn't run his mouth a lot, talk out of turn. He says what's on his mind, and that's it. If he doesn't have anything to say, he doesn't say anything. I don't think most guys know who Larry is, really. You don't even know that Larry is around, sometimes, but if you've ever been around him you know he's not missing anything that's going on around him. To me, he's in the same mold, but a little tougher, as Jim Gilliam.[9] I think Larry is underestimated as a player and as a person."[10]

As a husband and father of five children, Doby loved to stay home with his family in the off-season. But knowing that his chances of managing in the major leagues would be improved if he had some managerial experience, he accepted an arrangement made by Jim Fanning to manage Zulia of Maracaibo, Venezuela, in the winter of 1971–72.

Doby's experience in Maracaibo turned out to be a mixture of success and controversy. He managed the team into first place, and enjoyed working with players who achieved success in the major leagues, including Toby Harrah and Ben Oglivie, but had problems with the team's owners which led to his dismissal.

First, he objected to having the owners, their wives, and even their children sitting on the bench during games "because of the language we used." Next, he defied an order to use a pitcher out of turn, hearing rumors that the order was motivated by bets that the owners had placed on their team to lose. After the team won, strengthening its grip on first place and making it a favorite in the imminent postseason playoffs, Doby learned he had been fired when he got back to his hotel. He was replaced by a local hero, Luis Aparicio, his old teammate on the Chicago White Sox.

Yet the story had another page left in it. "I had a two-year contract," Doby says, "so there was a problem the next year because I was not the manager. But I took it to the Commissioner's office, which sanctioned Venezuelan baseball, and I got my money.

"That was a good experience in Venezuela, though. That's when I found out whether I could or could not manage. And of course I have to thank Jim Fanning, because he gave me the opportunity."

October 1972 proved to be a particularly eventful month for the nation in general, and Larry Doby in particular. National attention focused on the presidential race between Richard Nixon, running for reelection, and his challenger, Democrat George McGovern, riding the crest of a wave of political reform. But on the night of October 16, many Americans focused instead on Riverfront Stadium in Cincinnati, where professional baseball marked the twenty-fifth anniversary of the racial integration of the sport by honoring Doby and Jackie Robinson prior to the second game of the World Series between the Oakland Athletics and the local Reds.

Robinson, in failing health, just nine days from his death, threw out the first ball. In a special ceremony at the pitcher's mound, Commissioner Bowie Kuhn honored him for his work in combatting drug addiction.

"That's the last time I talked with Jackie," Doby recalls. "We were in the airport, coming home. Jackie was having a tough time seeing. People had to lead him around by the arm. But he had not lost any spirit. He wasn't looking for sympathy. He still had that toughness in him. You wouldn't know how much it bothered him to be almost blind unless you followed him around. . . . I found him to be nicer to strangers [than ever before]. You see, Jackie could be hard on strangers. I remember in that airport, people would walk up to him, and he'd say 'How are you?' and smile. He would never do that before. The change was good because people usually don't change. They die the same way they were."

After Robinson's death, six men significant in his life served as pallbearers. They were Doby, Pee Wee Reese, Don Newcombe, Jim Gilliam, and Ralph Branca from his years in baseball, and basketball player Bill Russell of the Boston Celtics. As they carried the casket to the hearse, Roy Campanella followed in his wheelchair.

With Robinson's death, Doby stood as the surviving pioneer of their historic contribution to the struggle for black equality in their country. "But I didn't think about that at the time," he said in 1981. "I've thought more about being the pioneer lately."

Doby continued to serve as batting instructor for the Expos in 1972. With the experience of managing under his belt, though, he began to make it plainer that he wanted to manage in the major leagues. He told Wendell Smith, the black sportswriter whose knowledge of baseball went back to the Negro leagues and his year as Jackie Robinson's first roommate with the Dodgers, "I give myself five years. If I don't make it by then, I'll give up the idea and get out of baseball altogether.

"I believe the time is ripe for a black manager. There's still some bigotry in baseball, of course, but I do not believe it's so prevalent that it would become a problem. The atmosphere is certainly much better now than it was in 1947 when Jackie Robinson and I came up to the majors as players."

Asked by Smith to identify the most important assets a manager must have, Doby named two. The first, he said, was "a matter of communication. You devote most of your time to keeping your 25 players contented and motivated."

The second attribute Doby identified was vintage Doby. "Respect," he said, "is the key to success in managing. You must respect the player, he must respect you. I am sure I can win the respect of any player who plays under me."[11]

A year later, still coaching first base and working with Montreal's hitters, Doby repeated his ambition to manage in the major leagues in an interview in the *Christian Science Monitor*. "I don't want it because I'm black, though. I never wanted any black tokenism, and I don't want any now. I believe I have the ability and the experience, and I want it on that basis."[12]

In November 1973, general manager Phil Seghi of the Cleveland Indians telephoned his counterpart in Montreal, Jim Fanning, to ask for permission to talk to Doby. Seghi claimed that he gave no indication at the time that the Indians had Doby in mind as the team's possible future field manager, and Seghi denied any such intention when interviewed in 1981. (Seghi died in January 1987.) But in view of what eventually happened in Cleveland, and in light of ample conflicting evidence, Seghi apparently would not be frank on the subject.[13] In any case, Seghi hired Doby to be a coach for the Indians in 1974.

"They [Seghi] told Mr. McHale that I had a good chance to become the manager if anything happened to Ken Aspromonte," Doby told a reporter for the Montreal *Gazette* after his 1974 season in Cleveland had ended. "Mr. McHale phoned me at home. I told him I was very happy working for Gene Mauch. I told him, 'Hey, I don't want to leave, not just for another coaching job, anyway.' Mr. McHale told me the value of being in the right place at the right time, that if I was in Cleveland when they made a change [of managers] then I would have the best chance. Still, I reminded him that Dick Williams and Don Zimmer went from coaching jobs with the Expos and Mauch to other managing jobs. I said I thought that I would have the same opportunity. Mr. McHale told me that I would be better off learning about the teams and players in the other league, just in case. Finally he said that if it didn't work out, I'd always have a job with the Expos. That was the clincher. But I didn't pick up and leave [Montreal], believe me."[14]

Fanning corroborated Doby's statement of 1974 during the baseball strike in 1981. "It's true," Fanning said. "When Phil Seghi talked to me, though he didn't come right out and say as much, he indicated as much—as a former Cleveland star, that that door [managing] may well open to him [Doby]. So it was a really difficult thing for me to handle then with Larry, because as I recall it I couldn't tell him everything I knew because if it didn't happen, he would then have, of course, great disappointment. But I think I implied it without really implying it, if you know what I mean."[15]

As he looked back in 1981 on the circumstances of his move to Cleveland from Montreal in 1974, Doby still had strong emotions: "If Seghi wanted me in Cleveland as a manager, why didn't they bring me in as manager, like they do in other places? In Cleveland, I had to coach for a year, and then they have to make their decision as to whether they wanted me as manager. Why did it have to be done in that fashion? In my thinking, it comes right back to color. If I had been white, and had done the things that I had done in Montreal, and they were looking for me, I would have been brought to Cleveland as a manager and not as a coach. So why did I have to be put on some sort of reviewing stand? It's another test. Why another test?"

Fanning claimed in 1981 that he had offered Doby a chance to manage in the minor leagues,[16] but Doby remembers no such offer. Instead, secure in McHale's promise that he could go back to Montreal, and more or less promised a shot at managing in Cleveland should Ken Aspromonte falter there, Doby accepted Seghi's offer. In a press release issued by the Indians on December 5, 1973, Seghi announced that Doby would join their coaching staff and have a "prominent position in front office operations. Doby will play a vital role on the Tribe's sales promotions and marketing teams."

The release quoted Seghi: "Larry will be a key contributor to what we hope to accomplish with the Indians, both on and off the field."[17]

The references to sales and marketing responsibilities were apparently intended to portray Cleveland as having a more integrated front office, where Jim "Mudcat" Grant, a black former major league pitcher, held a position, because Seghi never gave Doby a "prominent position" there.

Interviewed after the press release, Doby did not reveal that Seghi had discussed the manager's job with McHale and Fanning. Instead, he put just a whiff of intrigue into his change of teams when he said, "I'm very happy to be going back to Cleveland, although I want to make it clear I was not unhappy in Montreal."[18]

Anyone close to baseball didn't need a decoding device to figure out what that meant. Aspromonte, who had not proposed the addition of Doby to his staff, most especially knew from Doby's statement that Doby had more than coaching to lure him from Montreal. But Aspromonte, a loyal trouper, expressed his approval, and inserted a racial connotation as well. "Larry can be the 'middle man' between me and fellows like Charlie Spikes, George Hendrick, Chris Chambliss and others. A lot of young players are reluctant to talk to the manager, but not with a coach of Doby's stature."[19] The players Aspromonte cited are all black. He did not mention Jack Brohamer, Buddy Bell, or Frank Duffy, three front-line, young, white players.

Seghi, in his comments after the press release, added to the racial connotation by citing the same three black players, and stressed the importance of team unity in a racial, and therefore divisive, context: "Doby is a very qualified baseball man. He's qualified as both a coach and an instructor. I think a man of his caliber will add strength and fiber to the unity of our club.

"Certainly, he'll be able to relate to young men like Spikes, Hendrick, and Chambliss, and I think he can help bring everybody on the club together."[20] After the rhetoric subsided, Doby packed his bags and headed for Cleveland for the first time in a capacity other than that of player.

Spring training for Doby in 1974 proved to be a trip filled with comparisons. It brought him back to Tucson, where he had borne his segregation in the 1940's and 1950's. Now, 26 years after his first visit there as a player for the Indians, he could see how much Arizona had changed: hotel and dining accomodations were all fully integrated. The difference reinforced his belief that positive change could occur in his country. It also gave him immense satisfaction to know that he had been a principal agent of that change.

Throughout the spring, Doby worked with black and white players alike, as he had done in his five years with the Expos. A television reporter, however, perhaps mindful of the statements made by Aspromonte and Seghi, commented on camera, "I hear you were hired to handle Hendrick, Spikes, and other black players here." Doby, angry, the son of a man who groomed horses for a living, flashed back, still on camera, "You handle mules and plow horses, not people. If I thought I was hired only for that, I'd quit right now. I'm here to help everybody who needs it."[21]

When the American League season opened in April, the Indians stumbled. In May and June, rumors circulated that Doby would replace Aspromonte as manager. In July, the players saved Aspromonte's job. In a weekend series in Cleveland against the California Angels just before the mid-season All-Star game, with Aspromonte to be fired if the Indians did not win the series, his team swept the Angels. As they continued to win, the rumors subsided. Doby gradually learned, by roundabout means, that he would not take over the manager's position until after the season had ended. He had come within a weekend of becoming the first black manager in major league history.

As Doby continued to coach first, not third, base, and work with the hitters, he put his managerial aspirations on hold. In August, *Jet* magazine, in a story by Ronald E. Kisner, reviewed Doby's situation and quoted the deceased Jackie Robinson, who "stood before a capacity crowd at Cincinnati's Riverfront Stadium during the 1972 World Series, just weeks [*sic*] before he died, and proclaimed that he would not be happy until he saw a black manager running a major league team."

Kisner also reported a comment by Roland Hemond, general manager of the Chicago White Sox, who stated that he believed that three, four, or five years of managing in the minor leagues "is the best of all methods" to prepare a black man to manage in the major leagues.[22]

Actually, three men had already managed in the minor leagues, in varying degrees, but they were never promoted to the major league level. Gene Baker and Hector Lopez managed farm teams for the Pittsburgh Pirates and Washington Senators in the late 1960's. Tommie Aaron, brother of Hank, served as player-manager for the Atlanta Braves farm team at Savannah, Georgia, in the Southern League just the year before. A fourth, Frank Robinson, had managed the Santurce Crabbers in Puerto Rico for five winter seasons. And Doby had almost a full season in Venezuela. At the same time, though, many white men have had their first managerial experience in the major leagues, including Pete Rose, Lou Piniella, Whitey Herzog, Bobby Valentine, and the late Dick Howser.

During that same month of August 1974, Commissioner Kuhn told how he had been working on the problem behind the scenes, in a statement which foreshadowed one by his successor, Peter Ueberroth, in 1987. "Now is the time," Kuhn declared, "for the major leagues to have a black manager. It's more important now than ever. I can't order anybody to hire anybody but the two league presidents are working closely with me trying to exert pressure on the clubs. I could not function as Commissioner if I kept pushing and lost."[23] Thus, while baseball's executives, including Al Campanis of the Los Angeles Dodgers, were insisting that baseball had no barriers preventing black men from becoming managers, Kuhn was putting "pressure" on them to make such a move.

In September, although Cleveland had risen into contention for first place in the American League's Eastern Division, sounds of dissension emanated from the Indians' clubhouse.[24] On September 5, Seghi stunned everyone by purchasing the contract of 39-year-old Frank Robinson, a black outfielder at the end of one of the greatest careers in the history of baseball, from the California Angels for the $20,000 waiver price.[25] Suddenly another Robinson had entered Larry Doby's life.

Immediately, mysteriously, this Robinson replaced Doby as the favorite in the managerial rumors which had been reported in Cleveland's newspapers. To quell rumors of the shift to Robinson as heir-apparent to Aspromonte's job, Seghi denied them, and continued to deny them in 1981, as "mere speculation." Asked by a reporter if Robinson would be a player or a manager the following year, Seghi said, "Frank will be here next year, there's no doubt of that." Then he added, in a sentence whose verb was, significantly, in the present tense, "Frank is coming as a player."[26]

Asked about this in 1981, Seghi insisted that his acquisition of Robinson was "motivated by a chance to win our division. We needed a right-handed hitter, and Frank was available on waivers. I brought him here with the sole intention of trying to win the pennant."[27]

Few people believed Seghi then, or later. Hal Lebovitz opened his "Opinion" column in the *Plain Dealer* on the same day that the deal was announced by asserting, "Frank Robinson will be the next manager of the Indians. Every clue adds up to that conclusion."[28]

Doby agreed with Lebovitz, adding, in 1981, that "The thought of my being there as a manager didn't come from Seghi's own thinking. I think it came from outside thoughts and opinions, the Commissioner saying things. And Cleveland is a town where I had been accepted as a black player before. I wouldn't create any dislike, being a former Cleveland player, and it wouldn't require much of a transition. I think the one thing that turned Seghi off was that he found out that I was not a puppet."

The acquisition of Frank Robinson did little to help the Indians, either on or off the field. It split the Cleveland front office wide open, angered the players, and the team sank to fourth place in the pennant race.

Robinson told his side of the story in a book, *Frank: The First Year*, written with Dave Anderson:

Shortly after I joined the Cleveland Indians for the last three weeks of the 1974 season, I realized this was a ball club in trouble. The dugout was virtually segregated. On one side was the manager, Ken Aspromonte, with almost all the white players. On the other side was Larry Doby, a black coach, with all the black players. I sat here and there, mostly in the middle. Any ball club that's split along racial lines like that had to be in trouble.

Robinson laid further blame at Doby's door in his book. He justified firing Doby after Seghi had appointed Robinson as manager for the 1975 season:

I didn't keep any of Aspromonte's coaches, because I wanted to clear the air. In particular, I didn't keep Larry Doby because he had shown me he wasn't loyal to the manager. Doby was hoping to be the first black manager himself. But splitting the team racially wasn't the way to do it.[29]

In 1980, visiting Yankee Stadium as a coach with the Baltimore Orioles, Robinson repeated his charge that the Indians were a racially divided team, with Aspromonte and Doby on opposite sides.[30] But neither outfielder Oscar Gamble, pitcher Gaylord Perry, nor infielder Jack Brohamer agreed with Robinson.[31] As for Seghi, he hedged. Asked about Robinson's accusations against Doby, he said, "I don't think we had a split, but at the same time you can't expect men on a major league team to be lovey-dovey."[32]

In Doby's view, Seghi's comment "is a lot of bunk. Those were the closest guys that I can recall on any ball club. The Hendricks, the Spikes, the Brohamers, the Gambles, the Bells, the Duffys—they were great kids. Now John Ellis was different. And Perry was different. They hung out together a lot with Jim Kern and Milt Wilcox. They were all pitchers and catchers."

As for Doby's alleged disloyalty to Aspromonte, Seghi said, "Ken Aspromonte never said anything about disloyalty to me." Seghi attributed reports of a racial split to efforts to explain why the Indians finished in fourth place in 1974.[33]

Neither did Ted Bonda see evidence of a split in the team. From his vantage point as an investor and executive vice-president at that time, he said, in 1981, "No, I don't really think so. The Indians were no more split along racial lines than civilization itself." Nor did Bonda perceive Doby as disloyal to Aspromonte. "Larry is not pushy," he observed. "He would not advance himself. He never tried to sell himself."[34]

Player-coach Tom McCraw, a black man, also saw little merit in Robinson's charges of divisiveness and disloyalty. "There were some racial tensions," he said, "but they were not caused by Larry. They were more general in nature.

"I don't think Larry was disloyal to Aspromonte. Maybe Frank thought so because black players would go to Larry, and not to Kenny, for advice and with their problems. It was Larry's *job* to talk with them and save the manager from such things. Ken had enough on his mind just being manager."[35]

As Doby recalls it, "I was loyal to Aspromonte. Never did I mention the fact that the idea of managing was in the back of my mind. Never did I say anything against his managing, or try to disprove anything he did. I think if you're not loyal to a person, you create situations, you make statements.

"What Frank Robinson saw was that I had a better rapport with the players than he did. With Buddy Bell, with Oscar, and Brohamer, and Duffy, and John Lowenstein—they were a bunch of guys that were always kidding each other. I was always involved in it.

"This was dumb on Frank's part. If he had retained me as a coach I could have been much more helpful to him as an individual who could have relations with people and get production out of people."

After the 1974 season ended, Phil Seghi confirmed the rumors that he had spent three weeks denying. On October 3, he named Frank Robinson as field manager of the Indians for 1975, the first black man ever to manage a major league team.[36]

The appointment spawned a host of explanations, official and unofficial, and a variety of reactions. According to Seghi in 1981, "circumstances dictated the hiring of Frank Robinson. He had great energy, enthusiasm, intensity. We did consider Larry Doby, but the package was more enveloped in Frank Robinson."[37]

Nobody in Cleveland, however, bothered to call Doby and inform him of the appointment of Robinson, or to tell him that he was out as a coach as well. In 1981, in explaining why he did not renew Doby's contract as a coach, Seghi said that he and Robinson had discussed the matter and Robinson wanted changes. "In courtesy to Frank, we went along with him. We even let a close friend of mine, Tony Pacheco, go."

Did Seghi find Doby too direct, too abrasive at meetings between the field staff and the front office? "I never found that to be a problem. I follow the advice of Phil Wrigley: if two men agree, one of them is unnecessary."[38]

Ted Bonda, who was instrumental in bringing Doby to Cleveland, did not support Doby against Robinson. "Larry just didn't have the fire and charisma that Frank had," he noted. "I don't think it ever became a choice between Larry and Frank. Larry was not strongly considered for the job as manager. And I didn't have that much to say about the team's coaches, because Phil and I had an agreement that the ball club was his province and I would handle the business end."[39]

Tom McCraw, from his middle position as both a player and a coach in 1974, expressed little surprise that Doby didn't replace Aspromonte as manager. "He might have gotten it if he hadn't been such a bear, but more of a cub," McCraw explained. "I can understand why Larry found it hard to be diplomatic in the front office. He had paid his dues for over 20 years, and he may have run out of patience. I advised him about this, but he couldn't do it. Larry should have known that you don't make loud noises in the presence of the people who have the power. It scares them."[40]

When told about McCraw's comments, Doby questioned them. "I don't know what Tom is saying. I never made any loud noises. I think that what he's saying is that you don't disagree with these people, whatever they say."

McCraw found it hard to explain why Robinson didn't keep Doby as a coach. As he sat on his stool in the visitor's clubhouse in Yankee Stadium in 1980, still a coach for the Indians, he was reminded that Robinson had once said, in Doby's and McCraw's presence, words to the effect that "whichever one of us gets the manager's job, keeps the other one."

"I think he said that in a bar in Milwaukee," McCraw recalled, although Doby thinks it was in the clubhouse in Fenway Park in Boston. "But I'm not sure whether Frank was being humorous or serious," McCraw said.[41]

But Robinson remembered his intention. "I said that in a joking way," he explained. "As manager, I felt it necessary to clean house. If Larry feels bitter toward me because of that, I can understand it. I don't feel anything negative toward him."[42]

Doby, trying to avoid the bickering which has so often interfered with the progress of oppressed groups throughout history, expressed reluctance to respond any further to Robinson. "I cannot waste any time or energy to even think about being bitter toward Robinson," he says. "The best thing I can do for Robinson is wish him luck, period."

Dick Young, in his "Young Ideas" column in the New York *Sunday News* of September 28, five days before Seghi's appointment of Robinson, tried to attribute it to Doby's failure to improve the performance of George Hendrick, an outfielder described by Young as "loaded with talent, and black, and moody." Robinson, Young wrote, "is to be hired because he has shown [in winter baseball in Puerto Rico] he can get George Hendrick to put out."[43]

The record book, though, shows that the manager didn't make much difference to Hendrick. In 1973, before Doby, Hendrick batted .268 with 21 home runs and 61 runs batted in. In 1974, with Doby, Hendrick raised his average to .279, with 19 home runs and 67 runs batted in. In 1975, under Robinson, Hendrick batted .258 with 24 home runs and 86 RBIs. As a team, the Indians finished sixth and last in their division in 1973, and fourth in 1974 and 1975.[44]

Statistics and opinion aside, however, Doby has only warm memories of Hendrick: "My attitude toward George was that he was a young man who needed a chance to mature. George brought me to meet his family on our first trip into Los Angeles. I met his aunt, his mother, and ate dinner there. He and I got along real well. I'd go to his room [during road trips] and sit down and talk with him. The one thing I'd notice in his room when I'd go there, he reads a lot. He read all the militant black writers—Rap Brown, Stokely [Carmichael], Huey Newton. . . . If George and I hadn't gotten along well, I don't think George would have taken me to his house for dinner, or introduced me to his aunts and his mother."

Hendrick, approached for an interview when he played for the St. Louis Cardinals in 1980, politely declined, as he usually did when approached by sports reporters. "Look," he said firmly, "I respect Larry Doby. Let's just leave it at that."[45]

Bowie Kuhn didn't have an explanation for the choice of Robinson over Doby, but he did have a reaction. "It is something that was long overdue," he said. "I've been actively pressing for a long time for it to happen. . . . I've talked to a lot of people and a lot of clubs. I think the term 'jawboning' is an appropriate expression to use.

"But now that it has happened, I'm not going to get up and shout that this is something for baseball to be exceptionally proud of because it's so long overdue.

"About the best thing we can say is that we've finally got something straightened out, and I'm proud of that."

Although few people knew that Kuhn had been pivotal in bringing Monte Irvin and Doby back into baseball in 1969, there were rumors that he helped to maneuver Doby into the fluid situation in Cleveland before the 1974 season. Asked to comment about this, Kuhn said, "I have felt for a long time that Doby was a good candidate, and I'm sure I talked to a lot of people about him. But whether or not I talked to Cleveland about hiring Doby, I don't remember."[46]

Regardless of that seemingly evasive answer, Doby has only positive feelings toward Kuhn, who encouraged contact with him throughout his years as commissioner. "I can feel when somebody is sincere, when they mean it, and I always believed that with him," Doby says. "I never had a lot of conversation with him, but I always had that feeling about him."

In contrast to Kuhn's restrained reaction to the appointment of Robinson, Lee MacPhail, president of the American League and son of Larry MacPhail, allowed more enthusiasm to show. "The impact of Frank Robinson being named manager of the Indians, the first black manager in major league history, is second in importance only to Jackie Robinson's entry into baseball in 1947," he said.[47]

Bill Veeck, asked for a reaction, revealed both his disappointment and his satisfaction: "I was hoping Larry Doby would get the job but that is completely understandable because he is equally competent and we are close friends. Both are very qualified. I'm delighted somebody is finally becoming intelligent enough to select a manager on his ability rather than his color. I'm glad to find a club where an unknown doesn't frighten them to death. That is the only reason for the hesitancy in hiring a black manager. Frank is equipped, because of his managing in the winter. He was the leader of the Baltimore club [as a player], albeit unofficial."[48]

More bitter and disappointed than he would then publicly admit, Doby returned home to Montclair in October of 1974. For the second time in his life, he didn't have a job in baseball. But having come within one weekend of being the first black manager in the major leagues, carrying his reputation as one of the sport's greatest batting instructors, and with his pride somehow still fully intact, Doby returned to the Montreal Expos in 1975 to resume his quest to be a manager in the major leagues.

NOTES

1. Montreal Expos, press release, February 27, 1971.
2. *The Sporting News*, March 13, 1971.
3. Ibid.
4. Ibid.
5. Personal interview with Gene Mauch, June 10, 1980.
6. Personal interview with John Mayberry, September 9, 1980.
7. Personal interview with Mike Jorgensen, August 15, 1980.
8. Personal interview with Ken Singleton, August 9, 1980.
9. Gilliam played the infield and coached for the Brooklyn and Los Angeles Dodgers from 1953 until his death in 1978. He was an above-average player whose main asset was his intelligence, a quality widely recognized by other players, coaches, managers, and front-office executives such as Al Campanis, whose comments about blacks as managers caused him to be fired by the Dodgers in the spring of 1987.
10. Personal interview with Dusty Baker, June 11, 1980.
11. *Denver Post*, June 11, 1972.
12. *Christian Science Monitor* (Boston), September 26, 1973.
13. Personal interview with Phil Seghi, January 14, 1981.
14. *Gazette* (Montreal), October 4, 1974.
15. Telephone interview with Jim Fanning, July 15, 1981.
16. Ibid.
17. Cleveland Indians, press release, December 5, 1973.
18. *Plain Dealer*, December 22, 1973.
19. Ibid.
20. Ibid.
21. *Press*, April 3, 1974.
22. Ronald E. Kisner, *Jet*, August 15, 1974.
23. Bowie Kuhn, in Frank Robinson and Al Silverman, *My Life Is Baseball* (Garden City: Doubleday and Co., 1975), p. 236.
24. *Plain Dealer*, September 3, 1974.
25. Ibid., September 13, 1974.
26. Ibid.
27. Seghi, loc. cit.
28. Hal Lebovitz, "Opinion," *Plain Dealer*, September 13, 1974.
29. Frank Robinson with Dave Anderson, *Frank: The First Year* (New York: Holt, Rinehart and Winston, 1976), p. 11.
30. Personal interview with Frank Robinson, August 9, 1980.
31. Personal interview with Oscar Gamble, July 23, 1980; with Gaylord Perry, September 18, 1980; and with Jack Brohamer, September 22, 1980.
32. Seghi, loc. cit.
33. Ibid.
34. Personal interview with Ted Bonda, January 14, 1981.

35. Personal interview with Tom McCraw, September 22, 1980.
36. *Plain Dealer*, October 3, 1974.
37. Seghi, loc. cit.
38. Ibid.
39. Bonda, loc. cit.
40. McCraw, loc. cit.
41. Ibid.
42. Robinson, loc. cit.
43. Dick Young, "Young Ideas," *Sunday News* (New York), October 29, 1974.
44. Neft, Cohen, and Deutsch, *Baseball*, pp. 430, 436, and 442.
45. Personal interview with George Hendrick, September 26, 1980.
46. *Plain Dealer*, October 4, 1974.
47. Ibid.
48. Ibid., October 3, 1974.

12

Veeck, Again

Larry Doby's return to Montreal after his disappointment in Cleveland became public knowledge on April 25, 1975, when the Expos announced that he had "re-joined the Expos as a minor league batting instructor."[1] Immediately, Doby set out for Memphis of the Class AAA International League.

The assignment was another disappointment. Doby had been in the major leagues with Montreal for three seasons and with the Indians for another, always as a batting instructor. The transient life in a lonely motel in Memphis reminded him of the assassination of Dr. Martin Luther King, Jr., there in 1968. Living alone in Quebec City and West Palm Beach did not appeal to him either. Yet he went, sustained by a dream of his own, managing in the major leagues.

At all three levels of the Montreal organization, Doby succeeded again, as the testimonies of Tony Bernazard, Gary Roenicke, and Ellis Valentine demonstrate.[2] The three men are, respectively, Latin, white, and black.

The Expos promoted Doby back to their major league team in January of 1976. Under new manager Karl Kuehl, the season proved to be a mixture of success and controversy. Doby worked effectively with the hitters, especially Andre Dawson, who praised Doby as "a keen, quiet individual. I'm a very quiet person, and around Larry I could open up more. I knew he was talking to me from within his heart."[3]

But the behavior of shortstop Tim Foli dominated the Expos in 1976. According to catcher Larry Parrish, a dispute between Foli and Kuehl "set the season off on the wrong foot for us. Timmy tried to umpire, play shortstop, manage—all of it. Larry tried to smooth it over. The coaches were 100 percent behind Karl. When the management didn't back Karl up on Foli, then the players sort of went their own way."[4]

Eventually, the Expos fired Kuehl, placing Doby in line, again, to be named manager. After all, their president and general manager, John McHale and Jim Fanning, had, in effect, recommended him for the managerial post at Cleveland. But McHale had a different idea. Despite the team's location in the city which had accepted Jackie Robinson in 1946, he appointed the team's chief scout, Charlie Fox, to the position. Passed over again, as he had been in Cleveland the year before, Doby unburdened himself to Maury Allen of the *New York Post*:

I don't want to say it's prejudice, but what else can I think? I'm considering getting out of the game I've loved all my life and writing a book about what really has happened.

I've given this organization everything. I was with them when they started. I've done every job they've asked. . . . When they hired Kuehl, they told me to help him. If I'm good enough to help him, I should have been good enough to be offered the job. They weren't afraid I'd fail. They were afraid I'd succeed.[5]

Looking back, Doby "was surprised, and then again I wasn't surprised, when [McHale] named Karl Kuehl instead of me. I felt the same way when he named Charlie Fox instead of me. One feeling was in the back of my mind, and the other was in front of my mind. I guess I still had the hope that he'd appoint me to manage the Expos. I still thought that how I read McHale wasn't really the true McHale.

"But when Fox came, I had a total picture of McHale. I could see the true man. I think he did not want to see a black man in a power position."

A month later, the season over, McHale not only passed over Doby for the third time, naming Dick Williams as manager, but he did not renew Doby's contract as a coach, which Doby knew might happen when he spoke so frankly to Maury Allen.

After the announcement naming Williams, a reporter asked Doby if he thought that major league owners were using a quota system or engaging in black tokenism. "People have to live with their consciences," Doby replied. "If I shoot my mouth off too much, I would be boycotted. There is no job opportunity for a one-man crusader. I could write a book and say 'Goodbye to baseball,' but I want to stay in the game. It's in my blood."[6]

A few days later, 11 years before the racist remarks by Al Campanis of the Dodgers, and 11 years before the nostalgia and concern generated by observance of the fortieth anniversary of what Doby and Robinson had done in 1947, sportswriter Alan Richman evaluated Doby's comments:

Larry Doby, one of the many retired baseball players not named to manage a major league baseball team for the 1977 season, has taken the opportunity to remind us that his manhood has been dealt a severe blow and the black athletes of North America have been delivered another racial insult.

Larry Doby often brings up questions about his manhood and his black skin when denied a job. Not once has he raised any questions about his ability to manage.[7]

And finally, Richman wrote, Doby got into a dispute with Montreal management because Helyn Doby was not asked to model in a fashion show in August of 1976, implying racism as the cause, and in retaliation he refused to allow his daughter, Susan, to participate in a "father-son" game. When McHale learned of Doby's reaction, he called to deny that prejudice had anything to do with the incident. Doby told McHale that he had not raised the issue of prejudice, but that he objected to the team's not asking Helyn to participate in the fashion show while inviting Susan to participate in the game.[8]

Nevertheless, Richman wrote,

One of Doby's problems is that he does not say what he thinks. He hedges about the racial problems in baseball, alienating himself from both the white establishment and the black militant players. He seems to thrive on both real and imagined persecutions, a man living precariously on the edge of torment.

If there still is prejudice against blacks as major league managers—and there probably still is—it is an interesting and unique form of prejudice. It is not so much a prejudice against qualified blacks as it is a refusal to hire blacks who are no more qualified than many incompetent white managers. . . .

Baseball executives will continue to hire uninteresting, uncharismatic, uneducated white men to manage their teams. If they find a superbly qualified black man, he will be approached. Uncharismatic, uneducated, uninteresting black men will never be hired as major league managers, because they are not part of the crony system in baseball.

Larry Doby might be more qualified to manage than some white major league managers but he is not being deprived of what is rightfully his. There are other black men more deserving of a chance.[9]

Doby took up Richman's conclusions in turn. "How can he say that I don't say what I think, right after he quotes me for saying what I thought about the fashion show? Now in instances where I have expressed myself even more directly, I've been condemned for it. So a guy in my situation can't win.

"I don't follow Richman's statement that I'm living 'on the edge of torment.' I'm happy! I've always been happy! I think that's what shakes people up! A guy like Richman knows what's going on for black people in baseball. So he's more upset than I am, because I'm strong enough to deal with it.

"I'd like to know why he calls prejudice against blacks as major league managers 'unique.' Why is it unique? It's prejudice! What's so unique about it? Because it's a business where you're supposed to have equal opportunity? It's not unique—it's the same old thing. He doesn't know what he's talking about.

"Richman is also wrong about blacks not being part of the crony system. Frank Robinson is—he changed from being one way to being another way so he could be part of the system.

"At the end of what Richman wrote, he's saying I'm qualified but I'm not being deprived. Well, I am if I'm qualified! I am being deprived! Now it could be that there are some black men who are more qualified than I am. That could be. But for me, I was a pioneer in my field. How did that come about? Doesn't that give me a certain amount of qualification, with knowledge? If not, what does?

"Now that may be my opinion, that I'm qualified, which may not be Richman's. But who is he to say I'm not qualified? Has he ever been in the positions I've been in? I could not say that he's not qualified to be a writer. I've never been in that position.

"If I am qualified, it is my right to be a manager. Is baseball going to use merit to choose managers, or not? If not, then we can't even have a discussion like this.

"What makes me more angry than anything about what Richman wrote is that his column is not an example of logical thinking. But he has my reputation in his hands!"

Thirty years after he brought the American League into the interracial age, Bill Veeck rescued Larry Doby's career in 1977. In the same ball park where he introduced Doby to the major league world, Veeck became president of the Chicago White Sox and named Doby to a coaching staff led by manager Bob Lemon.

It was a joyous reunion for all three men. They had shared in that golden year of 1948, when the Indians of their youth won that dramatic playoff game from the Boston Red Sox, and went on to defeat the Boston Braves in the World Series. With new coaches Bobby Knoop and Stan Williams, and holdover Minnie Minoso, the trio of Veeck, Lemon, and Doby set out to recapture 1948.

In Chicago, Doby enhanced the reputation he had earned at Montreal and Cleveland as a batting instructor. Alan Bannister, Jorge Orta, Eric Soderholm, and Brian Downing all praised him: Bannister as "the best I ever had," Orta for Doby's "honesty," Soderholm for his own 25 home runs, and Downing for instruction which helped him to be the best right-handed hitter in the league the following season.[10]

Oscar Gamble, who had profited from Doby's coaching at Cleveland in 1974, once again enjoyed its benefits in 1977 in Chicago. "In the two years I played with Doby as my batting instructor," he said, "I hit .291 and .297. Without him I was hitting in the .260's and .270's. I'm a power hitter, and I used to brag about how far I could hit the ball. Then as we'd go around the league he'd show me some locations that he had reached. And they were farther."[11]

Although the White Sox had enjoyed a happy and successful season in 1977, they embarked on the 1978 season with less optimism than might have been expected for a team that had finished a strong third in its division. Six key players had sought larger salaries elsewhere in those early days of free agency, and there were no significant additions to the team's weak pitching staff.

As a result, the White Sox struggled for respectability through the early weeks of the season. Dissatisfaction spread from Veeck to the players on the field. Lemon remained calm, as always, and somehow the Sox began to play better baseball, winning 17 of 19 games during the middle weeks of June. Then, surprisingly, Veeck fired Lemon on June 30 and appointed Doby as the second black manager in major league history. Second, of course, to another Robinson, Frank.

The change "was not meant as any commentary on Lemon's ability," Veeck said in a statement that clarified nothing, "but rather as a result of unusual circumstances which seemed to make a change necessary."[12] It was the first in a long series of evasions by Veeck.

"There were two 'unusual circumstances' that Bill didn't like," Doby observed in 1981. "He disliked the decline in attendance below the previous year. And because of how well the White Sox did in 1977, he expected a miracle, a division winner, in 1978. But we had lost Zisk and Gamble. Those two guys hit 61 home runs and drove in 184 runs in 1977."

Veeck made his move on June 30, when the Sox had a road game scheduled against the Twins in Bloomington, Minnesota. While Doby sat in his hotel room watching a soap opera on television, Veeck telephoned, asking Doby to come down to his room. After the traditional "Hello Lawrence– Hello William" formalities that the two men had observed for 31 years, Veeck asked, "Would you like to manage this club?"

Suddenly, Doby's dream to manage in the major leagues had become a reality. Yet he expressed mixed feelings about the appointment he had worked so hard for since he began his coaching career with Montreal nine years before. "I was surprised and somewhat saddened," he told the press. "Bob [Lemon] and I have been friends since 1947.

"Although it's a happy moment for me, it's still not as happy as you would like for it to be. [Bob and I] had a long talk today and, of course, the first thing he said to me was, 'Don't feel that way, because we're still friends and these things happen in baseball.'

"If you work at baseball as long as I have, I think you want to go as high as you possibly can, and as high as your knowledge will possibly let you go. This certainly has been a thought in my mind for years, ever since I came to Chicago."[13]

But Doby restrained his ambition from the time he joined the White Sox in spring training in 1977, just as he had done at Montreal and Cleveland. "Never did Lawrence intimate, even remotely, or by indirection, that he was after this job," Veeck told Dave Nightingale of the Chicago *Tribune*. "I think Bob felt that, too, and that's why he was so quick to suggest Larry as his replacement."[14]

Asked by Charles Maher of the Los Angeles *Times* if he had any advance warning that he'd become the manager of the Sox, Doby replied, "No. Mr. Veeck is an intellectual, a mysterious man to me. I've never been able to tell what he was going to do."[15]

In the absence of a plausible explanation from Veeck about replacing Lemon with Doby, the Chicago baseball writers provided their own. A typical explanation came from Jerome Holtzman, who told the readers of *The Sporting News* that "Veeck . . . admitted he wasn't certain the Sox would win more games under Doby than they had won with Lemon. This admission seemed to underscore the belief that the change was made chiefly to hype the gate with the hope of achieving the unrealistic goal of a two-million home attendance."[16]

From Syracuse, New York, the *Tribune* reported the reaction of Doby's former rival, Frank Robinson. From his vantage point as ex-manager of the Indians and as manager of the Rochester Red Wings of the International League, Robinson said, "Any time something like this happens I'm always surprised. It's a step in the right direction."

Robinson expressed his hope to return to a managerial position in the major leagues, but not with the White Sox because "Doby's Bill Veeck's man." Asked to predict Doby's performance, Robinson replied, "You never know how someone will do until they're given a chance."[17]

The White Sox players, asked for their reactions to the appointment of Doby, expressed a variety of feelings. Black outfielder Ralph Garr saw the change as evidence that Veeck wanted a "tougher" manager than Lemon.[18] At least three other players approved of the change. Infielder Alan Bannister told a reporter, "We needed a change." Third baseman Eric Soderholm said, "I'm a Larry Doby man. I like his style. I think he's going to be a great manager." Black first baseman Lamar Johnson observed that the Sox had been "playing scared" under Lemon, taking too many pitches. He expected the team to be more aggressive under Doby. "I'm glad about the change," Johnson said. "It couldn't have happened to a nicer guy. I'm sure Larry will do a good job. I know it'll help the hitters." White pitcher Steve Stone, regarded as a "team elder," felt badly for Lemon, but said, "We're at the point where we needed something and I hope Larry Doby can find what it is."[19]

For civil rights leader and presidential aspirant Jesse Jackson, however, there were no reservations. Jackson, director of the Chicago-based Operation PUSH, told the *Tribune*, "My reaction is that I think it is in order.

It is a reflection of Larry Doby's expressed abilities and of Bill Veeck's courage. Unfortunately, many other owners have left the color barrier up at the managerial level. And so such qualified men as Maury Wills, Jim Gilliam, and Bill White have been denied the opportunity to manage. For Bill Veeck, this was another gallant step. Just as he did 30 years ago, Bill Veeck has gone a step beyond."[20]

NOTES

1. Montreal Expos, press release, April 25, 1975.

2. Personal interviews with Tony Bernazard, September 16, 1980; Gary Roenicke, August 9, 1980; and Ellis Valentine, September 16, 1980.

3. Personal interview with Andre Dawson, September 16, 1980.

4. Personal interview with Larry Parrish, September 16, 1980.

5. *New York Post*, September 22, 1976.

6. *Plain Dealer*, October 26, 1976.

7. Alan Richman, "Doby Strikes Out as Boss Material," *Gazette* (Montreal), October 27, 1976.

8. Ibid.

9. Ibid.

10. Personal interviews with Alan Bannister, September 22, 1980; Jorge Orta, September 22, 1980; Eric Soderholm, September 2, 1980; and Brian Downing, September 5, 1980.

11. Personal interview with Oscar Gamble, August 29, 1980.

12. *Chicago Tribune*, July 1, 1978.

13. Ibid.

14. Ibid.

15. *Times* (Los Angeles), July 3, 1978.

16. *The Sporting News*, July 22, 1978.

17. *Chicago Tribune*, July 1, 1978.

18. *The Sporting News*, July 22, 1978.

19. Ibid.

20. *Chicago Tribune*, July 2, 1978.

13

Major League Manager

As his first act as manager of the White Sox, Larry Doby invited the deposed Bob Lemon to a meeting with the players in the clubhouse, where Lemon uttered a brief farewell and introduced his successor. The sincerity of Lemon's remarks, and Doby's reaction, provided a rare exception to the usual boisterous camaraderie which typifies such places. The players were deeply touched at seeing these two old friends in a moment of emotional transition. "Larry took 10 minutes to compose himself," recalled Alan Bannister. "He was emotionally overcome. I liked that. It showed the feelings of the man."[1]

After recovering, and with Lemon sitting nearby, Doby spoke to the 25 players now under his leadership. "I tried to deal with the concept of winning as partly a state of mind," Doby said in 1981. "I spoke about physical and mental preparation to win. I told the players that I didn't want one blaming another for mishaps, because we're all human and we all make errors now and then."

As he prepared for the game against the Minnesota Twins, managed by his own old mentor, Gene Mauch, Doby decided to retain Bobby Knoop, a white man, as third base coach, and the popular Latin, Minnie Minoso, as first base coach. He also elected to bring in Sam Hairston, a black man from the minor leagues, as bullpen coach to capitalize on Hairston's knowledge of the organization's young pitchers. Doby released the pitching coach, Stan Williams, and sent for Bruce Dal Canton, who had been pitching and coaching for the team's Triple A farm team in Des Moines, Iowa. Both are white men.

Asked by the *Tribune* for any other ways in which he'd differ from Lemon, Doby said, "I don't necessarily intend to run a 'tighter' ship. . . . Let's call it a 'different' ship. In seeking improvements, it could mean extra work from the players or whatever it takes to get an individual to produce what I expect him to produce.

"I don't want to get into a game situation where I have to ask a man to do something that he is not equipped to do."[2]

As the White Sox took the field that Friday night against the Twins, they owned a record of 34 wins and 40 losses, good for fourth place (out of six) in the Western Division of the American League. But a rain storm forced postponement of Doby's debut as manager.

Under clearing skies on Saturday afternoon, the White Sox suffered a 10–0 defeat as Dave Goltz pitched a six-hitter for Minnesota and the Twins pounded Chicago pitchers for 15 hits.[3]

On Sunday, July 2, the Sox presented their new manager with his first victory, 8–5, in the first game of a doubleheader. Claudell Washington, Bill Naharodny, Lamar Johnson, and Chet Lemon provided the offensive power, while Jim Willoughby pitched shutout ball in relief of starting pitcher Wilbur Wood. Doby's pleasure did not last, however. Minnesota won the second game, 9–5.[4]

Following the Sunday doubleheader, the Sox returned home to Comiskey Park on the thirty-first anniversary of Bill Veeck's announcement that the Cleveland Indians would introduce Doby to the American League two days later at that very same ball park. Unmindful of the significance of the date, Doby began to dress for a Monday night game against the Texas Rangers when a telephone call from Danny Ozark, then the manager of the Philadelphia Phillies of the National League, interrupted him. The sincerity of Ozark's call was not the only reason Doby felt stunned. "Aside from the in-person congratulations I got from Gene Mauch in Minnesota," he said, "I'll always remember Danny's call because it was the only one I got from any major league manager."

That night the White Sox prolonged their manager's warm feelings by defeating Texas, 7–6, as Chet Lemon and Jorge Orta drove in five Chicago runs with a pair of home runs.[5]

The next morning, on the Fourth of July, Doby learned of Veeck's plan to assign the first base coach, Minoso, to the position of public relations manager. To replace Minoso, Doby decided that Tony LaRussa, who managed Knoxville to the first half championship in the Class AA Southern League, should be called up to the majors.[6]

Following the series against Texas, the White Sox went into a tailspin. At that point 5–7 under Doby, they lost nine straight games and sank into last place in the Western Division of the American League. But then they defeated the Milwaukee Brewers, 5–1, and went on to sweep the Rangers in a three-game series. With a record of 44–58, Chicago trailed the first-place Kansas City Royals by 14 and one-half games. Their record during the month of July under Doby stood at 10 wins and 18 losses.[7]

Things got even worse in the first ten days of August, when Chicago lost seven of nine games while Veeck and Doby tried to remain calm. The Sox continued to lose, however, dropping three of their next four games. On August 15, after six and one-half weeks under Doby, they had compiled a record of only 13 wins and 30 losses.[8]

On August 17, too soon to know that the Sox would win more than they would lose for the rest of the season, sportswriter David Israel assessed Doby's situation, deciding that "Larry Doby is no more responsible for the travesty . . . than any season ticket holder." Israel observed Doby to be calm, very much under control, and confident that he would prove himself to be a good manager. He ended his story prophetically: "The only problem is that if there is too much suffering, too much bad vaudevillian comedy, and too little winning between now and the end of the season, Larry Doby might not be given that opportunity on Chicago's South Side."[9]

Yet, slowly, with little notice from anyone, apparently including Veeck, the White Sox turned around. Over the last six and one-half weeks of the season they won 24 games and lost 20. It was far from a championship pace, but under Doby's leadership a team that had just one outstanding player, center fielder Chet Lemon, played better than .500 baseball. During those last six and one-half weeks of the 1978 season, Doby, given the quality of his team's talent, may have been one of the best managers in baseball.

Whatever anxiety may have arisen in the front office when the White Sox were losing receded when the team started winning. The *Tribune* reported on August 20 that a poll of the stockholders demonstrated majority support for Veeck's administration of the team. One, though, expressed his view that the appointment of Doby as field manager was "little more than a play for black attendance."[10]

Doby conceded that that may have been the case. "I'm not naive," he said in 1981. "In fact, there was an increase in black attendance. Bill's son Mike told me that."

As the calendar changed from August to September, Doby could look back on nine victories in 14 games, but Chicago then lost four out of five to the Baltimore Orioles. The next day, Labor Day, he was ejected from a game for the second time as manager. After the game, a 2–1 loss to Minnesota, he accused umpire Joe Brinkman of calling him an obscene name and lumping other black players with him in a racial slur. "They call him a representative of the flag and the national pastime," Doby fumed. "Wait till they get a copy of the letter I wrote to the American League office."[11]

In 1981 Doby still harbored resentment against Brinkman. "When he threw me out of the game, he said, 'I'll throw all you cock suckers out,' meaning the black players. Bill Veeck sent a letter about this to the American League office, and I was so right in my report that I never got fined.

Lee MacPhail [the league president] telephoned me and apologized to me for what Brinkman said, and said Brinkman knew he was wrong. He asked me to come to New York and sit with Brinkman. I refused. What did I need to go to New York for? They were afraid that I was going to carry this further. Then MacPhail said, 'Well, you know, he admitted he was wrong, and he apologized.' And I said, 'Well fine, that's good enough for me.'

"Brinkman is still umpiring, and still having trouble. He's an arrogant guy, and what comes out of his mouth depends on the nationality of the person he's dealing with."

With the Brinkman affair behind them, the White Sox regained their balance and won three of their next four games. Yet neither the players nor their manager knew that Veeck had long since begun a quiet search for a new manager. Privately, Veeck began to "spot check" orders for tickets and noticed that more than the usual number came from Chicago's North Side. Publicly, he announced that on Friday night, September 8, the White Sox would celebrate "Don Kessinger Night."

The connection between the trend in ticket orders and "Kessinger Night" is not hard to make. In Chicago, the Cubs dominate the north side of the city and the White Sox the south side. Kessinger, before joining the Sox in 1977, had been the popular shortstop for the Cubs for 12 seasons. Therefore, Veeck concluded, Kessinger accounted for most of those ticket orders from what he called "the other side of town." And so Veeck decided to capitalize on Kessinger's drawing power in his pursuit of ticket sales and the income his team needed to survive.

Of even greater importance for the tenure of Doby as manager, Veeck claimed in 1981 that his "spot checks" had revealed no discernible impact of Doby as manager on ticket sales in Chicago's huge black community, in contradiction of what Mike Veeck told Doby at the time. And because Doby had performed no miracles as manager, Bill Veeck had begun to make up his mind that Doby would be out, and someone else, possibly Kessinger, would be in for 1979.[12] Although Veeck denied that the attendance of 30,270 on "Kessinger Night" influenced him to appoint Kessinger as manager some 40 days later, his denial runs contrary to his developing pattern of thought on the subject.

Doby, unaware that Veeck had decided to replace him, guided the White Sox to a 3–2 victory over the Seattle Mariners after the ceremonies honoring Kessinger. Three nights later, as the result of a 3–1 loss to Minnesota, the Sox were mathematically eliminated from the pennant race. They had a 61–83 record, 18 games behind Kansas City.[13]

Their elimination did not demoralize the players, however. The White Sox won their next four games, and 10 of their next 18. On October 1, the final day of the season, they lost to the California Angels in Anaheim by 5–4 as Nolan Ryan pitched a five-hitter and struck out 13 Chicago batters.[14]

On October 2, the day after the final game of the 1978 baseball season, Bill Veeck privately informed Larry Doby that Doby would not be reappointed as manager for 1979. Although Veeck made no announcement of the decision, and Doby silently returned home to Helyn, their five children, and four grandchildren in Montclair, the Chicago press began to print rumors of Doby's successor. The rumors continued until October 19, when the *Tribune*, in a streamer across the top of Page One, announced that "Don Kessinger will manage '79 Sox." In their accompanying story, reporters Richard Dozer and David Condon revealed that Veeck would make an announcement to this effect at a press conference to be held that day in the Bard's Room at Comiskey Park.[15]

Thus Doby, who was ushered into major league baseball as a player at a press conference in the Bard's Room on July 5, 1947, was officially ushered out of his position as a manager in the same room on October 19, 1978.

"The impending announcement," wrote Dozer and Condon, "was all but verified by Larry Doby, the incumbent Sox manager, who confirmed that he had been notified by Veeck Wednesday he would not be retained as manager. Doby will serve as a minor league batting instructor, however, and plans to join the Florida Instructional League camp soon.

" 'I enjoyed my time with the White Sox,' Doby said by telephone from Montclair. 'It makes me feel good to think I did as well as could be done in that situation.' " Then, showing that he had not lost his sense of humor, he made reference to Bob Lemon's transformation from fired manager to World Series manager with the Yankees that season. "I'd like to get another opportunity—something like the one that came to Bob Lemon."[16]

At the press conference, Veeck explained that Kessinger was "the best choice possible—our only choice, really." "Last year," he continued, "after I so wisely made Bob Lemon available to take the New York Yankees to the World Series, I had hoped that the hiring of Larry Doby would shock our club into turning things around. It didn't work. Not the first mistake I've made, not the last I'll make.

"I took a man away from doing what he does best—instruct hitters—and asked him to manage. In Don, we have a qualified man and a popular man. I don't deny that his popularity in Chicago was a factor in his selection."[17]

Actually, Veeck admitted in 1981, some of the things he said at the press conference were made just so that he would have something to say.[18]

"I'm glad he admitted that," Doby said. "I was certainly more qualified than Kessinger. I had coached and managed. I knew more than Kessinger did about pitching and defense, except for infield defense. As for taking me away from what I did best, that's how every man becomes a manager.

"The only thing Bill said at that press conference which impresses me is that he said he had to survive. He loved that word 'survive.' As a matter of fact, I use it a lot."

After the press conference, Doby reported for duty with the White Sox team in the Florida Instructional League. There, he arrived at the batting cage early every day, waiting for the hitters to show up. "I think this shows the character of the man," commented Alan Bannister. "He didn't sulk. He was always out early for batting practice."[19]

In 1979, Doby served as batting coach for the White Sox when they were at home in Comiskey Park. When the club went on the road, he did too, visiting Chicago's minor league teams at Des Moines, Appleton, Wisconsin, and Knoxville, Tennessee.

"That had a lot to do with my leaving baseball," Doby points out. "It was not so much having to go down to the minors, but how it was done. You see, Kessinger didn't want me around at all. He knew doggone well that I had a tremendous rapport with those kids on the team. Regardless of how much I knew, how much I could teach, I was a threat to him. So the further he could get me out of the picture, the better.

"So at the end of the '79 season, I told Bill, 'I'm a little bitter, a little frustrated, because this is just like 1947 all over again. At this age, I'm not going through that again.'

"And then there was the money. I can't afford to work in the minor leagues for $25,000. But if they had said that I could later become the director of the farm system, I would have taken that in a minute. I like working with kids. And you'd be talking about more money, too.

"So after the '79 season, I told Bill, 'I need to leave this for a couple of years, to look at it from the outside.' And I left.

"A couple of weeks later, Bill called me and asked if I could go down to Florida to help out in the Instructional League. But I told him that I had been contacted by Joe Taub, the owner of the New Jersey Nets of the National Basketball Association, and that I had accepted a job with the Nets."

Veeck, asked to explain his firing of Doby in an interview in 1980, refused to discuss the subject. "That's the one area I won't talk about," he said.[20]

Approached again in 1981, Veeck was alternately voluble and restrained. "It's very difficult to discuss because Larry didn't really have much chance to manage," he said. "He only managed a short time, with adverse conditions. I wouldn't say he was either outstanding nor—either way. I just don't think he really had an opportunity."

Asked what his expectations were when he appointed Doby to manage, Veeck explained that he was "hopeful that the players who seemed to be playing less successfully than the year before, that the change might reduce some complacency. That's usually the reason, when you make cosmetic changes, you do it for some such reason. It wasn't as if I believed the ball club was going to win anything. I didn't. But I did think that they might play a little better.

"The reason that I selected him is that he knew the athletes. I felt that he had, particularly with the black players—well, he had a good rapport with all of them, but particularly with the black players. I thought this would be helpful. One never knows until the deed how you will play the actual game itself. I was not surprised either way. In other words, I did not think Larry was particularly outstanding, nor did I think he was particularly bad."

Actually, Veeck said, he expected more than he got from Doby because "I thought I knew something about the talent. What I was really hoping for was some small minor miracle would occur. They don't very often happen. But once in a while. Just often enough to keep hope alive. This time it didn't happen."

Asked to describe the "miracle" that would have caused him to reappoint Doby for 1979, Veeck hedged: "We were going to start on an interim basis, right? Then it would take something the other way to change the interim basis. In other words, I started out with the idea that it would be a temporary thing."[21]

"He never told me that," Doby said after learning of Veeck's statement. "It now seems as if Bill was looking for a miracle on a temporary basis. It seems that if I had been able to make an even better record, but less than a miracle, I still would have been fired. But then Bill would have a guilty conscience."

"The great change, or big change, that I hoped for, didn't occur," Veeck continued. "The team's 15–15 record in September was an improvement, obviously, but I don't think that if you took it in total, that you look and see the games, the clubs, and so on—sometimes you have to be able to interpret the figures."[22]

Veeck did not explain why he would want to "interpret" the most final numbers in baseball—the won-lost columns. Chicago's record of 24 wins and 20 losses during the last six and one-half weeks of the season is a fact that, given the quality of his players, speaks most favorably of Larry Doby as a manager.

In the only instance where Veeck did "interpret the figures," he said, "You find an interesting thing happened. The players that I thought Larry would inspire—if that be the word—worked in reverse. In other words, it was the white players who improved and the black players didn't. I don't know why. I really don't know. I was surprised. I thought it would be the other way. I thought the black players would rally to a greater degree. Maybe they were trying too hard."[23]

With respect to batting, Veeck's conclusions are demonstrably wrong. The batting records of the black and white players who played under both Doby and Lemon in 1978 show that the black players improved their averages by 14 points under Doby, while the averages of the white players declined by 13 points.[24]

In reaction to Veeck's evaluation, Doby said, "Statistically, there's no way for Bill to make those statements. But, if you don't have anything to say, you say that.

"But the thing I don't understand is, why did Bill even expect that the blacks would do better? I felt totally the opposite way about my relationships as a manager with the black players. I thought the blacks would have a tendency to take me for granted, because I'm black. A lot of black players have not gotten to the point where they respect the position of manager. The position that a manager is in, that should be respected. The blacks shouldn't feel that because you're a black manager, 'you're just another one of us.' Whites have a tendency to know more about that than blacks because whites have been exposed, or taught, or trained. Blacks haven't learned that, because they haven't seen enough blacks in positions which demand respect. It's not our fault that we might not respect a position. We haven't had enough experience to know.

"Also, the black players, before Bill named me as manager, didn't see me in a position of power. I was coaching first base, but the position of power in baseball is third base coach. That's the last step before you become a manager. First base is usually just a guy.

"I really thought that if I would have serious problems, it would not be with the white players, it would have been with the black players."

While Doby is disappointed that Veeck had reached such erroneous conclusions about the performances of the black and white hitters, he agrees with Veeck's view that you have to "interpret the figures." But Doby's interpretation is much more cautious. "Just because the figures show that the blacks improved and the whites declined," he said, "does not mean that the switch from Bob Lemon to me caused it. Lots of things could have caused these changes. The figures don't necessarily explain anything. What they do show, though, is that Bill was working with the wrong figures."

Surprisingly, given Connie Mack's long-accepted estimate that "pitching is 80 percent of baseball," Veeck made no reference to the performance of Chicago's pitching staff under Lemon and Doby. "I think Bill didn't want to bring that up," said Doby. "He doesn't miss too much."

Or perhaps Veeck failed to refer to pitching because he knew that no black-white comparisons are possible. With the exceptions of Francisco Barrios and Pablo Torrealba, who are, respectively, Mexican and Venezuelan, all members of the White Sox pitching staff in 1978 were white Americans. Their records show a marked rise in earned run averages after Doby took the reins on July 1.[25]

Although the black batters improved and the white batters declined under Doby, the relative batting averages of Chicago's white and black players under Lemon and Doby cancel each other out: the overall team batting average of .264 on the day Lemon was fired stood at an identical .264 when the season ended.

Thus one is forced to look elsewhere to explain Chicago's success under Doby during the final six and one-half weeks of the season. Yet Veeck did not mention that he had looked elsewhere, and he did not try to explain Doby's success during those final weeks. It would seem that his mind had been made up to replace Doby long before Doby turned the White Sox around, and almost no amount of success thereafter would have been sufficient, unless there had also been an improvement in gate receipts.

Two factors explaining Doby's success over the last six and one-half weeks can be found. First, Doby began to use his bench more effectively. Second, four new pitchers, all of them white—Mike Proly, Steve Trout, Rich Wortham, and Ross Baumgarten—joined the pitching staff and compiled a combined record of 13 wins and only six losses.

While most observers agree that a baseball team's manager does not make the difference between winning and losing more than a handful of games in any one season, Doby must deserve some of the credit for Chicago's improvement. His team had just one .300 hitter and just one outstanding defensive performer—center fielder Chet Lemon in both cases. The pitching staff had one established but ineffective star, aging knuckle-baller Wilbur Wood, then at the end of his career. The rest were journeymen, with the exceptions of Steve Trout, and Britt Burns, who came up late in the season.

Yet Bill Veeck, when asked about the White Sox record down the stretch, remembered that span as "slightly under .500." In fact, it was .545.

It would seem, then, that Veeck's style of operating the White Sox contributed to his decision to fire Doby. He evaluated Doby's performance by considering data that was incomplete or wrong. And he depended on "spot checks," not thorough market studies, to decide that Kessinger would sell more tickets than Doby, even though those same spot checks revealed that attendance by black fans increased under Doby.

For reasons not apparent, Veeck did not acknowledge what he probably knew, that few if any season-ticket holders were black. As American League president Bobby Brown explained to a correspondent of the *New York Times* in 1986, "The Chicago White Sox playing in Comiskey Park on the south side of Chicago do not have a single black season-ticket holder."[26] Such knowledge would undoubtedly have contributed to Veeck's decision to appoint Kessinger, a white man, as his field manager for 1979.

"So," Veeck continued, "I recognized that I was going to have to make a change. I didn't think I had been exactly fair [to Doby] in the matter. It bothered me. But it would have bothered me more to go busted.

"And Larry recognizes that he hadn't really a fair chance. And I made no bones about it. I think he'll tell you I told him exactly that. But it was expedient, and I hate to do things that are expedient. But sometimes you have to."[27]

If "Veeck the Expedient" is an easily understood character in the dismissal of Doby as manager, "Veeck the Humanist" is not. This most approachable man did not encourage Doby to discuss the matter with him, while knowing that Doby would not do so without encouragement. "But I had my own thoughts and opinions," Doby commented. "They came from my dealings with certain people, certain stockholders. I just don't think what Bill said is the whole thing. I think that what he said is just part of it."

One part of it is something that never occurred to Doby until he reflected on his dismissal three years later: "Bill said to me in 1976, before he owned the White Sox, when I was with Montreal, that he wanted me to manage some day. But he said, 'I want to get you a good ball club first.' Yet he gave me an opportunity with a bad ball club. But I just realized now that he knew he was going out of business when he made me manager. And once he goes out of business, there's no chance for me to manage. He wanted to wait, but I think he just ran out of time, because he was running out of money.

"A combination of things caused Bill to fire me," Doby concluded, "and he did not reveal all of them."

NOTES

1. Personal interview with Alan Bannister, September 22, 1980.
2. *Chicago Tribune*, July 1, 1978.
3. Ibid., July 2, 1978.
4. Ibid., July 3, 1978.
5. Ibid., July 4, 1978.
6. Ibid.
7. Ibid., passim.
8. Ibid., August 17, 1978.
9. Ibid.
10. Ibid., August 20, 1978.
11. Ibid., September 5, 1978.
12. Telephone interview with Bill Veeck, October 1, 1981.
13. *Chicago Tribune*, passim.
14. Ibid.
15. Ibid., October 19, 1978.
16. Ibid.

17. Ibid., October 20, 1978.
18. Veeck, telephone interview, loc. cit.
19. Bannister, loc. cit.
20. Personal interview with Bill Veeck, April 23–24, 1980.
21. Veeck, telephone interview, loc. cit.
22. Ibid.
23. Ibid.
24. *Chicago Tribune*, passim.
25. Ibid.
26. *New York Times*, March 23, 1986.
27. Veeck, telephone interview, loc. cit.

14

Pride Against Prejudice

The story of Larry Doby's lifelong use of pride against prejudice can best be understood by comparing him with Satchel Paige and Jackie Robinson, and by a glimpse of Doby at work for the New Jersey Nets.

Although Paige and Robinson shared the stage with Doby during those early years of the integration of baseball, neither of them ever shared the spotlight. Using vastly different methods of coping with daily life as black men in white America, Paige and Robinson kept the spotlight almost entirely on themselves. Doby, using a third method of coping, stood in a dimmer light away from center stage.

No argument will be developed here that one of the three men chose the best method, or even that they chose in a conscious sense at all. It will be argued, though, that of the three, Doby's method was the least understood.

It might seem surprising that this be so. Paige, who created a world of his own with his comic stories and legendary feats, became larger than life. To understand him required a long leap of faith, a suspension of disbelief. In comparison, Robinson, once unleashed by Branch Rickey, boldly divided the world in order to conquer it. In so doing, he subordinated himself to his noble cause. To understand him, one first had to understand one's own reaction to Robinson's pugnacity.

Doby neither enlarged his myth nor subordinated himself to a cause. He tried, instead, to live within himself. There seems to be little challenge in understanding that. But things are seldom what they seem. In evaluating black Americans, white Americans seem to understand the Paiges and Robinsons, to relate easily to fantasy and disputation.

In contrast, the photograph of Doby with Steve Gromek during the 1948 World Series symbolizes what Doby has sought—fusion and unity.

Why are these more difficult to understand than fantasy and disputation? A closer look at the three men reveals why.

Paige had been to baseball what the Harlem Globetrotters have been to basketball, the comic fool who first performs, magically, and then laughs all the way to the bank. Just as Globetrotters humor would not be nearly as funny to white audiences if the players were white and did not come from "Harlem," Paige would not have been quite as funny if he were white. It is impossible to separate race from the laughter.

Forty years before his induction into the Hall of Fame at Cooperstown in 1971, Paige had already become a comic legend. By 1971, he knew from long experience how to provoke laughs from audiences. During his seven-minute induction speech, the almost entirely white audience laughed 13 times. And they laughed where Paige knew they would, including eight times about his age. (Baseball fans told Bill Veeck in 1948 that he "could have got anybody but Satchel, he's too old to vote.")[1]

Paige brought his act with him when he became Larry Doby's roommate as a 42-year-old rookie pitcher with the Cleveland Indians. It was an act Doby did not always appreciate. "I didn't like it when guys laughed at Satch's stories," he says, "because I knew they were also laughing at Satch himself as a black man. So Satch and I didn't spend much time together.

"But I really enjoyed him during a game one day in Cleveland when Satch kept burping, more than he usually did, and Bob Lemon brought a glass of bicarbonate of soda out to the mound. Satch drank it, and said 'Thank you.' Now that was funny!"

Few who studied Paige would disagree with Mary Frances Veeck, who had ample opportunity to observe him when he pitched for her husband's St. Louis Browns in the early 1950's. "Satchel used to walk into a room," she said, "and I would crack up, because you could see the eyebrows do a little something, you saw a little thing happen with the mouth, and I'd think, 'Here he goes.' He did this with anybody and everybody. But Satchel was very smart, in total control."[2]

Harrison Dillard agreed. The 1948 and 1952 Olympic track star from Cleveland observed that "Satch knew he was putting people on. It was deliberate. From some of the things he said, you almost had to come to that conclusion. The guy had too much native intelligence not to know that he was having the last laugh."[3]

Doby and Paige had little influence on each other. Although Doby called him "roomie" and Paige referred to Doby as his "old lady" in 1948 and 1949, there was little likelihood that the rich and famous Paige would change his established style in the presence of his more serious 25-year-old roommate.

Nor did Doby change for Paige. When the Brooklyn Dodgers visited Cleveland for a charity exhibition game in 1949, Doby arranged for Robinson and Roy Campanella to assemble at the home of Arthur and Doris Grant, where Doby lived, before the game. Doby did not invite Paige to join them. In fact, as Arthur Grant remembered it, Robinson openly expressed his disdain for Paige. "I don't see how the hell you could stay with a guy like Satchel Paige," Robinson told Doby. "I just couldn't take it."[4]

"Jackie detested Satch, strongly," Doby says. "I never paid that much attention to him. In the clubhouse, when Satch would start to tell his stories and the guys would start laughing, I'd ease out.

"Satch was competition for Jack. Satch was funny, he was an outstanding athlete, and he was black. He had three things going. Jack and I wouldn't tell jokes. We weren't humorists. We tried to show that we were intelligent, and that's not what most white people expect from blacks. Satch gave whites what they wanted from blacks—joy."

By comparing Doby with Robinson, we may obtain a still clearer picture of Doby. If Paige's comedic style made Doby seem solemn and intense, Robinson's outspoken fury made Doby's demeanor seem mild and relaxed.

Few people knew both Robinson and Doby as well as Don Newcombe, Robinson's teammate on the Brooklyn Dodgers from 1949 until Robinson retired after the 1956 World Series, and his friend thereafter until Robinson's death in 1972. According to Newcombe, "Jackie had to win at everything he did. He had an intense desire to win, to be superior. And he was superior to other people—I don't care who it was. He would talk to President Kennedy like he'd talk to you. If he liked you, he would be nice to you. If he didn't like you, or if you said something to rile him, he would tell you about it.

"That's why I don't believe there's another man, other than Larry, who could have done the job that Jackie did. And I'm wondering if Larry could have done it, with his temper. Larry had a very volatile temper. Jackie did, too, but Jackie was able to control his. Larry couldn't harness his temper to his performance. That's my opinion of each man. And Larry is my best friend. He's my best friend."[5]

"Newk didn't put it quite right," Doby reacted. "I could never channel my temper into my performance consistently, like Jack, but I could from time to time. Sometimes, if a certain thing happened on the field, it would come out. I'd try to hit the white baseball a little farther, a little harder.

"But I always controlled my temper. The only time my temper took advantage of me was in 1957, when I had that fight with Art Ditmar. I probably could have fought every day if I had wanted to.

"I don't know where my angry feelings went. They must have gone inside. I got sick to my stomach. I wound up with an ulcer. But the main thing I'd want to do was to get away by myself so I could get myself back under control."

Ignoring the possibility that such behavior might have caused some people to call him a "loner," Doby went on. "Another difference between Jack and me is that I was never a public crusader. My way of fighting racism is to do it individually, privately. If I'm in a social situation and something comes up, then I talk about it.

"What would I have gained as a crusader in baseball? I wouldn't have gained anything. I don't think I'm a crusader for blacks. I think I'm an individual who knows about double standards, who knows about injustice.

"I think the thing that helps me now, but which I couldn't do when I was a player, is that a couple of times a week things come up and I can talk about them with individuals. But I don't have a long conversation, because what I say about double standards is true, and the person knows it's true. Most people still don't expect or want me to speak truthfully, though, and it upsets some people when I do."

Newcombe, who saw both the public and private sides of his two friends, saw parallels between them which few others could have seen: "They both had to keep their mouths shut, and they both had to keep all that venom inside them. Then, when they exploded, with whomever it was—it could be their wives, their kids, their friends—all of this would come out. And that's where you'd see a side of Larry Doby and Jackie Robinson that you didn't recognize, you didn't know.

"Larry developed an ulcer, Jackie had all these other things [high blood pressure, arthritis, diabetes, and blindness just before his death]."[6]

In sharp contrast to Paige, who took advantage of the fact that he was black, Robinson had opposite feelings. According to Newcombe, "Jackie used to sit in his room sometimes and rub his hands, hoping the black would go away. He'd say, 'Why can't the black go away so I can do what I'm capable of doing without all of these roadblocks being in my way? I want to play baseball. I want to do what I can for Jackie Robinson first, and my family, and my people.'

"But it seemed it was in reverse. He was doing it for his people more than he was doing it for Jackie Robinson and his family. And I think that helped to destroy him."[7]

Doby, unlike Robinson and Paige, neither regretted the color of his skin nor exploited it. Yet all of them, in their own ways, felt its hurt.

While touring with Robinson's barnstorming team in the off-season, Doby was content with the companionship of men like Newcombe and Roy Campanella. Robinson, meanwhile, "would go with the white guys who had booked the tour," Doby remembers.

"But for Jack that was a way of survival. To hang around with me or Newcombe, there would be no advancement for Jack. That was Jack's way of fighting against white feelings of superiority. He knew how to maneuver into areas where he had to maneuver in order for him to be successful. And it must have worked, because when Jack left baseball he worked for Chock Full O' Nuts and for Nelson Rockefeller."

Doby, meanwhile, walked a different path. Not driven to conquer, as Robinson was, Doby could establish more mutual relationships with people. "When I first got in the American League," Doby recalls, "Jack wanted exclusive attention. He wanted it all to himself. When we would go to different functions together, he would want the whole audience. If I got some of the audience, then you could see him move in to the area where I was standing and he'd take over." Doby, a man who would not admit to weakness, at the same time never felt compelled to prove that he was stronger than Robinson.

In fact, Doby would make no audible demands on anyone. As A. S. "Doc" Young so shrewdly noted in 1953, "It might be said that the major difference between Jackie and Larry was this: Jackie, as time was to prove, dressed himself in the cloak of humility and made it into a perfect fit through one of the greatest acting jobs in baseball history; Doby wore the cloak as a gift of nature."[8]

Robinson, and by implication Doby, has been assessed from a different perspective by the poet and dramatist Amiri Baraka (Leroi Jones). Expressing his loyalty to the black men who played on the Eagles of his youth in Newark, Jones regarded Robinson as a "synthetic colored guy" who was "imperfected" at the "California laboratories of USC."

Jones implies that he preferred Doby:

But the scarecrow J. R. for all his ersatz "blackness" could represent the shadow world of the Negro integrating into America. A farce. But many of us fell for that and felt for him, really. Even though a lot of us knew the wholly artificial disconnected thing that Jackie Robinson was.[9]

The words of John "Buck" O'Neill provide a touching conclusion for a comparison of Doby, Robinson, and Paige. O'Neill played first base for the Kansas City Monarchs in 1945 as a teammate of Robinson. In 1946, O'Neill and Paige were teammates on the Monarchs in their unsuccessful effort to defeat Doby's Newark Eagles in the Negro World Series. O'Neill maintained friendships with all three men in the years that followed. Elegant and handsome, he became a talent scout throughout the midwest for the Chicago Cubs. In an interview at Ashland, Kentucky, at a reunion for players from the old black leagues in 1980, O'Neill reflected on his knowledge of Doby, Robinson, and Paige:

"I believe I'd have made Larry one of the greatest players who ever lived. He might have been a kid I would have slept with. There were a whole lot of rough spots he had to face. He's a beautiful person, but few people know him.

"Jackie was a ball of fire. He was as fiery a person as I've ever seen. And he had the intelligence to know what things meant.

"Satchel never dealt in black and white. He was a star. He never took a back seat to Dizzy Dean or Bobby Feller.

"Satchel would say, 'Get outta my face,' but Jackie would take it home with him. But that was the catalyst that made Jackie such a great player— 'I'll show ya, I'll show ya, I'll show ya.'

"Larry would need me to take his hand at certain times, but with Satchel, I'd fraternize with him. We're gonna drink beer together. We enjoyed lyin' to each other.

"I loved Jackie as a person, I love Satchel as a friend, and I love Larry as a son." [10]

With reference to the fact that he never had a father at home, but without acknowledging that his mother required him to move from the warmth of his home with his Aunt Alice and Uncle James Cooke in South Carolina to be placed with her friends in Paterson just before starting ninth grade, Doby responds:

"I appreciate Buck's feelings. I was much younger than Jackie, in age and the kind of exposure Jackie had had at UCLA and as an officer in the Army. A man like Buck would have been a great help to me. I could have forgotten about a lot of things I took home at night. Going with Satch wasn't my thing because I wasn't drinking at that time.

"With a guy like Buck, who had a lot of exposure and who must have known how to deal in the world, and who was such a mature man, just the idea of having him around, I think, would have been a great help to me.

"If you go back to my childhood, I was alone most of the time. I never had that father-type image. That's nice for Buck to see that."

Among Doby, Robinson, and Paige, then, Doby's was the most typical of the black experience in baseball in the years from 1947 until the civil rights movement enabled and encouraged black players like Curt Flood and Dick Allen to speak up in the 1970's. [11] No black players during those early years of integration were as outspoken as Robinson or as antic as Paige. Most were like Doby—gifted athletes who forced their way onto major league rosters by means of their performance statistics, and who kept their mouths shut once they got there. "We couldn't appear uppity, and we couldn't allow our intelligence or knowledge to show," Doby says.

After Doby returned to baseball as a coach in 1969, on the crest of a civil rights movement which he and Robinson had, in effect, started, he began to speak more freely when asked questions by reporters, managers, and general managers. But by 1974, when he went from Montreal to Cleveland in expectation of becoming major league baseball's first black manager, his honest answers to questions prompted one of his black fellow coaches, Tom McCraw, to advise him to be "less of a bear and more of a cub" in the presence of general manager Phil Seghi.

"That would have been outside of Larry's personality," observed Don Newcombe. "Larry can't go outside of his personality. Otherwise he's not going to be honest, and Larry's an honest man. I don't think McCraw is on the right track in telling Larry to be a cub. Larry should be a bear, for what he's gone through. Why does he have to be a cub? Why do you have to be a cub all your life, because your skin is black?"

Noting that Robinson "would say things maybe too fast, sometimes," Newcombe said that, "Larry talks only if he's asked. He would rather not say anything to you at all, rather than say something that turned out to be wrong."[12]

When asked, Doby has apparently made his views clear to anyone who would take the time to understand them. "I no longer feel misunderstood," he says. "Now my problem is that I am understood, but there are people in baseball who don't like what I say. They seem to think that baseball's problems with racial prejudice were ended by Jackie Robinson in 1947."

But of course they weren't, as demonstrated by Al Campanis of the Los Angeles Dodgers, who concealed his prejudice from the public until 1987, when he told Ted Koppel, on network television, that black Americans "may not have some of the necessities to be, let's say, a field manager or perhaps a general manager."[13] It is virtually certain that these views are shared, privately, by other executives throughout baseball.

Doby has lingering regrets that he's been out of baseball since 1979, an estrangement that Newcombe understands: "I'm so glad to see Larry out of baseball I don't know what to do," he says sardonically. "Now isn't that something! Here's a man with all of this knowledge, intelligence, this ability to lend something constructive to baseball, and he's not being allowed to do it."

Newcombe is well aware that Doby will not try to "sell" himself to an owner or a general manager, and anticipated the reactions if Doby were to try. "If both a black man and a white man try to sell themselves," Newcombe said, "it's OK for the white man in terms of likeability. The black man is supposed to stay in his place, wherever his place is."[14]

In reaction, Doby says, "Newk told me a long time ago that I would not get as far as I wanted to get in baseball. He knows how much baseball means to me. In the beginning of my coaching at Montreal my hopes were very high because I felt I could go from the ground floor up, from the minor leagues to the big leagues. It's a shock when you get there and then you're knocked down. Newcombe saw this a long time before I did.

"One of the things that bothers me more than not reaching a certain point, is that any time you have knowledge to contribute and you're not allowed to do it, then there are a lot of people who are not getting the best from what you have to offer. It's tough for me when someone can dictate your life at that point.

"I don't think Newcombe is right when he tells me I want to make baseball different. I think I would just like people in baseball to have more respect for the contribution I can make as a coach or manager, and forget about the color of my skin."

But that, of course, *would* make baseball different.

In the 1980's, in his capacity as director of community relations for the New Jersey Nets, Larry Doby appears as the guest speaker at banquets, and runs inner-city basketball leagues for elementary school children. In a typical guest appearance, his remarks follow a familiar pattern: he speaks knowledgeably about the Nets and about their interest in promoting academics and good citizenship among the kids who play in the leagues the team sponsors. During the question-and-answer period, the questions eventually shift to Doby's views about baseball, which he answers before nudging his audience back to the Nets. At the end, after the applause, the baseball fans in the audience often line up for autographs, and a chance to tell him when and where they saw him during his playing career.

Occasionally, the aftermath of a guest appearance offends him. In one such instance, an obviously prosperous white man approached Doby and told him, "You handled yourself very well." His pride wounded, Doby bristled but remained silent. Oblivious to Doby's reaction, the white man expressed his thanks for Doby's appearance, received an answering nod, and left.

For many readers, especially black readers, the white man's remark needs no interpretation. For others, it might. To Doby, to any sensitive black person, the unspoken remainder of the remark is clear: "You handled yourself very well, *for a black man.*" No matter how well intentioned or sincere the person may have been, no matter how unconscious of his meaning, his remark is patronizing, and thus insulting.

For those who read the remark to be a compliment, the test is a simple one: would the man have made it to a white man of equal status whom he had just met for the first time? Of course not. It might be a compliment if addressed to someone who is a close friend or a co-worker, but Doby was neither of those. It is a remark delivered to someone regarded as inferior—a child, a woman, a handicapped person, a black person.

That Doby had to suffer the indignity of this remark in the 1980's demonstrates beyond any doubt that his life has been, and continues to be, lived in the shadow of a racial problem that will not go away.

Even worse, there have been people in the past who have said, and written, that the racial problem does not exist, except in Doby' mind. One of the many people interviewed for this book, a sportswriter with a national audience, declined to talk on the grounds that "Larry Doby sees things which are not there." Yet "You handled yourself very well" and "I won't lend my glove to no nigger" and "Nigger Heaven" at the Majestic Theater in Paterson and the segregation of Arizona, Florida, and South Carolina are realities which span Doby's entire life. To call reality imaginary is to inflict the ultimate injury on a person: it is an attempt to destroy his mind.

There, in an unexpected instant after a guest appearance, moments removed from approving applause, Larry Doby's race was once again thrown in his face. And, once again, he did not disarm the man with humor, as Satchel Paige would have done, or attack him verbally, as Jackie Robinson would have done. Instead, as usual, he depended upon his inexhaustible pride as private protection against public prejudice.

In the 1980's, out of baseball, Larry Doby reflects on his life. He is proud of what he has accomplished and proud that he has done so, as he says, "within the system." He has few regrets.

"I miss baseball, but I don't miss it to the point where it upsets me. I miss it in February, just before spring training. And I miss it when I see so many changes in coaches and managers and nobody makes me an offer I would accept. I don't want to think about it too much, though, because it might distract me from what I have to do now. I don't dwell on the past. To me, the past is learning to be applied to the future, to make it better. You remember the bad part of the past so as not to repeat the bad. I thank God that although I'm not involved in baseball, I survive.

"That's why I'd like to see this book end in positive hopes. Whatever the struggle has been, I've been able to overcome it. If you look you'll see that it's not been done with one particular race or nationality, but all races and nationalities. Don't forget that I had success in Japan, too.

"I'd like to look at myself as a person that can give the reader a little different insight as to what he might think, or what he might go up against, or what he is up against.

"The bottom line, of course, is that there are good people and there are bad people. If you let your mind dwell on people who are racists, or bigots, you might become negative in your thinking. I'm comfortable because I don't look at people as white or Irish or Jewish or Italian or whatever. I just look at people as people. So I think I'm a much happier fellow.

"There's one thing I've had to do because of the double standard: I've had to have almost a perfect record. That's why I've always asked, where would Billy Martin have managed if he were black? If he were black, he would never have gotten the chance to prove that he's such a smart manager.

"I feel privileged to have worked for Bill Veeck and Joe Taub [former owner of the Nets]. It's amazing how Veeck and Taub were alike. I never thought that I would meet two people in my life that would be almost identical in terms of their inner feelings for people.

"What I'm trying to say is that for black and white youngsters, there are some good people in this world. Everywhere I've been, I've met good people—black and white and yellow. I don't want to think about prejudice any more. I'd rather think positively about tomorrow."

In that succession of days which constituted "tomorrow," 1987 brought a wave of recognition to Doby. Prompted by the fortieth anniversary of his integration of the American League, Montclair State College and the State of New Jersey honored him—the college with the degree of Doctor of Humane Letters, the state legislature with resolutions declaring July 15, 1987, as "Larry Doby Day."

Baseball Commissioner Peter Ueberroth, embarrassed by the Al Campanis incident, appointed Doby to an advisory committee headed by Dr. Harry Edwards to find ways to increase the number of black managers and executives in the sport. Ueberroth, perhaps still motivated as much by embarrassment as by baseball's tradition of commemorating its past, later invited Doby to throw out the first ball at the All-Star Game in Oakland.

The Cleveland Indians dedicated their Old Timers Day game to him. With Helyn and their children looking on as guests of the Indians, the team gave him a videotape of the ceremonies and the camera used to film them; a portrait of him in action during his days of glory as an active player; an eight-day trip to play golf in Scotland; and, best of all, in Doby's view, the team auctioned his Indians shirt, with "Doby 14" on its back, for the benefit of the Cleveland State University Hospital. Already a member of the Indians Hall of Fame, the Chicago White Sox named him to their Hall of Fame.

The Congress and the President of the United States may soon bestow the ultimate accolade. A recent bill sponsored by Senator Frank Lautenberg of New Jersey, and co-sponsored by 22 other senators, reads:

The President of the United States is authorized and requested to present, on behalf of the Congress, a gold medal to Lawrence Eugene Doby in recognition of his achievements in baseball and contribution to the advancement of civil rights in this country, and to the wife of Jack Roosevelt Robinson in recognition of Jackie Robinson's achievements in baseball and his contribution to the advancement of civil rights in this country.

The bill would also "authorize the Secretary of the Treasury to sell bronze duplicates of those medals." [15]

And so, after a lifetime in the shadow of Jackie Robinson, Larry Doby has been accorded, however briefly, the exalted status which Robinson has had for so very long. Yet it is a status which Doby has not sought, and does not believe in. Rather, his lifelong habit of somehow combining humility with pride, of feeling proud while remaining "plain me," enables him to say that these recent events "rank right up there with that picture of me and Steve Gromek in 1948."

NOTES

1. Transcript, Hall of Fame Library, Cooperstown, N.Y.

2. Personal interview with Mary Frances Veeck, April 24, 1980.

3. Personal interview with Harrison Dillard, January 12, 1981.

4. Personal interview with Arthur Grant, January 9, 1981.

5. Personal interview with Don Newcombe, April 10, 1982.

6. Ibid.

7. Ibid.

8. Doc Young, *Great Negro Baseball Stars and How They Made the Major Leagues* (New York: A. S. Barnes and Co., 1953), p. 80.

9. Amiri Baraka, *Autobiography* (New York: Freundlich Books, 1984), p. 35.

10. Personal interview with John "Buck" O'Neill, June 24, 1980.

11. Curt Flood, one of baseball's finest outfielders in the 1960's, sued to invalidate baseball's reserve clause in 1970. In 1972, the U.S. Supreme Court ruled against him. Dick Allen, who became baseball's highest paid player in 1970, often spoke his mind on the subject of racial prejudice and other "political" matters. Both men quit baseball for other pursuits, although both could have played for several more seasons.

12. Newcombe, loc. cit.

13. *New York Times*, April 9, 1987.

14. Newcombe, loc. cit.

15. S. 1519, 100th Congress, First Session, July 21, 1987.

Appendix:
Larry Doby's Career Statistics

REGULAR SEASON

Year	Games	AB	R	H	2B	3B	HR	RBI	BB	SO	SB	BA	SA
1947	29	32	3	5	1	0	0	2	1	11	0	.156	.188
1948	121	439	83	132	23	9	14	66	54	77	9	.301	.490
1949	147	547	106	153	25	3	24	85	91	90	10	.280	.468
1950	142	503	110	164	25	5	25	102	98	71	8	.326	.545
1951	134	447	84	132	27	5	20	69	101	81	4	.295	.512
1952	140	519	104*	143	26	8	32*	104	90	111*	5	.276	.541**
1953	149	513	92	135	18	5	29	102	96	121*	3	.263	.487
1954	153	577	94	157	18	4	32*	126*	85	94	3	.272	.484
1955	131	491	91	143	17	5	26	75	61	100	2	.291	.505
1956	140	504	89	135	22	3	24	102	102	105	0	.268	.466
1957	119	416	57	120	27	2	14	79	56	79	2	.288	.464
1958	89	247	41	70	10	1	13	45	26	49	0	.283	.490
1959 Det	18	55	5	12	3	1	0	3	8	9	0	.218	.309
1959 Chi	21	58	1	14	1	1	0	9	2	13	1	.241	.293
Totals	1533	5348	960	1515	243	52	253	969	871	1011	47	.283	.490

*--Led American League

**--Led major leagues

WORLD SERIES

Year	Games	AB	R	H	2B	3B	HR	RBI	BB	SO	SB	BA	SA
1948	6	22	1	7*	1	0	1	2	2	4	0	.318	.500
1954	4	16	0	2	0	0	0	0	2	4	0	.125	.125
Totals	10	38	1	9	1	0	1	2	4	8	0	.237	.342

*--Tied for most hits with Earl Torgeson and Bob Elliott of Boston Braves

ALL-STAR GAMES

Year	Games	AB	R	H	2B	3B	HR	RBI	BB	SO	SB	BA	SA
1949	1	1	0	0	0	0	0	0	0	0	0	.000	.000
1950	1	6	1	2	1	0	0	0	0	0	0	.333	.500
1951	1	1	0	0	0	0	0	0	0	0	0	.000	.000
1952	1	0	0	0	0	0	0	0	0	0	0	.000	.000
1953	1	1	0	0	0	0	0	0	0	0	0	.000	.000
1954	1	1	1	1	0	0	1	1	1	0	0	1.000	1.000
1955*	-	-	-	-	-	-	-	-	-	-	-	---	---
Totals	6	10	2	3	1	0	1	1	1	0	0	.300	.700

*--Named to team, but did not play.

Bibliographical Notes

The principal source for the contents of this book is its subject, Larry Doby. In a series of tape recorded interviews lasting many hours, he reviewed his life in great detail, providing information which became the foundation for all subsequent research. Upon completion of that research, and the writing of a first draft incorporating his recollections and the fruits of research, Doby read the manuscript in my presence. This proved to be a vital step, because the material stimulated memories long since buried by time. His reactions were then cross-checked against other sources, and a second draft took shape. Thereafter, a long and often painful process of pruning gradually reduced a massive manuscript to its present form in this book. Other significant sources are cited in the remainder of this essay, and of course in the notes that follow each chapter.

Chapter 2, which traces Doby's ancestry back to slavery and describes his boyhood in Camden, South Carolina, is based upon the records of the United States Census, housed in the Military Ocean Terminal at Bayonne, New Jersey; upon estate packets stored in the Kershaw County Court House in Camden; upon interviews with Betty Lytelle Cooke and Kathryn Cooke Johnson, with whom he lived after his maternal grandmother was institutionalized; upon an interview with Richard DuBose, a central figure in black baseball in South Carolina when Doby was a boy; and upon an interview with Doby's mother, Etta Walker.

Chapter 3, chronicling Doby's life in Paterson, New Jersey, is based upon interviews with many of his contemporaries in the local playgrounds and at Eastside High School. In addition, Paterson's two newspapers at that time, the *Morning Call* and the *Evenings News*, were found to be in close agreement as to the facts of Doby's exploits as an athlete in football, basketball, baseball and track. Although little of the material about his years at Eastside found its way into the final manuscript, it did provide corroboration of the memories of those who were interviewed.

Doby's entry into the Negro National League, and his season and a half with the Newark Eagles after World War II, were reported by weekly black newspapers in 1942, 1946, and 1947, and are described here in Chapters 4 and 5. Microfilm of the *New Jersey Afro-American* is on file at the Public Library in Newark. The Schomburg Museum in New York City, as a major repository of material about black history in the United States, houses microfilm of many other black weeklies. It also has a file of clippings about Larry Doby which, although not extensive, did prove useful. The spirit of those days is difficult to find in such sources, however. For that, interviews with veterans of the black baseball leagues, gathered for a reunion at Ashland, Kentucky, provided ample proof of the vitality of this phase of Doby's life.

As the movement to integrate baseball after World War II gained momentum, the black press continued to provide the most complete coverage of events, and so provides a substantial portion of the material in Chapter 5. In addition, the papers of Albert B. Chandler, the man who became the Commissioner of Baseball in 1945, are available at the library of the University of Kentucky in Lexington. They furnish a valuable behind-the-scenes view of the pressures brought to bear on Chandler.

The events that enabled Doby to integrate the American League, reported in Chapter 6, were reported in detail in the *Morning Call*, stored in the files of the Public Library in Paterson. Of course, the Cleveland *Plain Dealer* and the Cleveland *Call and Post*, the latter a black weekly, are also indispensable to anyone wishing to follow Doby in an almost step-by-step manner. The *Plain Dealer*, as a leading American newspaper, can be found in many libraries. The files of the *Call and Post* are well maintained in that paper's editorial offices in Cleveland. In addition, interviews with Bill Veeck, Lou Boudreau, traveling secretary Spud Goldstein, and the players who sat in the dugout when Doby made his debut provided information which was not reported at the time.

Doby's years as a major league player, described in Chapters 7, 8, and 9, were reported in their fullest detail in the *Plain Dealer* and the *Call and Post*. Personal perspectives were provided by interviews with many of the players on the Cleveland Indians and Chicago White Sox of those days. Harrison Dillard, Al Rosen, and Boudreau all provided valuable material; but Al Lopez, who was both teammate and manager of Larry Doby, proved less than candid. These years are also preserved by a thick file of clippings in the Hall of Fame Library at Cooperstown, New York.

The years 1961 through 1969 were years of transition for Doby, coming between his years as a player and his years as a major league coach and manager. They are described in Chapter 9. Don Newcombe, who played with Doby in Japan and has been a lifelong friend of Doby, spoke freely about their year there. Helyn Doby also contributed heavily to this portion of the book.

The activities of major league coaches are seldom reported on the sports pages. Chapters 11 and 12 thus depend on the testimony of players whom Doby coached on the major and minor league teams of the Montreal Expos, the Cleveland Indians, and the Chicago White Sox. For the sections on Doby's aspirations to manage a major league team, interviews with Jim Fanning of the Expos and Phil Seghi of the Indians were most informative.

The sequence of events which led to Doby's being named the manager of the White Sox were reported in the greatest detail in the Chicago *Tribune*, available in many libraries. But the key figure in these events, Bill Veeck, at first refused to comment, later relented, and ultimately proved to be either less than frank and open or unclear about the facts and his own thinking. He is quoted at length in this section of the book, but his remarks are qualified by editorial comments by the author.

For the final chapter, an attempt to synthesize and summarize Doby's life, personal interviews with Buck O'Neill, Harrison Dillard, Bill and Mary Frances Veeck, and Don Newcombe produced insights that can be found nowhere else.

Index

Aaron, Hank, 133
Aaron, Tommie, 138
Adelis, Pete, 90
Alexander, Grover Cleveland, 89
Allen, Dick, 172
Allen, Maury, 148
Allison, Augusta Brooks, 7-9
Allison, Charles, 7
All-Star Game: 1947, 41, 44, 57; 1949, 89; 1950, 93-94; 1951, 96; 1952, 98; 1953, 99-100; 1954, 102; 1955, 109; 1987, 176
All-Star Game, Negro Leagues, 34
Altrock, Nick, 95
Alvarez, Ossie, 117
American Youth for Democracy, 59
"Amos 'n' Andy," 8, 71-72, 89
Amsterdam Star-News, 20, 22
Anderson, Dave, 139
Aparicio, Luis, 111, 134
Armstrong, David W., 25
Aspromonte, Ken, 135, 136-38, 139-40
Avila, Bobby, 105

Bagli, Adolph, 14, 17
Baker, Dusty, 133
Baker, Gene, 138
Baltimore Elite Giants, 32, 33, 37
Baltimore Orioles (American League), 100, 115-16, 118, 133, 157

Baltimore Orioles (International League), 33
Bankhead, Dan, 61
Bannister, Alan, 150, 152, 155, 160
Baraka, Amiri, 32-33, 43, 171
Barney, Rex, 78
Barnhill, Dave, 21
Barrios, Francisco, 162
Bartell, Dick, 74
Baumgarten, Ross, 163
Bearden, Gene, 80, 82
Bee, Clair, 23
Bell, Buddy, 137, 141
Bell, Cool Papa, 33
Bennett, Dr. George, 119
Bennett, Zelma and John, 69, 100
Benswanger, William E., 21
Berardino, Johnny, 58
Bernazard, Tony, 147
Berra, Yogi, 90, 102, 104, 105
Black, Don, 48
Black Bottom, 7-8, 11. See also Camden, South Carolina
Blease, Cole L., 8
Bonda, Ted, 140, 141
Bostic, Joe, 31
Boston Braves, 80, 82-83
Boston Red Sox, 35, 79, 80-81
Boudreau, Lou: decides to switch Doby to outfield, 58; excuses Do-

Boudreau, Lou (*continued*)
by's lataeness, 60; handles Doby's
first day, 45–50, 52; hears radio report on Doby, 42; manages Doby in
1947, 62; not consulted on Doby,
40; playoff game in 1948, 80–82; puts
Doby in starting lineup, 53–54, 57;
regular season in 1948, 74–76; regu-
lar season in 1949, 89–90; replaces
self with Doby, 59; in spring train-
ing in 1948, 70–73; statement on Do-
by's arrival, 42–43; substitutes Flem-
ing for Eddie Robinson, 61; views
on integration, 22; World Series in
1948, 82
Bozza, Sam, 67
Bradenton, Florida, 131
Bradley, Alva T., 22
Bradley, Tom, 71
Bragan, Bobby, 116
Branca, Ralph, 134
Braves Field (Boston), 82
Brent, George, 91
Brewer, Tom, 118
Briggs Stadium (Detroit), 60, 74, 96
Brinkman, Joe, 157–58
Brissie, Lou, 95
Brohamer, Jack, 137, 140
Brown, Barney, 29
Brown, Dr. Bobby, 163
Brown, Butts, 21
Brown, Ralph, 123
Brown, Rap, 142
Brown, Willard, 30, 58, 60–61
Browning Home. *See* Mather Acad-
emy
Brown v. Board of Education of Topeka,
100
Buffalo Stadium (Houston), 73, 88
Burke, Mayor Thomas A., 77
Burns, Britt, 163
Busby, Jim, 100, 102, 110, 113
Byrne, Brendan, 126
Byrnes, James F., 112

Calhoun, John C., 8
California Angels, 138, 158
Camden, South Carolina, 5–11. *See
also* Black Bottom

Campanella, Roy, 19, 35–36, 78, 89,
125, 134, 169, 170
Campanis, Al, 35, 128, 138, 148, 173
Camp Robert Smalls, 25–26, 56
Carmichael, Stokely, 142
Carrasquel, Chico, 110, 113
Center Field Lounge, 123, 125–26
Central League (Japan), 124
Chambliss, Chris, 137
Chandler, Albert B., 30–31
Clark, Allie, 68, 81
Cleveland Buckeyes, 56
Cobbledick, Gordon, 46–47, 49, 68,
69, 97–98
Colavito, Rocco, 116
Colored Intercollegiate Athletic Asso-
ciation, 24
Comiskey, Chuck, 115, 118
Comiskey, Grace, 55–56
Comiskey Park (Chicago): Doby ends
major league playing career, 118;
Doby fights with Art Ditmar, 113–
14; Doby fired as manager, 159; Do-
by's first American League game,
45–49; Doby's first appearance as
manager of home team, 156; Doby's
first full game, 53; Negro League
All-Star game in 1946, 34; Negro
League World Series in 1946, 34; key
game in 1948 season, 79; post-season
barnstorming game in 1946, 35
Conley, Gene, 102
Conn, Billy, 33, 34, 36
Connors, Chuck, 67
Cooke, Alice and James, 69, 172
Cooke, Alice Lytelle Doby, 6, 9–10, 69
Cooke, Betty Lytelle, 5, 6
Cooke, James, 9–10
Correll, Charlie, 71–72
Cory Methodist Church, 76
Crosley Field (Cincinnati), 100
Curvy, Emily, 84
Curvy family, 33, 123

Daily Worker, 20–21, 44
Dal Canton, Bruce, 155
Daley, Bud, 116
Dandridge, Ray, 20, 30
Dark, Alvin, 82

Davis, Piper, 30, 58, 61
Davis, Tommy, 117
Dawson, Andre, 147
Day, Leon, 20, 23, 30, 34
Dean, Dizzy, 103
Detroit Tigers, 74, 80, 110, 117
Deutsch, Dutch, 121
DeVita, Mayor Michael U., 83-84, 87, 96
Dewey, Thomas E., 4
Dillard, Harrison, 92-93, 98, 168
DiMaggio, Dom, 80, 93, 98
DiMaggio, Joe, 54, 59, 78-79, 80, 93
DiMaggio, Vince, 100
Dimond, Bob, 84
Ditmar, Art, 113-15, 169
Dixiecrats. See States Rights Party
Doby, Alfred English, 5
Doby, Burrell, 5-6
Doby, Christina, 87, 91-92, 98, 115
Doby, David Jonathan, 6-7, 9, 59
Doby, Helyn Curvy: acknowledged for contributions, xi; alleged to control Doby, 97-98; attends first spring training in 1949, 69; attends Old Timers game in 1987, 176; comments on rumor of Doby's joining Indians, 41; marries Doby, 33; not invited to participate in fashion show, 149; object of discrimination, 91-92; operates Center Field Lounge, 123; reason for Doby to attend L.I.U., 23
Doby, James Cureton, 5
Doby, Joseph William, 5
Doby, Kim, 87
Doby, Larry, Jr., 87
Doby, Leslie, 87
Doby, Molly Bailey, 6, 10
Doby, Susan, 88, 149
Dobys, amateur baseball team, 77
Doerr, Bobby, 81
Donovan, Dick, 111
Downing, Brian, 150
Dropo, Walt, 111, 113
Du Bois, W.E.B., 15, 62-63
Du Bose, Richard, 10, 59
Duffy, Frank, 137
Durocher, Leo, 20-21

Easter, Luke, 92-93, 95, 101, 113
Eastside High School, 11-14, 83-84, 96
Ebbets Field (Brooklyn), 20, 89
Edwards, Hank, 48, 49, 68, 74, 76
Edwards, Dr. Harry, 176
Ehlers, Art, 100
Einhorn, Eddie, 95
Eisenhower, Dwight D., 112
Ellis, John, 140
Embree, Red, 48, 68
Erskine, Carl, 102
Essex County Board of Freeholders, 126
Evers, Walt, 93

Fanning, Jim, 131, 133-34, 135-37, 148
Feller, Bob, 48, 60, 79, 80, 82, 99
Fenway Park (Boston), 75, 80, 118
Ferrarese, Don, 116
Ferriss, Dave, 75
Fielding record, 109-10
Flaherty, John, 102
Fleming, Les, 48, 53, 61
Flood, Curt, 172
Foli, Tim, 147
Forbes Field (Pittsburgh), 35
Fox, Charlie, 148
Fox, Nellie, 102, 111
Foxx, Jimmie, 73
Francona, Tito, 117
Frick, Ford, 22, 31

Gamble, Oscar, 140, 150-51
Garcia, Mike, 92
Garr, Ralph, 152
Garvey, Marcus, 15
Gehrig, Lou, 89
Gentry, Rufus, 74
Gettel, Al, 48, 58, 60
Gibson, Josh, 20, 30, 33, 37, 75
Gilliam, Jim, 133, 153
Goldstein, Spud: arranges housing in Los Angeles in 1949, 88; arranges housing in Texarkana in 1948, 72; arranges housing in Tucson in 1948, 68-69; arranges housing in Tucson in 1954, 100; assigns Doby to first hotel, 52; meets Doby, 46; participant in glove incident, 53-55; participates

Goldstein, Spud (*continued*)
   in contract negotiations in 1954, 101;
   rebuked by Doby in Los Angeles in
   1954, 100; witness to clubhouse in-
   troductions in 1947, 48
Goltz, Dave, 156
Gomez, Ruben, 104
Goodman, Billy, 29
Gordon, Joe: becomes Doby's manager, 116–17; befriends Doby in
   1947, 62; compared with Doby as
   batting instructor, 132; in film with
   Doby, 91; meets Doby, 48; needles
   Doby, 79; relieved by Doby, 61;
   warms up with Doby, 49
Gosden, Freeman, 71–72
Grant, Arthur, 26
Grant, Doris and Arthur, 77, 98, 169
Grant, Mudcat, 136
Great Lakes Naval Training Center, 25
Greenberg, Hank: asks Doby to apolo-
   gize to Lopez, 98; negotiates 1954
   contract with Doby, 101; negotiates
   1955 contract with Doby, 109; permits "Day" for Doby, 96; instructs
   Doby on hitting in 1948, 75; ru-
   mored to have black quota system,
   95; rumored to want to trade Doby,
   99; sprayed by Doby's champagne,
   103; votes to send Doby to San
   Diego, 118
Griffith, Clark, 26, 44, 59, 99
Griffith Stadium (Washington, D.C.),
   34, 59, 75, 89
Gromek, Steve, 1–4, 48, 79, 82, 103,
   167, 177
Grove, Orval, 55

Hairston, Sam, 155
Hall of Fame, Cleveland Indians, 129
Hapgood, Russell, 14, 17
Harder, Mel, 48, 59, 95
Harlem Globetrotters, 39, 168
Harlem Renaissance, 15
Harrah, Toby, 133
Harridge, Will, 31, 94, 113
Harrist, Earl, 49, 50–51
Hatfield, Fred, 115

Havana Sugar Kings, 120
Heath, Jeff, 58
Hegan, Jim, 48, 62, 68, 79, 81, 83, 103
Hemond, Roland, 138
Hendrick, George, 137, 142–43
Henrich, Tommy, 59, 67
Hiroshima Carps, 124
Ho, George (Ho Sing Ping), 20
Holmes, Benjamin F., 34
Holmes, Tommy, 83
Homestead Grays, 31, 33, 37
Honda, Carl, 124, 125
Horne, Lena, 39, 91
Hoskins, Dave, 101
Hotels: Biltmore, 71, 88; Book-Cadil-
   lac, 103; Del Prado, 42, 52; Du Sa-
   ble, 52; Kenmore, 59, 81; Majestic,
   56; Santa Rita, 68–69, 88, 91–92, 95,
   100; Statler, 59; Stevens, 52; War-
   rick, 59; Watkins, 71, 88
Houtteman, Art, 74, 103
Lowser, Dick, 138
Hucles, Henry B., 24
Hudson, Sid, 75, 89
Hughes, Sam, 21
Humphrey, Hubert H., 2, 129
Hutchinson, Fred, 74

Ikeda, Hayato, 125
Irish, Ned, 24
Irvin, Monte: barnstorms with black
   team, 35; invites Doby to play in
   Puerto Rico, 29; leading batsman for
   1946 Newark Eagles, 33; Negro
   League All-Star, 34; player for Smart
   Sets, 15; refused by Veeck, 40–41;
   Rheingold representative, 125–26;
   star of 1946 Negro World Series, 34;
   star of 1954 World Series, 104; takes
   job in Kuhn's office, 129

Jackson, Cleveland, 40, 46, 49–50, 52
Jackson, Jesse, 152–53
Jackson, Perry B., 76
Jamieson, Charlie, 14, 83–84
Jansen, Larry, 73, 88, 94
Jensen, Jackie, 99
Johns Hopkins Hospital, 119, 120

Johnson, John W., 36
Johnson, Lamar, 152, 156
Johnson, Mary Kathryn Cooke, 5, 6, 7, 8
Jones, Aldona, 92
Jones, Leroi. *See* Amiri Baraka
Jones, Louis: accompanies Doby to clubhouse in Chicago, 46–47; arranges Doby's hotel in Cleveland, 56; checks on Doby's character, 40; escorts Doby to Chicago, 44; escorts Doby to hotel after first game, 52; fired by Veeck, 68; hired by Veeck, 39; informs Doby of contract, 42; introduces Doby to Veeck, 45; plans to escort Doby to Chicago, 43
Joost, Eddie, 57
Jorgensen, Mike, 132-33
Judnich, Walt, 68, 72, 81

Kachadurian, Al, 15-16, 17
Kaline, Al, 110
Kansas City Monarchs, 34, 78, 171
Kazuo, Takada, 125
Keck, Harry, 21
Kell, George, 93
Keltner, Ken, 48, 49, 54, 57, 61, 80, 81
Kennedy, Bob, 80, 81, 83
Kennedy, John F., 123
Kern, Jim, 140
Kessinger, Don, 158-59, 159-60, 163
"The Kid from Cleveland," 90-91
Killefer, Bill, 39-40
Kiner, Ralph, 93-94, 101, 119
King, Dolly, 23
King, Dr. Martin Luther, Jr., 97, 111-12, 127
Klieman, Ed, 48, 69
Knoop, Bobby, 150, 155
Koppel, Ted, 128, 173
Koslo, Dave, 73
Kuehl, Karl, 147-48
Kuhn, Bowie, 127, 128-29, 134, 138, 143

Lakeland, Florida, 117
Landis, Jim, 118

Landis, Kenesaw Mountain, 19, 21, 22-23, 30, 39, 127
Lane, Frank, 116
LaRussa, Tony, 156
Lautenberg, Senator Frank, 176
Lehner, Paul, 58, 60, 95
Lemon, Bob: accepts Doby as coach, 150; befriends Doby, 62; brings bicarbonate of soda to Paige, 168; compared with Doby as manager, 152; fired as manager by Veeck, 151; invited by Doby to clubhouse meeting, 155; member of 1947 Indians, 48; Most Valuable Player candidate, 105; replaced by Doby as manager, 151-52
Lemon, Chet, 156-57, 163
Leonard, Buck, 20, 30, 34
Litwhiler, Danny, 109
Livingstone, Al, 84
Lockman, Whitey, 104
Lollar, Sherm, 111
Lopat, Eddie, 96
Lopez, Al: benches Doby in 1952, 98; comments on Doby's first at bat, 50; comments on trade of Doby, 113; evaluates Doby's 1954 season, 104; manages White Sox, 115; names Doby to 1955 All-Star team, 109; orders Doby to rest injury, 96; replaced by Doby at bat, 60; southern origins, 48; trades Doby to White Sox, 110; votes to send Doby to San Diego, 118
Lopez, Hector, 109-10, 138
Louis, Joe, 26, 33, 34, 36, 62
Lowenstein, John, 141
Lubbock, Texas, 72, 74, 83

McCraw, Tom, 140, 141-42, 173
McCulley, Jim, 105
McGovern, George, 134
McHale, John, 128-29, 135-37, 148
Mack, Connie, 162
McKechnie, Bill, 61, 67, 79, 95
Mackey, Biz, 30
McKinley, Bill, 76
MacPhail, Lee, 143, 158

MacPhail, Leland S., 21-22, 30, 44
McQuinn, George, 78
Manley, Abe, 40
Manley, Effa, 20, 32, 40-43, 83
Mantle, Mickey, 89, 99, 100, 102, 110
Maracaibo Zulia team, 133
Marion, Marty, 111, 115
Maris, Roger, 116
Marmo, Ben, x, 96
Martin, Billy, 113-14, 175
Martin, J. B., 31
Mather Academy, 10-11
Mauch, Gene, 132, 136, 155, 156
Mayberry, John, 131, 132
Mays, Willie, 104
Menendez, Danny, 120
Memphis, Tennessee, 131, 147
Meridian, Mississippi, 112
Merson, Len, 67
Metkovich, George, 48, 57, 119
Michaels, Cass, 55
Mills Brothers, 71
Milwaukee Brewers (American Association), 39
Minoso, Minnie, 88, 95-96, 99, 102, 105, 111, 150, 155
Mitchell, Dale, 46, 48, 55, 68, 81, 82, 83, 103
Mize, Johnny, 96
Mog-Mog Atoll, 26, 29, 60, 116. See also Ulithi Atoll
Montclair, New Jersey, 87-88, 117, 143
Montclair State College, 176
Montgomery bus boycott, 97, 111
Montreal Expos, 129, 131, 132-33, 135, 144, 147
Montreal Royals (International League), 29, 31, 35
Moore, Ray, 118
Moore, Terry, 103
Moses, Wally, 132
Motley, Marion, 26, 56
Motley, Marion and Eula, 76-77
Muckerman, Richard, 58
Murphy, Mayor Vincent J., 32

Nagoya Chunichi Dragons, 123-25
Naharodny, Bill, 156

Narleski, Ray, 103
Negro American League, 31
Negro National League, 31, 33, 35
Newark Eagles: Doby's debut, 19; Doby's first salary, 20; new bus, 36; 1946 World Series, 34-35; opposed by Buck O'Neill, 171-72; reaction of players to future integration, 23; recalled by Amiri Baraka, 171; sale of Doby's contract, 40-42; spring training in 1946, 31-32
Newcombe, Don: barnstorms with Jackie Robinson, 35; called up to Dodgers, 36; comments on Doby and Robinson, 169-71, 173-74; exhibition game at Brooklyn, 89; at Jackie Robinson's funeral, 134; plays with Doby in Japan, 123-25; signs contract with Dodgers, 31-32
Newhouser, Hal, 74, 80
New Jersey State Legislature, 176
New Jersey Nets, 160, 167, 174
Newton, Huey, 142
New York Black Yankees, 35, 36
New York Cubans, 35, 37
New York Giants, 70, 72-73, 88, 103-5, 113
New York Yankees, 59, 60, 78-79, 89-90, 94, 96, 103, 110, 113
Nixon, Richard M., 134
Norman, Bill, 40, 48-49, 117
Nozinski, Mike, 35
Nugent, Gerry, 22-23

O'Connor, Leslie, 46
Oglivie, Ben, 133
Old Timers Athletic Association (Paterson), 43, 59
O'Neill, Buck, 171-72
O'Neill, Steve, 90
Orta, Jorge, 150, 156
Owens, Jesse, 3, 62
Oxford, Mississippi, 112
Ozark, Danny, 156

Pacheco, Tony, 141
Page, Joe, 90
Paige, Satchel: compared with Jackie Robinson, 167-69; Doby's room-

mate, 77–78; exhibition game in 1948, 78; joins Indians, 77; judged by Doby, 30; judged by Buck O'Neill, 171–72; released by Indians, 92; restrains Doby, 79; segregated in 1948, 88; sense of humor, 175; sings in quartet, 79

Pappas, Milt, 118

Parks, Rosa, 111

Parrish, Larry, 147

Partlow, Roy, 36

Paterson, New Jersey, 7, 11–12, 13, 16, 87, 117, 123

Paterson Crescents, 67

Patterson, Pat, 32

Pearson, Len, 32, 35, 36

Peck, Hal, 48, 68, 76, 79

Pellagrini, Eddie, 70

Perry, Gaylord, 140

Philadelphia Athletics, 56, 58, 76, 78, 79, 80, 90

Philadelphia Phillies, 39, 156

Philadelphia SPHA's, 67

Philadelphia Stars, 32, 37, 41

Philley, Dave, 95

Piniella, Lou, 138

Pittsburgh Pirates, 35, 138

Players Fraternity, 56

Pope, Dave, 101

Porterfield, Bob, 89

Proly, Mike, 163

Rackley, Marv, 35

Raschi, Vic, 90

Reese, Peewee, 58, 134

Reischauer, William O., 125

Renna, Hal, 109

Rhodes, Dusty, 104

Richards, Paul, 115, 116

Richardson, Thomas H., 31

Rickey, Branch, 29, 31–32, 35, 36, 44

Rivera, Jim, 111

Rizzuto, Phil, 93

Robeson, Paul, 15

Robinson, Bill "Bojangles," 60

Robinson, Eddie: fractures ankle, 61; glove incident, 53–55; hit seven times by pitches, 91; identified as southerner, 48; improves performance in 1948, 58; kicks Jackie Robinson at Montreal, 33; sings in quartet, 79

Robinson, Frank, 138–42, 143, 150, 152

Robinson, Jackie: after 11 weeks with Dodgers, 43; barnstorms in 1947, 62; compared with Doby and Cleveland infield, 58; compared with Doby and Paige, 168–75; demeaned in editorial, 57; described by Mauch, 132; evaluated by Dusty Baker, 133; evaluated by *Jet* and *Ebony,* 114; first black to appear in All-Star game, 89; forms barnstorming team, 35; games against Doby in 1948, 78; gets Bankhead as roommate, 61; honored at World Series in 1972, 134; kicked by Eddie Robinson, 33; leads International League in batting, 34; in Little World Series, 35; named foremost black athlete, 36; in 1947 World Series, 61–62; overshadows Doby, ix; plays with Campanis, 128; preparation compared with Doby's, 47; releases feelings of blacks, 30; salary for 1947 and 1948, 67; shares news coverage with Louis, 33; shares popularity with Louis, 26; signs contract with Montreal, 29; stays with team in Chicago, 52; watched by Veeck, 40

Robinson, Rachel, 47

Rockefeller, Nelson, 171

Roenicke, Gary, 147

Rommel, Ed, 75

Rose, Pete, 138

Rosen, Al: compares Doby with Easter, 92, 93; defends Doby in cab, 88; hits grand slam on "Doby Day," 96; hits two homers in 1954 All-Star game, 102; in fistfight with Doby, 94; joins Indians in 1947, 61; named Most Valuable Player, 100

Ruel, Muddy, 58, 60, 95

Rumana, Henry, 16–17, 84

Ruppert Stadium (Newark), 32, 34, 43

Russell, Bill, 134

Russell, Fred, 57
Ruszkowski, Hank, 48
Ruth, Babe, 75, 89
Ryan, Nolan, 159

Sacramento Solons, 119, 120
Sain, Johnny, 82
St. Louis Browns, 70, 71, 79, 94, 97
St. Petersburg, Florida, 131
Salinger, Pierre, 123-24
Samuels, Marshall, 43, 46
San Diego Padres (Pacific Coast
    League), 118
San Juan Senators, 29, 35, 36
Santurce Crabbers, 138
Saperstein, Abe, 39-40
Sarasota, Florida, 120
Schaffer, Rudie, 76
Schmeling, Max, 36
Schoendienst, Red, 94
Score, Herb, 112
Scottsdale, Arizona, 116
Seay, Dick, 30
Seerey, Pat, 48, 68, 73
Seghi, Phil, 135-37, 138-40, 141-42,
    173
Simmons, Ozzie, 25
Simpson, Harry, 95
Singleton, Ken, 133
Slaughter, Enos, 113
Smith, Al, 101, 102, 110
Smith, Edgar, 49
Smith, Robert, 17
Smith, Wendell, 40, 135
Soderholm, Eric, 150, 152
Speaker, Tris, 69, 75, 79, 95, 103
Spikes, Charlie, 137
Spink, J. G. Taylor, 30-31, 57
Stanky, Eddie, 58, 83
States' Rights Party, 2, 4, 112
Stengel, Casey, 93, 98, 100
Stephens, Bryan, 48, 49-50
Stephens, Vern, 80
Stone, Ed, 30
Stone, Steve, 152
Summers, Bill, 55, 76
Suttles, Mule, 30

Tamblyn, Rusty, 91
Tampa, Florida, 112
Taub, Joe, 17, 160, 175-76
Taylor, Candy Jim, 56
Tebbetts, Birdie, 81
Texarkana, 72-73, 74, 83
Thompson, Hank, 58, 60, 61, 104
Thurmond, J. Strom, 2
Tillman, Ben, 8
Torgeson, Earl, 83
Toronto Maple Leafs (International
    League), 48, 61, 120
Torrealba, Pablo, 162-63
Trouppe, Quincy, 56
Trout, Steve, 163
Trucks, Virgil, 74
Truman, Harry S, 2, 4, 97
Tucker, Thurman, 68, 71, 79, 81
Tucson, Arizona, 68, 69, 70, 88, 91,
    95, 102, 117, 137

Ueberroth, Peter, 138, 176
Ulithi Atoll, 26, 29. See also Mog-Mog
    Atoll
Umphlett, Tom, 102
Umpiring, 75-76
U.S. Navy, 24-26

Valentine, Bobby, 138
Valentine, Ellis, 147
Veal, Dr. Benjamin, 14, 16-17
Veeck, Bill: appoints Doby as man-
    ager, 151-53; assigns scouts to evalu-
    ate Doby, 39; assigns Speaker to
    teach Doby, 69; buys Doby's con-
    tract for White Sox, 117-18; buys
    Doby's contract from Eagles, 42;
    buys St. Louis Browns, 97; cele-
    brates 1948 pennant, 81; conceals
    Doby plans from Boudreau, 42-43;
    confirms reports about scouting
    Doby, 40; considers assignment of
    Doby to minor league, 61-62; con-
    sults Wendell Smith, 40; cooperates
    on presence of plainclothes police,
    55; dismisses Jones, 68; evaluated by
    Doby, 175-76; evaluates Doby's
    ability, 60-61; fires Doby as man-

ager, 159; fires Lemon as manager, 151; hires Doby as coach, 150; hires Doby as scout, 121; introduces Doby to press in 1947, 44–46; invites Doby to coach White Sox in 1979, 160; justifies appointment of Kessinger, 169; justifies firing Doby as manager, 161–62; negotiates with Effa Manley, 40; permits Doby to make public appearances, 76; plans to buy Phillies, 19, 22–23; plans to introduce Doby at Cleveland in 1947, 47; plays role in movie, 91; ponders dilemma of southern minor league teams, 48–49; praised by Doby, 94; praised for appointing Doby as manager, 152–53; protects Doby from public, 53; reacts to naming of Frank Robinson as major league manager, 143; reassigns Minoso in 1978, 156; refuses to buy Irvin's contract, 40–41; and role in integration at Cleveland, 101; and Santa Rita Hotel, 69; sends Doby to San Diego, 118–19; signs Doby for 1948, 67; "suggests" insertion of Doby into starting lineup in 1947, 54–55; switches Doby to outfield, 58; tells false strikeout story, 51–52; turns down proposal for Doby Day, 59; unaware of segregation in Los Angeles, 71; willing source for biography of Doby, x
Veeck, Mary Frances, x, 168
Veeck, Mike, 157, 158
Veeck, William, Sr., 39
Vernon, Mickey, 26, 29, 60, 102, 116, 117

Wagner, Honus, 35
Walker, Etta Doby, 7, 10, 84, 96
Walker, Harry, 132
Walker, Larry (pseud.), 19–20
Wallaesa, Jack, 55
Waner, Lloyd, 103
Washington, Booker T., 6
Washington, Claudell, 156

Washington, D.C., 89
Washington, Kenny, 31, 71
Washington, Leon H., 71
Weissman, Lefty, 74, 76
Wells, Willie, 20, 30
Welmaker, Roy, 88
Wertz, Vic, 100, 104, 105, 110
White, Bill, 153
White Citizens Councils, 111, 112
Whiting, Bob, x, 41–42, 43, 44
Wilcox, Milt, 140
Wilhelm, Hoyt, 104
Wilkes-Barre, Pennsylvania, 56, 117
Williams, Davey, 104
Williams, Dick, 116, 136, 148
Williams, Stan, 150, 155
Williams, Ted, 75, 80, 93, 97, 103
Williams, Wendell, 14, 15, 16–17, 24
Willis, Bill, 56
Willis, Lucille and Chester, 69, 88
Willoughby, Jim, 156
Wills, Maury, 117, 153
Wilson, Artie, 88
Wilson, Hack, 88
Wilson, Pat, 15, 84
Wilson, Tom, 31
Wood, Wilbur, 156
Woodling, Gene, 110, 116
World Series: 1948, 82–83; 1954, 103–5; 1956, 113; 1959, 120; 1972, 134
Wortham, Rich, 163
Wright, Johnny, 31
Wynn, Early, 103

Yankee Stadium (New York), 89, 91, 94, 96, 109
Yonamine, Wally, 124–25
York, Rudy, 55
Young, Buddy, 26
Young, Cy, 94
Younger, Eddie, 23

Zarilla, Al, 58
Zernial, Gus, 95
Zimmer, Don, 136
Zisk, Richie, 151
Zoldak, Sam, 76, 80, 95

About the Author

JOSEPH THOMAS MOORE is Professor of History at Montclair State College, New Jersey. He is the author of *The Problem of War* and *War and War Prevention*, and numerous scholarly papers and articles in various textbooks and journals.